Date Due

WRITERS
AT
WORK

CANADIAN WRITERS AT WORK

Interviews with Geoff Hancock

Toronto
Oxford University Press
1987

Canadian Cataloguing in Publication Data

Main entry under title:
Canadian writers at work

ISBN 0-19-540638-9

1. Novelists, Canadian (English) — 20th century —
Interviews.*   2. Canadian fiction (English) —
20th century — History and criticism.*
I. Hancock, Geoff, 1946-

© Geoff Hancock 1987

OXFORD is a trademark of Oxford University Press

1 2 3 4 — 0 9 8 7

Printed in Canada by Webcom Limited

Contents

Introduction

These interviews began as a regular feature in *Canadian Fiction Magazine* over a decade ago, when Canadian writers were rarely interviewed at length. I talked to writers about their writing and the possibilities of contemporary fiction. I asked what it means to live in and write about contemporary Canada. I explored the sources of the Canadian imagination: how it creates, what it represents. What makes Canadian fiction "Canadian"? What might Canadian fiction aspire to be?

At the same time, I talked to authors about how they deal with the blank page. What pressures were placed on their art by the contemporary world? My special interest and expertise is the short story, and it is here that Canadian writing has made its greatest formal advances. I was not interested in explication — other resources are available for that method of dealing with a writer's text. But I was interested in the narrative strategies that informed their work. I spoke to writers who had an impact on Canadian literature, often at the moment of their impact.

It was a pleasure to meet some of my favourite authors and discuss their creative processes. I met Leon Rooke soon after I began my editorship of *CFM,* and his work appeared in the magazine as early as the fourth issue. I spent two months in Paris getting to know Mavis Gallant. Alice Munro and I became friends as part of Canada's first literary delegation to the People's Republic of China. Josef Skvorecky's company, Sixty-Eight Publishers, does the typesetting and layout of *CFM.* I knew Jane Rule as a creative-writing instructor at UBC; she was also my next-door neighbour. I have interviewed Robert Kroetsch several times, and admire the way his exuberant inventions challenge surface verisimilitude. I've also admired Jack Hodgins' work from his first publication in *CFM.* When I interviewed him, I had just returned from several months in South America, and was excited by the magic realism I saw in his work. We spent an hour in his car, in the rain, at the Nanaimo ferry terminal, talking about Latin American writers. I have many other special recollections — sitting in Bharati Mukherjee's New York apartment, discussing India, or speaking with Clark Blaise about new short-story writers, or swapping literary gossip with Margaret Atwood — para-literary concerns that are the writer's life. These, however, are the context — not the substance of the literary interview.

What exactly is the literary interview? As a form in and of itself, the interview intrigues me. It's partly the quality of talk — but can we consider conversation a literary form? Is it a primary or secondary text, a spectrum with ideas converging in a state of unresolved tension? As Coleridge asks in his *Biographia Literaria,* is there a distinction to be made between the primary imagination, the secondary imagination, and mere fancy?

The interview is a flexible form. It can be a reflection on contemporary fiction, an imaginary construct, a genre with its own techniques. It can be an extension of criticism, a manifesto, a biographical device, an insight into how writers view their work, a forum for debate on aesthetic ideas or technical short cuts. It's talk that preserves the creator's views, which makes it different from the critic's opinion. An interview is elusive because it is partly philosophical, partly biographical, partly theatrical. It creates mental images of concepts, an understanding of sensory perception. The interview as we know it is a product of our times. (The magnetic tape recorder was a post-war invention; the miniature tape recorder with cassette a technological breakthrough of the 1970s.) The interview satisfies part of our appetite for glamour and celebrity. Like a TV or radio show, it is fragmented, and can be entered and exited at will and at any point. The interview is discontinuous, and so it becomes post-modern. Replies come in clusters, answers compete for space and meaning. Not all questions and answers have equal weight — it is up to the reader to decide.

As a collaboration, an interview is gossipy at one extreme and philosophical at the other. The interviewer discovers opinions here and aesthetics there. An interview can make connections between a writer's books and can often correct and contradict critical commentary. It also creates an image of the writer, an authorial presence different from the one met in the novels and stories, and one that may very well be a fabrication. An interview is referential on the one hand, pointing to facts of interest, and fictional on the other, a mental structure created by the author and the interviewer in the play of give and take. Sometimes slight personality shifts occur, as the author's persona and my own intertwine. A performance takes place for the microphone, for the future audience. Finally, an interview is also composed, by the interviewer and the author, especially in revisions. As Joe David Bellamy has written, an interview is like a fiction; it deals in abstract ideas, but with a dramatic ambience.

Although many writers doubt the value of the interview, they use the occasion to engage in open and thoughtful discussion about the values of writing. They discuss in detail the way imagination plays with experience, they compare various narrative strategies, the way places and societies influence story-line and character. All of these interviews have been revised, some extensively. Here the interview becomes most fictional. The writer presents a self-portrait, revealing through layers the public self, the private self, the working self. Sometimes these selves overlap and contradict each other. In a sense interviews are like letters, only more public. As a view of the author as presented by the author, the interview is a form of self-creation, reminding us of the "fiction" of fiction, though it may seem like good honest talk. How can it be otherwise? Through struggle, the writer tries to fix and define, to re-create. A personality is created through dialogue. It's a sort of memory, with a strange two-ring action taking place. The writer tries to imagine the creation, and the reader reconstructs the imagining, with the interviewer as ringmaster.

A list of possible questions is sent to each author in advance, usually variations on the same themes: writers and writing, formative experiences, the imagination, literary traditions (Canadian and otherwise). The 1970s and 1980s raised questions about the morality of fiction, the use of allegory, fabulation, the overlap between the end of modernism and emergence of post-modernism, how books find their forms. These basic questions are where the magic of creation is located. How is it done? That's what I want to know. The essential questions are simple ones, about the daily writing routine, methods of revision, early attempts at writing, and favourite authors. Simple questions lead to profound subjects like symbolism, post-modernism, and surrealism. Often what writers say about their work is more perceptive than most criticism.

I approach writers with total curiosity, after reading their books and gathering data in clipping files. Sometimes an interview can be undermined in the discussion or during the revisions — who says what to whom? can we believe either? — but I try to avoid role reversal, and don't let the questions get turned around so that I become the subject. Focusing on a specific time, space, and presence, and my own impressions, I may add a physical description of the writer, his or her home, some characteristic activity. Usually I go to the author, but I recognize limits to an invasion of privacy. I never ask for an interview during a promotion tour, when any writer is bound to be worn out by stale questions and set responses.

The pieces in this book weren't planned as a collection. Some interviews were for an occasion — a special issue of the magazine, a new book — but often I just admired the author's work. I called up and asked for several hours of his or her time. Then I had questions I asked of myself. Interviews thrive in the gap between "speech art" and "written text." Is an interview an independent text? A performance? Does it exist only in a particular context — of a new book, a special issue, a new aesthetic thrust in the arts? How does it find a shape, a direction? What makes an interview dynamic? The logic of questions and answers is not the key to an interview. It's the undercurrent of understanding and response, as American interviewer Charles Ruas says. But sometimes the momentum of an interview means that a challenge to a question, a follow-up, is missed or consciously overlooked. Interviews can never be comprehensive or truly definitive.

My first interviews were partly influenced by those in *Paris Review*. The best of these were brilliant, but even they had their limitations: Americans and Europeans seldom had to explain where they were in the world. Joe David Bellamy's *Interviews with Innovative American Writers* made a bigger impact on me. Bellamy drew attention to the disruptive elements in American fiction — the fantastic, gothic, surreal, grotesque as elements of the new fiction. Fiction, he suggested, had to be re-evaluated to be vital. Likewise, a decade later, Tom LeClair's and Larry McCaffery's *Anything Can Happen* claimed new aesthetic perceptions in short fiction. I was stimulated by Graeme Gibson's *Eleven Canadian Novelists* (1973), a collection of interviews originally taped for broadcast on the CBC. Donald Cameron's two-volume *Interviews with Canadian Novelists* (1975) also revealed that Canadian writers had much to say about their fiction and the context of its production.

I saw that Canadian fiction had changed. Traditional forms and subjects had given way to new sensibilities and new modes of perception. With them came a new use of language, new formal structures, and a new style of criticism. Canadian writing was adventurous, idiosyncratic, exciting, personal.

These interviews are in part an explanation of new directions that have emerged in Canadian writing. The period of the 1960s and 1970s in Canada was a great cultural moment. A canon, however, was prematurely established at a time of major developments in Canadian writing. In this canonization of certain writers, others were often ignored or excluded. Nationalism was over. Bilingualism, multiculturalism, transculturalization, and translations gave Canadian fiction new characteristics. I worried that some writers I admired would be ignored completely.

A number of the writers I interviewed are new Canadians — from Europe, America, India — or Canadians who live abroad. They have new perspectives on the nature and purpose of Canadian fiction. Many teach creative writing, an important post-war development that emphasizes theory and technique — craft at the service of art. Canada has new literary models drawn from sources neither British, American, nor French. Latin American writing is cited several times in these interviews. In an age of translation and transculturalization, Gabriel Garcia Marquez and Jorge Luis Borges, as well as other Canadian writers, are mentioned more frequently than Samuel Beckett, T. S. Eliot, James Joyce, or Saul Bellow. Other writers are professors of literature, who speak articulately and at length about the dynamics of composition. Several, including Mavis Gallant, Leon Rooke, Josef Skvorecky, Jack Hodgins, and Bharati Mukherjee, said they had never before had the chance to discuss their writing in detail. Perhaps that is why their interviews have a particularly dynamic freshness.

These interviews are among the most requested by teachers and students of creative writing and Canadian literature. *Canadian Writers at Work* is an ongoing dialogue between creative artists and a literature-in-process. I was privileged, for a few hours, to interrupt this conversation with one of my own.

Many people contributed to this book. I would especially like to thank the writing and publication section of the Canada Council and the Ontario Arts Council for their continued support of *Canadian Fiction Magazine*. In particular, I would like to thank Steve Stevorovic, André Renaud, Luc Jutras, and Katherine Bery for continued personal and professional encouragement. Friends and colleagues who provided support include Thea DeVos, Linda Leitch, Elizabeth Brewitt, Alison Lane, and Zdena Skvorecky.

Special thanks must be given to Gay Allison and Meagan Julia, who enrich my own narrative with emotional nuance and story-lines too wondrous to unravel. Finally, I must thank the authors themselves, for their writings, and for their generosity in talking to me.

JANE RULE

Jane Rule's works include the novels *Desert of the Heart* (1964; filmed as *Desert Hearts*), *This Is Not for You* (1970), *Against the Season* (1971), *The Young in One Another's Arms* (1977), and *Inland Passages* (1986) and the short-story collections *Theme for Diverse Instruments* (1975) and *Outlander* (1981). Her essays have been collected in *Lesbian Images* (1975), on women writers, and *A Hot-Eyed Moderate* (1986).

This interview was taped on a Saturday afternoon and evening in October 1976 at Jane's home on Galiano Island. Though she was born in Plainfield, N.J., in 1931, she had lived in Vancouver for over twenty years and recently moved to the island. To get there, I had to take the Gulf Island ferry from Tsawwassen, and my overnight visit was scheduled around its twice-daily winter sailings. The Gulf Islands — Galiano, Mayne, Pender, Saltspring, and others — are, of course, British Columbia's heaven on earth, and even a weekend there convinces one books are somehow easier to write. The clear air is curiously Mediterranean, partly because the rainfall is less than a third that of Vancouver, some twenty miles across the Straits of Georgia, and partly because the peeling red bark of the arbutus trees gives the islands a mellow glow even on chilly days. A warm sun breaking through the overcast autumn sky, the smell of the sea, cormorants on rocks in the harbour drying their wings like parodies of imperial eagles, and Jane waiting at the dock with her friend Helen Sonthoff convinced me I was arriving someplace special.

Their house was a Pan-Abode, with large cedar timbers and every wall lined with paintings and drawings by their friends. A space above the view window contained a fine Hopi basket collection, an heirloom from Jane's grandmother and a reminder of the deserts of Arizona and Nevada where Jane and Helen holidayed in winter. The stereo was massive, and a space about the size of a large cupboard was filled with tapes of classical chamber music. Every room had its own set of speakers hooked up to the central controls and, no vulgarity here, the wires were well hidden. The house, like Jane and Helen, was gracious and classy, with the virtues of civility fairly abounding.

After exploring beach trails and the local cemetery (an offensive gravestone read, "Her marriage was her monument"), Jane and I retired to her well-ordered and comfortable downstairs study. Besides the only photocopier on Galiano — a crippling arthritic spine deterioration forced her to wear a neck brace much of the time, and excess typing was painful — the study had a wall of books, a great stone fireplace, two Judy Lodge paintings, a Scandinavian sofa, and a knockout view across the water. The three-

5

hour interview was interrupted only by Helen's delicious crab-and-artichoke salad and homemade wine.

Though she was very tired after a summer of houseguests and two previous interviews that week, Jane's answers were always direct. We raced the clock towards the end, since she had promised that, as of midnight, this was the last interview she would ever do.

HANCOCK

Do you like to do interviews?

RULE

No. Most interviewers ask questions that I've answered so many times before that, even though it's an interesting question, the answer gets stale. That's one of the problems. If it's a short interview, it's very hard on the interviewer to expect anything else. It's very difficult to stay lively in the standard interview.

And of course, I've had a lot of hostile interviews which I don't suppose anyone likes. I'm not at all good at countering hostility. I don't know what to do with it and I have no cleverness of any sort. What I do is go into my big dumb, gentle animal act which is pretty deadly dull. Then I lie in bed at night like a good fiction writer making up all the right answers.

In accepting an interview when you don't know what the questions are going to be, when it's a "live" performance and somebody asks you a question, whether you know anything about the subject or not, you somehow feel socially obliged to answer. I can remember once listening to myself sound off about Canadian politics in a way that absolutely amazed me. I really didn't know what I was talking about. I swore off interviews for a couple of years after that.

HANCOCK

Do you mind the tape recorder?

RULE

No. I don't. I work with a lot of gadgets. I use the tape recorder myself and have done for years. Not to write with. My whole family is wired for sound. My father is a gadget maniac and he had given us all tape recorders. We communicate with each other around the world with cassettes. Mother and Dad travel a lot and sometimes, instead of writing them a letter, I'll send them a tape. So it's more like a phone for me.

HANCOCK

So you don't feel, as Auden did, that machines create sorrow?

RULE

Not the kinds of machines I use. Anything that cleans up the room frightens me; anything that drives down the road frightens me. But if I can

6

push a button and get a copy of a manuscript, or plug in a typewriter, those don't bother me at all.

Do you like privacy?

Yes. I had a really interesting discussion with John Hofsess the other day about the difference between what is public and what is private. His view is that nothing is private except time and in a sense, I agree with him. I don't feel secretive about my life, but I feel very self-protective about my "time." I want plenty of time to get my own work done. The difficulty of not necessarily putting a wall around certain aspects of your life, and therefore making them seem secretive — if you don't do that, you find you are required more and more by people so that it is very difficult to protect the fact of privacy, simply that privacy as "time alone," rather than as secrecy.

You mentioned at one time you would burn all your letters, diaries, and other archival material.

That's certainly a thing I contemplate doing. I suppose part of that has to do with my own sense that the made work is the work that's shareable and I am embarrassed by the number of unimportant private papers accumulating for writers. It's perhaps to save some poor sod the problem of going through my laundry lists. That's in one frame of mind.

When an archivist came from UBC to ask about buying my papers, we talked a fair amount about some of the real problems. When I say that I don't feel secretive about my life, I mean it. But I also don't feel that I could make the choice for somebody else. There are very few papers that *I* have that wouldn't involve other people's privacy as well as my own. I am very protective about other people's privacy. People don't write to me with the notion their letters are going to end up in the archives of the University of British Columbia.

Back to this notion of vulnerability. Was there anything you were particularly afraid of as a child?

The dark. Very much afraid of the dark. To the point that finally when I was about twelve I got fed up. I remember exactly the night. "I'm sick of not being able to sleep." I got up and walked out on the back terrace through French doors that went right off my bedroom. A horrible room for a kid who was afraid of the dark. With a stream running down, the wind blowing and the trees bashing each other. I walked all the way around a lake. About two miles. It was simply such a shock to my system that I never have been frightened again. I think it started with a sense of not being able to distinguish what was a dream and what was real.

7

Where did you go to school?

Dad worked for a national company. So I went to my first school in New Jersey, then to California, then to Illinois, then to Missouri, then back to California with short stretches in other places as well.

HANCOCK
How did this affect you as a writer?

RULE
I think the moving around was very good in one sense. I learned very early that what a great many people thought of as "values" were really "manners," and that "manners" shifted radically from community to community. When I was in California I was in a multi-racial school, but when I was in St. Louis I didn't go to school with blacks. Though there were a lot of black children in that world, they walked in the street and I walked on the sidewalk. In all kinds of less obvious ways the sense of how you behaved in somebody's house, what kind of language you used, what kind of *accent* you used, all seemed to the people who had always been there the way you always did it. For me, it was being a foreigner and figuring out what the rules of the game were. It forced me to evaluate details of living which were very useful by the time I started writing.

HANCOCK
Did you have good teachers when you started writing?

RULE
When I started writing, yes. By this time I was in my early teens in private school. Before that I was in one enormous classroom after another. I didn't begin to read until I was about ten. Nobody knew it because I was very tall and I sat in the back row. I came into school about November and, if I didn't understand the book, the teacher felt it was because I hadn't read the first ten chapters because I hadn't been in school. I bluffed and stumbled and was so stupid I didn't understand why the boy across the aisle from me could read the board and I couldn't. I also didn't see anything that was going on. I didn't know that I needed glasses.

Until I came back to California at the age of twelve and went to private school. My teacher discovered not only that I couldn't read but that I had also skipped multiplication tables entirely. I didn't know what they were and I was trying to do long division. So I had a revelatory year, finding out that it wasn't magic: math was perfectly understandable, the English language was locked up in the marks on the page. It was grand.

HANCOCK
Were you a talkative child?

RULE
I don't think so. These questions came when my mother and father were here. I showed them the questions and they were quite interested. So I said,

8

"I don't really remember that kind of thing about myself." My mother said, "You were a frank child, and you were an outspoken child. But I don't think you were a talkative child."

HANCOCK

When did you begin writing fiction?

RULE

I suppose when I was around thirteen or fourteen. At that point I was much more interested in the sciences and I wanted to go into medicine. That was before I took chemistry which changed my life for the better. I was the kind of student who not only never did an experiment right, but got sponges stuck in the bottoms of test tubes. Just the housekeeping of chemistry was beyond me, never mind the experiment. I thought, if I fail chemistry in high school I probably wouldn't do well in medicine. By that time I was also beginning to realize that, of course, medicine was not a science that dealt with people, but with parts of bodies. Though I didn't mind cutting up chickens and cleaning pigeons, it was not really a life work.

I was already writing just for fun. When I was fifteen or sixteen, I decided I really wanted to write.

HANCOCK

You've had a number of very interesting jobs. Has that influenced your fiction?

RULE

Yes, I think so. Some of the jobs I've taken because I was a writer and wanted information. The blurb on *Desert Of The Heart* says I actually was a change girl at Harold's Club. And I was. For six nights to get the information to write the book. In a sense it wouldn't be true to say my time at Harold's Club inspired me to write the book. I went to Harold's Club to do the job, to get the information for the book I had in mind.

Teaching has been my other profession. When I was in college, I taught in a handicapped school. I didn't do that because I was a writer but because I was needed. I learned an enormous amount there about what it is to be without language.

I had one student who had cerebral palsy. Now this was a wing of a public school, a day school. This boy turned up in the class, just registered by his parents at age sixteen. He couldn't talk. He was such a bad case that he was sandbagged to his wheelchair because he couldn't control his hands. You could get yes or no out of him if he wasn't excited, but the moment he got excited he lost any control of communication. We thought he could read. We used to watch him when we were teaching some of the other students and he seemed to be able to follow words. But we couldn't ask him, and he couldn't really show us. We got an electric typewriter. We bound leather straps onto the table and put his wrists in those straps. He made a lot of mistakes, but he typed "I can read." And then he cried and

I cried and the master teacher cried. I thought, sixteen years locked in yourself and not able to give even a sense of your basic needs. Well, experiences like that have done something very important to me in terms of what language means, which are very different from an academic knowledge of language.

HANCOCK

You've also travelled a good many places. England, Greece, the U.S.A. and now you're a Canadian citizen. Has that had an influence on your fiction? The variety of human types? That sort of thing?

RULE

Yes, certainly. And landscapes as well. Setting is very important to me. When I first began to write, I felt such a stranger in any environment I was in I didn't use settings at all. I didn't know the names of plants, or flowers, or streets. In school I never knew where the washroom was. So when I wrote, I wrote as if particular flowers, streets, rooms didn't exist. I think that *Desert Of The Heart* was the first time I risked a landscape. I did an enormous amount of research for that. To be able to know the names of hills, roads. And I was what? In my late twenties. But I felt I had to deal with the landscape as a scholar would.

Read Virginia Woolf. Somebody wrote to her in high fury that she had a flower blooming in southern England that didn't bloom anywhere but Scotland. Virginia Woolf's answer was "It's my garden." I like that beautiful arrogance of somebody who owns a landscape, who is born to it, doesn't feel caught out or exposed as ignorant as a stranger or a foreigner. But I am still very careful to be accurate. I am still a stranger in landscapes.

As for types of people, I don't think in those ways. Though I realize I couldn't have made a Dina character as I did in *Against The Season* with a Greek character confidently unless I'd been to Greece. I felt as if I knew twenty times as much about the character as got into the book. Which is about the right balance. I feel freer to draw upon various cultural experiences from having been as many places as I have.

HANCOCK

What academic training have you had?

RULE

I have a B.A. in English from Mills, then I did a year as an occasional student at U.C. — University College, London (England) — and that's a beautiful term, an official term, and I think we should use it more on this continent because I think many of us are occasional students and that's really the way we want to use the university. I wasn't there for an advanced degree. I was simply there to take courses in Shakespeare and seventeenth century. Then I went back for one quarter at Stanford (1954) with Wallace Stegner. And that's the extent of my academic training.

HANCOCK

Does the influence of this academic training consciously appear in your fiction?

10

I suppose occasionally. One of the characters in *Desert Of The Heart* is a W.B. Yeats scholar. I'm not a Yeats scholar, but I feel competent enough about what I know to manifest it in the book.

But much of what I learned in my formal training, I had to unlearn as a writer. It's been very good training for teaching and I've been very grateful for it. But a great deal of what I was taught at the university was very rigid, was not the kind of thing that I needed to know about language to be a writer. In a way I'm grateful all the issues were raised because I could define what I had to unlearn.

That's a funny way of going about learning. For instance, all the academic training that I had about point of view seemed to me suspect. Such concepts were certainly suspect as taught by people who didn't write. So I was given a lot of bad advice. I studied under people who had rigid notions of what was good literature and what wasn't, and a great many of the writers who mattered to me, such as Gertrude Stein, Charles Williams, John Steinbeck, and Christopher Fry weren't being taught at the university, of course. But the whole sense of an academic stamp of approval is very limiting, as well as nourishing.

Are there any political, religious, or psychological traditions that are important to you?

That's an interesting grouping, to put them all together, because they seem to me very separate.

I'm not what most people would consider political. People in the women's movement object to my work because I'm not political in that sense. The women's movement matters enormously to me and I'm interested in the political part of it as well, but as a human being who happens to be a woman. I've done a fair amount of work in the women's movement with daycare centres and equal scholarships and equal pay and abortion reform, that sort of thing. I am a — off the top of my head — a socialist. I don't feel very well informed about my political stances and I guess one of the reasons I'm not is because I have a deep mistrust of any system as an answer. It seems to me socialism, as I understand it, is probably closer to a humane way to live than anything else I've ever seen. But I don't think of it as an answer. I don't think of politics as an answer.

In religious matters, I can't imagine anyone growing up in the tradition I grew up in not being enormously influenced by the Judaeo-Christian tradition. Our literature is full of it. The very cadences of our language are given to us in ritual form. Or were given to me, anyway. You go to church. The first novel I ever wrote was entitled after a phrase in the General Confession. The language is just there and the rhythms are very deep. I am not a practising Christian. I think a lot that shocks me about the world we live in is rooted in Christian teaching. It shocks me, for instance, that people think their children are something they own, that they can give to the world. We have solved the problem of nineteen-year-old boys for all these years by simply concocting another war to kill them off in and then we get stars put in the window for them. Then I hear "And God so loved the world He gave His only Son." And I think embedded in that mythology is what terrifies me most about the values of our culture. So it's very important, negatively important.

HANCOCK

And psychological traditions?

RULE

I really don't have much respect for psychology. I used to feel patient about it. I used to think it's young like an education faculty; it's trying to make itself a respectable academic subject. If it's pompous, if it develops a mystifying jargon, that's part of its inferiority complex. By now psychology's done far too much damage for me to feel any kind of patience with it. I really think we will see most of what we call psychology as a twentieth-century fad. A huge fad.

HANCOCK

Would you tell me a bit more about your involvement in women's groups?

RULE

Of course, now I am not as involved, because I've moved over to Galiano. I spent a couple of years at UBC working with various groups there. Helen and I were in on the beginning of the first groups for the women's movement at UBC, a group primarily of graduate students, some clerical staff, a few undergraduates and some faculty. The group began the research that eventually produced the *Status Of Women Report* that Shelagh Day got together for the university. Of course, what's happened with that is predictable. The very few women on faculty have benefited from it. A special fund has been set up. A special committee has been set up to ensure the few women on faculty do get equal pay. It doesn't cost the university very much. There are only a couple of hundred women on faculty. But the clerical workers and women students have not benefited at all, although two-thirds of the Report was devoted to their problems.

Of course, to change anything for the clerical workers would cost the university a great deal because all the housekeeping is done by women, and all the real running of the hard details of the department is done by women. For students the important change must come in attitudes in the classroom. Attitudes encouraging students to go on, supplying a kind of course that's meaningful to women students so they don't really feel they're simply second-class citizens allowed to stay a little longer on the track before they get rail-roaded off into something that's useful to men. I think that's where the work has to be done. No report can change that.

12

Then I moved on and went into the non-credit women's studies course and helped push it towards a credited course and ran seminars.

I've done a fair amount of book reviewing and article writing for various magazines on issues raised by the women's movement; a good deal, of course, writing on lesbian themes. And I intend to go on writing about that.

HANCOCK

Are you interested in sports? Kate, in *This Is Not For You,* is a championship swimmer.

RULE

Yes. In my books, somebody always gets in a good swim. I like swimming very much. When I was a youngster. Volleyball, basketball, badminton. I can remember going to a very small private school and often we would compete in Interstate meets. I should have been given a medal for getting from one event to the next. We were such a small school, that maybe ten of us would deal with volleyball, badminton and swimming.

HANCOCK

Judy Lodge's drawings elsewhere in this issue have a strong affinity with what I feel is a typical relationship between your characters. That is, far apart on a canvas, yet reaching out for each other. That same feeling appears in your prose as well. You have a very strong visual sense. Would you like to have been a painter, a graphic artist, or a musician? Or maybe another way of putting this, how much do painting and music influence your prose?

RULE

Both very much. I have never been interested at all in being a painter or graphic artist. Nor seriously a musician. As a youngster I played clarinet in the school band, but nothing serious. I was raised in a musical family and I really use music, perhaps more than I use literature to teach myself what I want to do in my own style. I listen to a great deal of chamber music and I listen to the voices of the instruments. I don't think I pay a great deal of attention to transforming form from one art to the other. But the tonal controls, the balance of voices, and the relationships that instruments express together seem to me much closer to the way my characters, anyway, relate to each other. That's where I learn. And I think of the *timbre* of a character. I think of the range of a character. I think as you might of an instrument, that a certain character can play a certain tonal part in a novel. A tuba cannot do certain kinds of things. A violin cannot do certain kinds of things. When I'm working to make a concert of characters, I listen to chamber music and think about relationships. It's something I do in every piece of work I do. There will be certain pieces of music I associate with certain books simply because the conflicts, the resolving harmonies, the movements and tonalities *belong* to the problems that are in the book.

Painting is something I didn't know about until I was grown. I saw

13

paintings. There were portraits and paintings in my family's house. But I didn't know about paintings, begin to look at paintings seriously until I was in my early twenties. I used to go to London, England to go to the theatre. That was one of the things that drew me to that city and I still love the theatre there, but now the selling galleries are as important to me as going to the theatre.

I feel an even greater affinity with some painters and their work than I do with writers. A great many of our friends in Vancouver are painters and I live, in a sense, in the development of their work. Judy Lodge, John Korner, Tak Tanabe, Jack Shadbolt, Gordon Smith, all this work says a great deal to me about the place I'm in and about the deep values, aesthetic values, I live in terms of.

HANCOCK

Do you find that affects you as a writer, that you become a constant observer, looking hard and close? Or conversely, you look a little bit farther ahead?

RULE

I've always said that nine-tenths of the time I am functionally blind. I rarely notice a lot of details unless I sit down and force myself to. I can take a walk and not see anything. I'm lost in what I'm thinking about. I can be riding in a car and not know where I am. I think part of the importance of painting for me is to keep making me look. It's something I'm limited in so the art of painting becomes somebody else teaching me to see. Sometimes very reluctantly. The Bridget Riley restrospective in London. I didn't get over to it for six months because it's so terribly demanding an experience in thinking about light. Bridget Riley obviously does that by wandering around in the world. I really need to be broken out of my habit of obsessive concentration.

HANCOCK

Do you not learn any of that from some contemporary writers?

RULE

I can't think of any writer who jars me awake in perception as I think of music and painting jarring me awake. It's not always a jar. Often I feel interested, technically interested in other writers. I don't suppose it feels to me something I can't do for myself. I don't mean I don't learn from other writers, I certainly do. But it's a quieter, less conscious and self-conscious process.

HANCOCK

Which writers then, classic or contemporary, have you learned from?

RULE

It's hard for me to know, I have never been a person with conscious models. Once I tried to have conscious models. I went through a phase where I thought I ought to learn from Gertrude Stein. And I suppose I have

14

learned from Gertrude Stein. Probably the most influential period for me was seventeenth-century English literature, and that had to do with the long rhythmic control of prose. I don't suppose anybody reading my prose would think it sounds like a John Donne sermon. But that's where I learned how a sentence was made.

HANCOCK

Which other writers do you value, not necessarily as influences?

RULE

William Butler Yeats, Shakespeare. The contemporary novelist I read with the most excitement is Patrick White because he's doing something with language that concerns me. That is, he doesn't lose any of the rich texture and imagery, yet at the same time he's using a lot of speech rhythms. And they're Australian. There's an extraordinary flavour. I was interested to hear he wanted to live in England — that was his spiritual home obviously. He felt much more comfortable there than in raw Australia. But he couldn't live outside the sound of his own language. I feel very much that way. The sound of the spoken language is very important to me. And he teaches me all sorts of ways to use it.

I also care enormously about Harold Pinter. Again, on the stage you are dealing with sound all the time. But what he's doing with language, what he's doing with silence, what he's doing with what is *not* said is something I'm interested in learning.

HANCOCK

How do you feel about the fact that many of Canada's leading writers are women?

RULE

I don't suppose I feel any way about it. I think literature is one of the provinces where women have been allowed to work; so it's not surprising that you find more women competent at writing that you find women who can play in the orchestra or women who can paint. Writing doesn't cost any money, you can do it in a very small space and you can do it secretly. You can't sing secretly, you can't hide an enormous canvas. I think because it can be a secret activity women have been able to participate in it.

It may sound odd now, but there are still real constrictions on women doing anything but what they're supposed to be doing. You'll hear our finest women writers worried about not spending enough time with their children or not entertaining their husband's business colleagues. Stealing time. Alice Munro has a marvellous short story, where she has a woman go off and rent a room to write in. Immediately she gets involved with the landlord and his problems and feels terribly guilty and cruel that she shuts the door and won't pay attention. Even this craft is a hard one for women to practise given their training as people who help other people and don't lock themselves up and do their own thing.

15

Do these writers have enough in common to be considered as a group or generation? Or a new literary frontier?

I don't think as a literary group. It's interesting to see how many are friends, and the women's movement may have made us more conscious of that friendship. A lot of the women writing in Canada know each other, communicate with each other, share each other's work. Not necessarily in manuscript, but really read each other with interest and pleasure.

I suppose if you step back, there is one generation. But, for instance, Margaret Atwood seems to me to be a different generation from Margaret Laurence. They're not. But in the short term it seems so. They're doing very different things. Margaret Atwood is a writer with much more concern with the manipulation of language than I think any of the others but Marie-Claire Blais. But of course, we also have language to divide us so that it would be very hard to see us as a group.

Let's talk about you: do you smoke or drink too much when you work?

I don't ever drink when I work and I smoke too much all the time.

Tea, coffee, drugs?

There's a rumour about me which is true. I drink Coca-Cola for breakfast.

Was there ever a moment when you were afraid of publishing your fiction? Fear of losing friends, family, job? Or to put it another way, as an art form the novel can be particularly dangerous because it demands such a total commitment. The writer is sometimes pitted against the world in a confrontation that is more than aesthetic or intellectual. Has the novel ever been dangerous to you in that way?

I don't think of the artist as in an adversary position to his or her culture. That's alien to my whole sense of art as celebration. To think of the activity of writing the novel or the novel itself as a dangerous weapon is nothing that is in my consciousness at all. Nor do I think of myself as artist in relation to my culture as enemy, adversary, at all. Lover, more like. If there is a relationship at all and I'm not sure there is. Except perhaps my own relationship to my work while it's being done.

But back to the first part of the question. Have I ever been frightened of publishing? It's in some ways hard to look back and remember. I certainly must have been frightened because the kind of work I do was going to be a problem. I think I have been concerned to protect the people closest to me from having to take on anything that I had to take on. But there isn't any way you can protect people close to you. So you simply have to learn to relinquish that responsibility because you can't do anything about it.

I can remember a question being asked of Audrey Thomas and me: "What do you do about family and friends if you're essentially an auto-biographical novelist?" This is a question Audrey speaks to. I tried to answer in a different way because I'm not an autobiographical novelist in that sense. But I can remember writing a story that was about two people my parents' age. That's where the likeness stopped. They had a daughter who came home, thinking she wanted to break up her marriage, and, while she was home talking with her parents she discovered she was pregnant. As she discusses this with her mother, her mother tells her that she married her father because she was pregnant. This is a small point in the story. But after the story was published, someone came up to my mother and said, "I didn't know you and Art had to get married." My mother wasn't vulnerable. But there's not a thing on this earth that I can do to protect my mother from that. To be afraid for other people is something you go on doing whether you know it's your responsibility or not. I've been very fortunate in the people around me. None of them felt it was my job to protect them. They feel that's their job and that's been a great relief to me.

As far as worrying about losing a job, I have always, not only from writing, but in any other circumstances, wanted to feel that there never was a question of being worried about losing a job. I've always been a fairly good worker in whatever I've done, and I've always been able to do jobs. I mean, I have so many ghastly skills that there never would be a time that I would worry. If I needed a job, I could walk into a gambling casino and be a change girl. I'd sling hash. I'd be a clerk. I could do any number of things. I've never been afraid of work. If somebody would say, "Publish this book and you'll lose your job at the university," well, fair enough, if that's going to be the case. Life wouldn't be worth living if you lived in that kind of nervousness.

HANCOCK

Has that happened to you? You mentioned something along those lines in the introduction to *Lesbian Images*.

RULE

No. I had friends in the meetings that took place when I was considered for reappointment. I know that the issue of *Desert Of The Heart* came up after it was published. One person on the committee said "How can you hire the person who's written this terrible book?" All the other people on the committee said, "Have you read it?" That was the first question. This person hadn't. His only knowledge of it was reading Jack Wasserman's review in the *Vancouver Sun*. I felt rather sorry for him. His colleagues took a dim view of him taking his literary judgements, or any other, from the *Sun*. So, I think I was defended as I said in the introduction to *Lesbian Images*, along the lines that a murder-story writer doesn't necessarily murder people, which is a silly argument.

17

Have you had censorship problems? The *Canadian Fiction Magazine* had censorship problems this year. In fact, our printer in Manitoba refused to print us. They objected to "certain language and descriptive material," none of which they would define or specify, though I gather several men at their plant were Mennonites. Have you had censorship problems also?

RULE

Yes. When *Desert Of The Heart* was accepted in England, where it first found a publisher, at the last minute they decided to send the manuscript to their solicitors. The solicior sent me a libel report on each character and publication was stopped.

HANCOCK

What's a libel report?

RULE

A libel report is a report on each one of the characters as if they were real people. Well, it's only libellous if the people are real. But in England the libel laws are so severe the onus is on the writer to prove the people aren't real. Well, if you stop to think about that, that's a pretty difficult thing to do. It would be easy to prove a character is based on fact, but to prove a character isn't is baffling. There is no method for doing it. I had to take the date out of the book. I wasn't allowed to say it was a particular year. The book had been set in Harold's Club and I had been very particular to get all the details accurately. I had to change the name of the club. I had to change all the slogans that are identified with Harold's Club. I had to look up all the names of my characters in the Reno phone book and I found one. I wanted to call her up and say, "You don't exist; leave town at once." So I had to change the name right there in the downtown office of the Vancouver telephone company. Then I had to look up *that* name to make sure it wasn't in the Reno telephone book.

The solicitors argued that even if all the characters were fictional characters, as I claimed, if there was a specific date and a specific place of employment, anybody who had the job of a change apron at Harold's Club at that time on that floor could claim I had represented them scurrilously; that any character as tall as Silver was easily identifiable, particularly when married to a little man. I had to write back and say, "Look, to my certain knowledge there was no one in Harold's Club as tall as Silver except myself, and I promise not to sue either you or me."

Well, they said change the date of her birth. I said I made it up in the first place. There's no point in changing all this stuff which is fictional to begin with. The book was held up for months. And the final changes were, in a sense, minor. But it's too bad to have the date out of the book because there's a lot of very specific detail. By the time the book was published, it was, I should think, six or seven years out of date in terms of the setting of Reno, Nevada. The review of the book in Reno was heartbreaking. They were outraged that I was representing Reno as having a piddling little airport when they had a brand new one; that their public library was so awful when they had a brand new one. And I didn't blame them. That's very hard to deal with. What I had to do didn't essentially change the book, but it was very irritating and very stupid.

Have similar circumstances happened to your other books?

No. I know a lot of places won't buy them, but a lot of places won't buy any books, especially with the subject matter as it's described.

Do you like to teach writing?

I don't suppose I ever have. I was at UBC as a visiting lecturer in the Creative Writing Department, but it didn't feel to me like teaching, as teaching in the English Department did. I did a lot of listening, and a lot of directing traffic in discussion. I did a lot of teaching people to read because I found that was the one thing the students were poor at generally. They didn't read each other's work with very good critical perception. So I spent a lot of my time talking about what it was to be a reader and a critic. But I don't think I did very much about teaching writing. I think I don't know how. A creative-writing class is a marvellous thing. I took them when I was in college. I don't remember much I was taught, but I do remember that was the meeting place and the growing place and the sharing place of my college life. Sometimes the comments were good, sometimes they were stupid. I learned to write by writing. The more time and the better environment you create for that, the better for the young writer. I don't suppose what I have to say about writing is very important to any student except in the most extraordinarily simple specifics. There may be one moment when you can talk about a stylistic problem when it will mean something to a particular student. If you teach at all, you have to have a sympathetic enough, empathetic enough, perceptive enough awareness of where the other writer is so that what you have to say is useful.

And what you have to say may be useful. Have you ever really thought about the fact that the subject and verb should, usually, carry the weight of the sentence? Someone said that to me when I was a sophomore in college and it was a total revelation. I went around as if I'd seen God! I don't see why no one had told me that in the third grade, but no one had. I'd learned Latin, with all those marvellous ways to build, I had so many dependent clauses you couldn't believe it and I was a genius at them. So just the *notion* of how to use the subject and verb . . .

Can you teach and write at the same time?

I can't. Certainly lots of people have. I tried to, but my students made me resent my writing and my writing made me resent my students. The same kind of energy goes into both. Usually I tried to teach every other year so I could give myself entirely to that job which I love and then have an entire year to spend on my own work. It's the same sort of energy, but it's almost inside out. Even trying to do magazine articles was difficult. Not anywhere as difficult as trying to write fiction, but you still write without any skin. To do that for two hours, then walk into a classroom where a teacher should be so invulnerable that any kind of test can go on. You're there to be one of those round-bottom toys that people can really bash. Being a punching bag is part of your job. It's very difficult to move from having no skin, then walk into a classroom to say now I'm a punching bag. It's hard on the nervous system.

HANCOCK

Malcolm Lowry said that Gabriola Island, just north of here, was Paradise. Do you feel the same way about Galiano?

RULE

No. Galiano is a convenient place for me to be. It's more isolated than I have been and I need a privacy of time. I like it. But it doesn't have any of the magic implied in a Paradise.

HANCOCK

Do you have a reader in mind when you write?

RULE

Myself five years hence. I say that because the process of writing for me is a process of discovering and disciplining and requiring my mind and imagination. That's why I do it. I want to be absolutely sure that no marvellous image or stylistic twirl which I can admire right now as "wow!" gets left in and doesn't carry the clarity that will make sense to me coming to that work as a stranger five years hence. I want to know what I thought. I want to know what I meant and it may be pretty, it may be eloquent, it may be funny. Those are things I can admire at the moment and know that five years hence the reader is going to look at it and say, what? Were you showing off there? What do you mean? I want to know. And I want to write for a reader who really wants to know so that I can really say as clearly as I can.

HANCOCK

That must take a great deal of testing of your pages.

RULE

I don't do as much revising as I used to. Partly because I have learned certain limits and certain skills and I keep learning new ones. I don't imagine I ever will not. But when I first started writing! I think I must have written the first chapter of *Desert Of The Heart* thirty-five times. It was partly because I didn't know how to write the first chapter. I just had to keep trying different points of view. Is this where the story really begins? I didn't know how to decide any of those things ahead of time. I didn't have enough experience to be able to see the pitfalls until they were right there on the page. So some of the rewriting I've done was simply to learn on paper what I didn't know before.

HANCOCK

Do you keep a notebook?

RULE

Yes, I keep extensive notebooks when I'm working on a particular piece of work.

At the end of the working day, when I'm working on a novel, I almost always sit down and write down the problems I'm having, the questions I'm having, the things I ought to go back and figure out, the projected work. I really talk to myself about where I am.

I can go, however, two or three weeks without turning to that notebook. But then there might be a week when I do notebook work and nothing else. Usually when I'm stuck on something.

HANCOCK

When you start on something, are you like a surfer, sitting at your desk, waiting for that big surge of emotion to carry you to the page?

RULE

No.

HANCOCK

Do you have a regular discipline?

RULE

Absolutely. If I waited for the surge I'd never write anything. I sit down and get to work. I'm not really aware of time once I'm at my desk. I think this is going to be a problem for me now because I can't spend the hours at my desk that I used to because my spine has been weakened with arthritis.

I would suppose that the first hour at my desk I do very little writing but I'm not really aware of time. I'm going to have to start being aware of time now. I can probably do the first hour lying on my back on the couch and be at the desk only when I actually need to be. But five hours can go by and I'm not aware of it at all. I don't move once I start to work. I'm just there.

HANCOCK

Are you a night writer or a day writer?

RULE

By temperament I would be a night writer and in the early days that was the only time I had to write. But that's socially very inconvenient and once I had full days to write, I taught myself to start, not terribly early in the morning, but from say ten to around three. I never work more than five hours. If I do, I'm sure to wreck what I'm doing.

HANCOCK

Do you get writer's blocks, the feeling as John Steinbeck put it, "that your work is like a raw egg on the kitchen floor and just won't coagulate"?

RULE

That's an awful image! I don't think I do get writer's blocks. I dread that time between pieces of work when I know that, if I'm to find the next subject, I'm going to do what Jack Shadbolt calls "creative loafing." I'm not very good at that. If I don't have anything specific in mind, I would far rather do the wash or go for a walk, or talk with a friend. I know there's a certain amount of time I have to be absolutely still and absolutely un-distracted and simply let my mind open to what is next. I'm much happier once a work is going.

HANCOCK

Do you type? Or write with pen or pencil?

RULE

I almost always compose on the typewriter. I sometimes, for reasons I don't understand, do longhand for articles. Maybe because an article starts while I'm reading a book and I'm not actually at my desk. My handwriting is very bad. I guess I'm one of the last generation where to be left-handed was not acceptable. In some schools it was perfectly fine to be left-handed and in others you weren't allowed to be so. I was shifted back and forth. I not only didn't know how to multiply or read, I couldn't write either. A basket case. When I was twelve, my father brought home a typewriter and plunked it down and said use both hands and tell them to go to hell. So I've been typing since I was twelve.

HANCOCK

Do you imagine everything or write from memory?

RULE

I don't think I make a very clear distinction between imagining and remembering. I think of imagining as "imaging forth," and a great deal of what goes on in my books is *planned*. I am not simply saying I'm writing this down because this is actually what happened. I'm writing this down because I planned. Which doesn't seem to me imagining. It's more like making a blueprint. The actual making of it is imagining, but it's "im-agining forth the plan." Some of this comes from memory; most of it comes from a kind of conglomerate.

HANCOCK

Is there a unique process by which this comes to you?

RULE

I'm not quite sure I know what you mean.

HANCOCK

To put it another way, is there a starting place for a fiction?

RULE

Not that I could pinpoint. Sometimes the oddest thing happens to me. I will be doing notebook work and I will hear a kind of attitude – I call it a voice, a quarrelling voice, or an ecstatic voice, or a lecturing voice – that isn't really something I'm thinking about. But I hear the tonalities and I begin to play around with it. It's like hearing a melody and I write it down. I don't know who the character is. That may sit, all two paragraphs of it, for months. Then, when I'm looking through notebooks during this in-between period which I like so little, that voice sound can connect with an idea I've had. I think, "Oh, that really is the minor character I've been looking for in this particular slot in the book." And there it sits. Very few things come to me all at once. They come in bits and pieces and gradually fit together. Then it's time to write.

HANCOCK

How long does it take to write a book? Do you plan a certain length of time?

RULE

If I have the free time to work, I can usually anticipate how long it's going to take. Sometimes it's hard for me to know how long it's going to take me to write a particular section, or how long it's going to be, I don't always have the sense that this is a ten-page part of the book. It may turn out to be a fifty-page section and then my time is different. But I usually expect to write two or three pages a day. I work seven days a week and I don't keep all those pages.

HANCOCK

Do titles come easily?

RULE

Some. And some don't come at all. I'm better at titles than I used to be. They don't seem to me as baffling. At first, writing titles absolutely dumbfounded me. What is this thing's *name*? I know that I've been criticized by publishers for titles. But they loved the latest. They think it will sell the book.

HANCOCK

What is it?

RULE

The Young In One Another's Arms and most people who approve of it don't know the Yeats poem it comes from and how dark the implication is. It'll look fine in cheap paperback.

But my sense of a title is — the thing I want a title to do is to say something about the experience of reading after you've read the book or story. So that you look back at the title and say. "Uh huh, that's right."

Of course, a publisher wants a title to be a come-on and I'm just not interested in a title as that at all. I can see why they are. I don't have any quarrel with publishers. But it's just not my sense of what a title does.

HANCOCK

Your style depends very heavily on conversation, and almost in a Pinter sense, is very tight. You use the spaces between the words and lines. I felt as I was reading that the words were almost the ends of sentences embedded deeply in the dramatic action. The prose, as a result, is very difficult to

23

skim. The words, in fact, have to be read line on line. Do you find dialogue easier to write than narrative?

RULE

Quicker. It either has to be going right or I throw the whole conversation out and begin again.

With a narrative part it seems I'm far more able to fix something inside, a paragraph that isn't quite working. But if I've got a tonality that's gone off in a dialogue, I've got to start all over again.

HANCOCK

Would you comment on the source of this style?

RULE

I don't really know. I think a lot about what dialogue does, what its jobs are. I know dialogue is the least informational part of a work. Other writers use dialogue to carry a lot of the freight of the work. I don't. There's very little information exchanged between characters in my work. All of the information in the dialogue I write is emotional information.

HANCOCK

Do you read it aloud?

RULE

I don't read it aloud at all. I have been conned into doing it occasionally. But everything I write is read to me by at least two other people. Out loud. That's part of my working process. The minute I finish a draft of a chapter, Helen reads it aloud. I don't want her to read it beforehand. I want her to read it as she first sees it. And Shelagh Day reads aloud to me. Also several other people. But I need at least two other people so I can hear it when my voice isn't controlling it. I know that I want this next exchange to be angry. I wrote it. I know the stage directions. They're in my head. Well, I have to find out for sure that the tone is implicit in the sentences on the page. There's no use in my reading, even to a tape recorder, and playing it back. Because I'm directing the traffic of those sentences.

By now the danger is Helen knows my work so well she can anticipate certain things. She can guess where the emotional tonality will be next. So I always look for at least one new reader.

Most people only read a book or story once. What's coming at them has to be there if they'll pay attention. I know a lot of people find my dialogue difficult because you really have to *listen*, you really have to *hear* what people are saying. You can't glance through it to see what time breakfast is.

HANCOCK

Is the emotional load the only load the dialogue carries?

RULE

That's the main load. That's a big one because it is the whole tonality of relationships.

HANCOCK

How many drafts do you do?

24

Basically three. And the last one is nearly always a very minor touch-up. In a book I don't go on to the next chapter until I've got the one right. So a lot of my revision is revision in process.

HANCOCK

Is there anything now, five years later, that you dislike in your books?

RULE

Oh yes, I can look back on certain extravagances of image, or simply ignorance of how to do a transition. I think, my goodness, it took a long time to learn how to stop those people talking and start writing a description. Simple basic things like that. I hope I'm better at it.

HANCOCK

Do you use stylistic tricks? Inverting word orders, phrases?

RULE

I think that I always hope for, strive for, a clarity. I try to work away from mannerisms. That's very difficult.

HANCOCK

What do you mean by mannerisms?

RULE

Favourite devices, favourite words. There's a stylistic trick that I'm currently trying to kill like a fly in my study. I add "or not" to an observation or general statement, liking the rhythms, liking the small challenge. It's got to be a habit and habits in writing are terrible. And the older you get the more mannerisms are natural to you and the more you have to fight them.

HANCOCK

When you're writing a book, do you do big scenes first, or do you blueprint the entire book, complete with names and synopsis?

RULE

I'm a blueprint writer. It's a tight weave that I work with. I couldn't possibly write a tight scene until I prepared all the ingredients, were sure they were there. There isn't a big scene for me really. Whatever scene it is, is so dependent on what has gone before that it's tightened into the fabric of the narrative. I was fascinated when Joyce Cary talked about picking out the important scenes in a book for him and rewriting them from three or four different points of view to see how they'd come out. He worked that way a good deal. I never could. There wouldn't be anything to say until I got there. So much of it for me is on the way. All of it, in a way.

HANCOCK

How do you communicate the emotional essence of a scene to the reader?

RULE

In all sorts of ways. One of the most important things for me is to make a character clear enough in the emotional position he or she is in so that I can have characters speak "angrily" or "happily" without having to give those stage directions. Part of this is preparation so that a reader who is paying close attention would know how this character is feeling at that moment. And I work very carefully with spoken language, vocabulary and rhythms that manifest the emotion so I don't have to direct.

I run into trouble every now and again. Occasionally I write a story that's suitable for *Chatelaine* or *Redbook*. *Redbook* is particularly bewildering in the questions they ask about my fiction. I'll write a story that seems to me so simple-minded as almost to be embarrassing. I'll get a four-page letter back that says, "When the young mother picks up the baby, does that indicate she's spoiling the baby, or loving the baby?" Everything I've learned to leave out is supposed to go back in. "She picked up the baby and clutched it possessively." Those awful stage directions! And at the end of this letter — "If we can't understand it, think of the poor reader." I thought, I *am* thinking of the poor reader.

But a lot of people do feel my work is not obvious in tonality. It seems to me totally obvious. But again, that's working with an effect of image, of landscape, of moment, of building character. All those things working together all the time.

HANCOCK

Do you sometimes get the feeling you're juggling too many things in the air?

RULE

I can dread things that I feel will be hard to pull off. I find the scenes I dread most are the easiest to write, because I've obviously been worried about them long enough to really prepare for them. The ones that I think are going to be a lead-pipe cinch turn out to be just ghastly in difficulty.

HANCOCK

When you blueprint a novel, are you conscious of "novelistic form," a plot development working itself out, a rising action, climax, dénouement? Or do you use those terms?

RULE

I don't think in those terms. I don't think of myself as a dramatic writer. I think of myself as far more interested in rhythms in a book that are closer to music — not Beethoven — closer to chamber music which has moments of intensity. I don't think in terms of plot.

HANCOCK

More like fast movement, slow movement?

RULE

Yes.

HANCOCK

Could you give me some examples of what might be called "dramatic" or "intense" moments in your fiction?

RULE

I'm not at all certain I know what that is in my fiction. I said to somebody the other day, "You know, I don't think there are any dramatic moments in my writing." Well, what do I mean by drama? Then I hear I have a prejudice against the word, that I don't like drama, that it means melodrama — fist fights and car crashes and late-night nightmares. Those are things I'm not really interested in experiencing or writing about.

In the rhythms of my work where the intensity is most evident to me — and whether this is true for the reader or not, I don't know — is in moments of insight, or emotional revelation. This can be not very important at all in the action structure. Action in my work isn't really the significant part of it. It's the minor bone structure. Somebody wrote a review of *This Is Not For You* saying, "I read this book and I have to go back ten pages to see that what happened was very important to the character, but it went by so quietly, it was as if it were my own life." And I thought, that's *exactly* the texture I want. Not, "And suddenly she *knew* . . ." I don't think people suddenly know anything. We finally realize things. So I don't think about dramatic moments very much.

HANCOCK

In another context, you said that the engagement was more important than the wedding.

RULE

Yes. The wedding is simply the outward manifestation. The wedding is the dénouement. I had to find that out when I was writing *Desert Of The Heart*. I was still thinking about great occasions as the dramatic arrival point. And every great occasion I've written about was the dénouement when I thought it was supposed to be the climax. I've just had to learn I don't think that way. I don't see living that way. I see most ceremony as boring, embarrassing, difficult and if I'm going to deal with it, I'm going to deal with it like that rather than as the great occasion we're taught to think. It's like graduating from college. If you think about your very important moments, very few of them are those that we designate as important. Most of the time we get through those in a, well, near-catatonic state.

HANCOCK

You once used the expression, "backtracking the drama." What do you mean by that?

RULE

Precisely the same thing. This business of thinking the arrival point is the wedding, when in fact, the revelation of that relationship happened sometime long before that. The wedding is the symbolic representation of something that happened before. Don't think of the wedding, the funeral, the graduation as the arrival, as the obvious thing happening outside, when the important things are happening inside. In order to understand the real rhythm you have to backtrack it first and find out where it really happened and what really happened.

Do you find the concept of a book changes from the original idea?
Not very much. This book I've just finished — it's coming out in March, 1977 — I have changed the concept of it on purpose. I started to write it, I don't know how many years ago, say eight — and I saw the shape of it. I simply looked at it and I thought I'm not going to write that — that is going to make the kind of statement that may or may not be true. I don't want to make it. It's bleak, in a way that is not anything for me to say. So, I said this is a book I'm not going to write and that's that.

But the characters kept tugging at my sleeve. They were fairly far along in development by the time I decided to desert them. As if they were saying if you want to play that game, you go ahead and play, but I'm not playing with you. The original end of that book is in the middle of the book now. So I've taken them all past the structure that I first imagined. It's the only time I've ever done that. It was a very conscious decision and basically a moral decision.

HANCOCK

Is the novel to be an emotional experience for the reader, in the sense of a well-told story having an elegantly constructed form and the right moral values?

RULE

I don't know what a book is supposed to be for the reader. That's something outside my control and outside my interest even. There are ways people use my books that I don't like. I have books used as if they were propaganda and I don't like that. But there's nothing I can do about it. Each book is so particular in its experience that I suppose a book is written for a reader to experience it as I do, sentence by sentence. That's the only experience we share, the sentences.

HANCOCK

So it isn't the writer's duty, as you see it, to perpetuate moral values?

RULE

No, no. I don't really believe a moral value is a shared thing in the sense that you can teach it or preach it. I think you can communicate qualities and values that you yourself perceive. But whether or not someone else takes those is not my business.

HANCOCK

So as a writer you just have to perceive things as clearly and as truthfully as you can.

RULE

I think the difference between art and propaganda is this. The business of art is to manifest what is and propaganda is working at trying to make what ought to be. I'm not even interested in what ought to be most of the time. Now, I can get on a band wagon, but I know perfectly well it's a frivolous activity compared to manifesting what is.

HANCOCK

When you're constructing your novels, do you consciously work cycles into them? *Against The Season* has the death and birth ending . . .

RULE

As does the new book . . .

HANCOCK

. . . and in *Theme For Diverse Instruments*, every story seems to suggest the house is a potential prison. Are these consciously worked in or do you just arrive at them?

RULE

They certainly aren't in *Theme For Diverse Instruments*. That's a collection of stories that spreads over twenty years. The first thing I noticed was how many stories I liked that had "house" in the title. Then, David Robinson (publisher of Talonbooks) asked me to find a painting for the cover — and he was determined it was to be a painting — and I was reluctant to use one because I don't like using a painting as if it were an illustration. I get very nervous about that. But then I remembered a painting of Judy Lodge's that seemed to me just right. It's the interior of a house. Obviously interiors are very important to me. There are an awful lot of them in *This Is Not For You*. I didn't plan it that way, of course. Each one of the stories is a thing in itself.

As for the rhythm of seasons, I'm sure that will always be there. When I'm dealing with a group of people, if there is a long enough span of time, it's just one of the natural rhythms that you do deal with. It's just *there*.

HANCOCK

When your characters can't communicate their feelings, how does your "novel-language," if there is such a term, reveal the loneliness or the guilt or even the happiness of women who can love other women? I refer to just the prose itself. How is the prose controlled?

RULE

I don't deal very often with the circumstances of characters who can't communicate with each other. You're probably thinking of *This Is Not For You* in your question. There the whole device is of someone talking to herself, apparently writing a letter to somebody else as a way of articulating what is otherwise silence. If you pose a problem of someone who will not communicate, you've got to find a form that will both express the refusal to say and express what hasn't been said.

Now, in *This Is Not For You*, there's an awful lot that Kate never does say. So you have to work with irony. I mean she never does say she's appalled at what she has done. But over and over again, in ironies you set this up so that you know she must be appalled or she wouldn't be trying to justify. So justification becomes a tonal way of saying what isn't said. "Methinks the lady doth protest too much."

29

HANCOCK

Yes, I see. Your major characters are often well educated, intelligent, professionals. Evelyn in *Desert Of The Heart* has a PhD in English, Ann is a professional cartoonist. In *This Is Not For You*, Kate studies economics and Esther ultimately becomes a nun. As a result your prose in places becomes abstract and intellectual. *Desert Of The Heart*, in fact, even includes an essay on Nevada and the flaws in human nature — at least I read it as an essay.

RULE

Yes.

HANCOCK

And in *This Is Not For You*, in several places you question the "moral sickness of a conservative Church." In *Against The Season*, you touch, though less overtly, upon myth and the many varieties of human relationships. A comment on this?

RULE

One of the things that troubles me about a lot of accessible fiction is that it is important not to use your head, as if ideas were not part and parcel of real experience. That there is the ivory tower and then there is real life. Certainly in my own living, I have known, and lived with, and moved among people who are educated, intelligent and in dealing with parts of their own life use ideas. It's very important to incorporate intelligence, abstract intelligence. To me it's as important as the seasons. It's part of real living. I don't think that ideas govern life. I don't think that morality governs life, but it's part of the fabric of living which our society has set apart. You have to be a scholar, or, you're a creative writer. A scholar functions with his or her intelligence and a creative writer functions in an emotional, intuitive and aesthetic way. That seems to me a silly division. I can't think of people functioning without their training or intelligence. Some of the characters I deal with are highly trained people and highly trained people use what they know.

HANCOCK

Do you like to experiment with prose?

RULE

Yes. It's an important thing for me to do. I don't publish very much of the experimenting because I do it to push to whatever extreme limits I need, to find out how a device will work. Very occasionally I publish an experimental piece like "Theme For Diverse Instruments," the title story in the collection. And there are one or two other stories in that collection I consider experimental. But experimenting for me is primarily an exercise to learn something about the language.

A great deal — I suppose half my writing time — is my very private writing time and stuff that I don't send out. It doesn't seem to me necessarily sharable. I think of experimentation as an important part of my technical experience, not necessarily an important part of the shared experience.

You have the deepest respect and concern for your characters. Where do they come from? And how do you get them beyond stereotypes?

When I'm conceiving a character it's a conglomerate, not just people I've known, but of experiences I've watched people deal with. I wouldn't do a portrait of someone I know. Occasionally there's a fictionalized portrait, but mostly it's a conglomerate. I'm not interested in creating a character and living with a character unless I am really interested in and respectful of the experience that's involved. I would be bored creating characters I felt condescending to. You have to live with characters for a long time and I don't want to spend a great deal of time with people or ideas that I don't honour.

Now, I disagree violently with some of my characters. The most extreme example is the main character in *This Is Not For You*. Her vision is entirely opposed to my own. But she was an intelligent adversary. I tried not to be in an adversary position. Instead, I shut up my own sense and tried to get inside hers. It was a requirement, sometimes a tiring one. By the time I finished that book, I felt I had lockjaw because Kate is so *tight*. But it was worth it. It was an important requirement, an important concern. I don't think I'd ever want to write dealing with concepts or people for whom I had no respect. There would be no point for me.

And in doing so, you can get away from the concept of women in motorcycle jackets?

It's not a concept that I've ever had. I think it's important to talk about the lesbian material in my books. It's certainly there, it's there very strongly and I suspect it always will be. I don't think of it, as I'm sure a great deal of my audience does, as a kind of special ghetto group in the world. I have never lived in a subculture, I have never felt excluded from the human family or job or social life. I feel as if the popular attitude toward lesbian experience does make clichés, does make ghettoes. Most of the homosexuals I know live in the ordinary community, working, having dinner parties, being themselves and being known. And yet there's the persistent sense that homosexuals are defined by their sexuality and excluded by their sexuality. I never have been, nor have numbers of my friends. The sense that homosexuality had to do with the bars downtown or motorcycles or costumes. There are a number of people who are homosexuals, who are heterosexuals, who like motorcycles and leather jackets. I would imagine if you lived in that world and knew those people, you would write about them as people, just as I write about people.

31

The sense, however, in society, is that special sexuality is totally defining and limiting. I'm not writing to try to prove that isn't so. I'm simply writing out of my sense of the world as I live in it. But there are so many misconceptions. One of the difficulties of my fiction is getting through to a sensibility that expects, first of all, it ought to be erotic because that's the only point in writing about people who are homosexual, and second, there is something morally depraved about it. Or, conversely, my fiction should connect readers with a whole sense of love, wonder and liberation.

I certainly don't write about love, wonder and liberation in any circumstance because we're all hedged around with requirements, bewilderments and questions. Many of the characters I write about are not homosexual. I think one of the most offensive things in my work for people who are defensive about it is that the people I write about who are homosexual, are not ghettoized, are not excluded, are not strange, peculiar, sick people. That's very scary. It's like saying, "These are human beings." And that's the one thing you musn't say. You can say, "These are depraved, wild people," and everyone will buy the book. You can say, "These are the liberated people who are going to teach us how to live in zero population and why don't you all get on the band-wagon?" And that's perfectly acceptable. But when I say Rosemary and Dina live in a little city, or a big town and move about in a community with all different kinds of people, and have dinner with people and go to restaurants and buy property and worry about their own needs and concerns, then that's really scary. I don't know why. But I think that's where a lot of the distorted criticism comes from.

HANCOCK

So you write to explore character?

RULE

Yes.

HANCOCK

As a result of that, do you contrive situations to reveal character?

RULE

Yes, certainly.

HANCOCK

For example, how do you get all your characters together at a party? *Against The Season* has a big party at the end.

RULE

Yes, it's one of those dénouements, isn't it? It's not the place where everything is revealed. It's the place where everything is celebrated.

I think of the gathering of people as a kind of formal dance. Every now and again you want to hear all the instruments play together. A large group, a party — and that's hard to handle in prose, isn't it? Because you have only that one thin line. You don't have all the instruments playing together and I can sometimes feel very envious of a composer. He can gather all his instruments together, all his musicians together and they

32

can all blow at the same time, or bow at the same time. But essentially, it's wanting to get all those tonalities together. And they all have to give space to each other because in prose they can only appear one at a time. But to try to create the illusion of all together is an interesting technical problem.

HANCOCK

Do you find party scenes difficult?

RULE

Fascinating technically. It's a slow business of working everything out so it balances.

HANCOCK

I have favourite characters in your books. Agate, Silver, Grace Hardwick. Do you have favourites?

RULE

I have holiday characters in my books. Agate is one, Silver is one. Monk is the holiday character in *This Is Not For You,* the character who can break the tension when everything gets very earnest and very uptight.

I *always* need a character who can badmouth a bit, who can cool it, who can clown it. These are characters I find very easy to write.

HANCOCK

What do you mean by a "holiday character"?

RULE

Well, I can take a holiday from the earnestness and tension and whatever is going on with the other characters.

In the new book, the best character for me, the holiday character, doesn't appear for five chapters. The first chapter doesn't produce him. His name is Boy Wonder and he's the most bad-mouthing character I've ever created. At the moment he's my favourite character because I've most recently lived with him. He really does restore a kind of sanity which I think the comic characters do.

I always liked Monk. *This Is Not For You* is the most earnest, intense of the books I've written and I found it the most tedious. Though Monk doesn't come into it as much as some of the holiday characters in other books, she was an *enormous* relief every time she arrived to get a little levity into the atmosphere.

HANCOCK

Your physical descriptions of characters are very sparse.

RULE

Yes, I suppose that goes along with what I call my functional blindness. I don't often notice physical detail in itself unless it's a strong signal. But the person who is concerned, upset about something, or shy about coming into the room — these human and emotional messages are very vivid to me.

I'm not particularly interested in physical description. Occasionally it's important. But it's lip service for me. I give characters physical tags because other people seem to think that physical reality is very important. For me, the "vibrations" of a character are very important and I spend a lot of time on that. It doesn't seem to me to matter very much what length their fingers are or what their clothes look like.

Now occasionally it does. For example, Dina (in *Against The Season*) is encased in her clothes. The physical description is there to say this person is very physically self-protective.

I think now I do more physical description than I used to. My eyes rest on the physical person more, and perhaps that's age. I begin to think the physical presence we walk around in is a frail, mortal thing. I see it as lovelier now.

But I've been bored by what our culture has taught us about physical appearance. I've been bored by people being read by their appearance, by the limitations of the cliché responses. Using physical description would often mean putting a barrier between the reader and what I want to say about the character.

HANCOCK

Have you had problems creating characters, male or female? I noticed several of your male characters seem very indecisive, that they can be pushed around quite easily. Or am I reading them wrong?

RULE

I was particularly interested in the criticism of characters in *Against The Season*. This book deals with a great range of characters, male and female. People seemed to think the male characters were weak and indecisive. I think, Carl? Weak and indecisive? He's grieving about his wife and he's uncertain about what he wants to do with his life. Amelia is grieving about her sister and nobody says she's weak and indecisive. I have a feeling people also think Cole is weak and indecisive. I think Cole is young and I don't expect nineteen-, twenty-, twenty-one-year-old males to be confident of who they are, absolutely in control of everything. Agate *is* weak and indecisive. She can't make up her mind about the abortion, or what to do with the baby. But Agate is female. She's allowed to be indecisive. Cole is the same age. He's got his kinds of hang-ups. I think of Cole as a strong character. He's endearing, he's bewildered. He handles an enormous amount of emotional freight by the time the book is through and he grows very strongly.

But our culture says that if you admit a man misses his wife, you admit that a man or boy is a bit frightened of sex and isn't quite sure how you deal with people and even wonders whether you shake hands or stand with your hands to your sides, you've got a Caspar Milquetoast because boys are born confident. People are oddly unsympathetic to the emotional insides of males. I don't feel as if I've created any weak males. I've created people who have doubts. The bank manager in that book is a perfectly confident man out there in public. He happens to be very bewildered in some of his interior choices. Name me a man who is not.

34

But I am a woman, I am a lesbian, so if I write a male character and he is uncertain, I'm doing something bad to men. I'm ruining their image. I feel as if all the male characters in that book are strong, perceptive, open and growing people. I think Carl is a beauty. He can go to the old people's home, he can hold Amelia's hand, he can say, "We don't grieve well, either one of us. We don't know how to do it." He has the guts to propose to Ida and to go through the embarrassment of that and face his own needs. I think he's one of the strongest people in the book. So, indecisive about what? About the things one ought to be indecisive about, about the things one doesn't know.

And Cole is funny. He's vulnerable. But think of the things he copes with as a kid. My youngest crew in the creative-writing seminar always had the same first comment whenever a story was read. "This character is immature." Well I'd say, "This character is only eighteen." But they were eighteen and you're not supposed to be immature when you're eighteen.

But I feel people take male characters and say, "Either they conquer the world, or they're weak characters." When you say they're indecisive, are they really and truly indecisive compared to the people you know? In what ways?

HANCOCK
Do you judge your characters?

RULE
Not in any conventional way, no. I suppose I judge them before I make them and the ones I feel judgemental about I don't write.

HANCOCK
So you don't have control over your characters?

RULE
Oh, ultimately yes. One of the scariest things about writing, and one of the things that frightens me about plot is that you can be entirely unjudgemental in your comment, but you kill certain people and you let other people have a nice time. So that the whole process of just exposing people to things is a terrifyingly judgemental business.

One of the things in plot that frightens me so, and that I find so reprehensible in Dickens is that he's perfectly proud to go around killing small children so we all will be better social beings, and, if he wants to marry a woman to someone her social superior, he's got to figure out his audience will think that wrong unless he gives her smallpox first and then it's ok.

Well, I withdraw from that. But there is no way a novelist escapes final judgement of a character, or a judgement of the whole environment they live in, by what happens to those characters. Some of them live; some of them die. Some get born; some don't. Some of them lose arms and eyes. Some don't get the people they want. So who's doing that? I am.

HANCOCK
Could you tell me a bit about the germination of your first novel, *Desert Of The Heart*?

35

Gosh, that's so far back . . . I think I knew the thematic structure of the book before I knew the package of the book. I wanted to write a book that dealt with what the world said was pointless, purposeless, sterile. I wanted to write about how people worked, how people loved, how people dealt with the land. And take those values that we get in western culture. The claim, or the justification is, what you do is productive. You marry and have children. You make a product that is important and you transform the land into land that works for you. You grow your crops and you produce a living. I'd lived in the desert. I'd lived in the environment of business. It seemed the gambling business was a kind of metaphor for Ford Motor Co., or the university or anything else. But there it was, perfectly clear to me. It was just there as a kind of ingenious way to spend time, that provided a living. I wanted to write a book about activities, ways of life, that had no justification inside our value system.

HANCOCK

What problems, technical or otherwise, did *Desert Of The Heart* create?

RULE

Oh, point of view. It's a ping-pong match finally, as I conceived it. I wrote about fifty pages of the book from Ann's point of view. I wrote fifty pages from Evelyn's point of view. I wrote fifty pages of the book from an omniscient author point of view. God knows what else. I started the book five years too early in the story. Then I condensed it in time to six weeks, just trying to hang onto it. The form of it. Narrowing it down to what I could get hold of. I had many too many ideas. Much too much for a book. I remember thinking, "I'll just get a form that traps me so I can't go off in all these directions." I still wrote some essays. I still got some of this stuff into it.

HANCOCK

Do you think now it was a technical mistake to slip an essay or two into the book?

RULE

No. I wish I'd known how to solve it. I could solve it better now than I did then. But I excluded a lot from the book which was rightly there. Though most people feel I put too much in that I shouldn't have. But there were many more goodies that I was very disciplined and left out. It was a rich book for me.

HANCOCK

Would you comment on your attitude towards characters who keep relationships at a distance? Orphans, overseas foster children, adopted children are common motifs throughout your fiction.

RULE

What I'm interested in in relationships is suggested there. The novel has importantly dealt with families, with the structures of a small town where you really inherit your concerns and your cares. But most of us have moved into an urban world where we leave our families behind and where we leave the small town or farm values behind. We're left free to choose for ourselves. It is no longer important for any human being's survival that he or she marry; we're all free to marry or not, to have children or not. We have the mechanization to be able to do that. You can take away all of the requirements of human connection, of human interdependence, all the structures for it anyway.

What interests me is watching people detached from all those requirements, figuring out ways to build a human community that is satisfying and nourishing to them. I am often concerned with voluntary relationships, with the choice. Because I think that's where we are. I think it's a much more common experience.

We don't think of it as the common experience, but look about, particularly in urban worlds. How many people do we adopt as sister, as brother, as child, as friend, as surrogate-parent? How do we recreate the generations, not so close and demanding and genetically owing? We still want human community and we create it in all sorts of different ways.

For instance, in *Against The Season*, the only blood relationship is one with the dead. Amelia's sister is dead. All the other relationships are voluntary. There isn't one that is a simple requirement. You have to say, "No, I don't want to take care of my mother for the rest of my life. I want to be free. I don't want to be like my Daddy. I want to be free." All those characters have left that world behind. So how do they build a community of human care? The next book is about the same thing. That's what I'm interested in writing about. Voluntary human relationships.

HANCOCK

Would you tell me how *This Is Not For You* began?

RULE

That came more out of anger than any book I've ever written. Having known an awful lot of people like Kate, intelligent, articulate and self-protective, who seemed to me very ungenerous in the way they lived. But I think the exercise was not so much to express anger, but to get inside the character to understand that point of view. Kate is a composite of half a dozen people.

HANCOCK

What was the source behind the entire novel as an unmailed letter? Why this structure?

RULE

Well, if there is somebody who refuses to admit the position she is in and wants to justify, you've got to have her free to justify, and at the same time self-indulgent because there isn't going to be any audience. In a way, wanting to say, but not.

HANCOCK

Letters and diaries reoccur very prominently in your work. Like Cousin B's diaries in *Against The Season*. Is that meant for the same purpose?

RULE

Those diaries in *Against The Season* are part of the legacy of the "requiring past." One of the ways to set the new society we live in so we can understand it, is to have a representation of the past, of blood kinship. That dead sister felt absolutely trapped in the environment she was in, and in love with it, and bitter about it. She is one of the ones who thought she had no choices and she's a motif to set against the very tentative.

Rosemary has chosen not to bury her mother, to go off and only comes back when her parents are dead. But I wanted the backdrop of that kind of requirement.

In Amelia it's loving. Amelia never felt trapped and she has an emotional generosity, the greatest ease in creating a new community. So those diaries function as a past. Which is a requiring voice; it grieves people.

HANCOCK

Using the second person "you," or at least the version of it in *This Is Not For You,* is rare in English. Did that present technical problems?

RULE

Oh, terrible. Very simple, but terrible. Apparently Kate is writing to Esther though she knows she's not going to mail the letter. But if the reader is going to understand all of the experiences Kate wants to talk about – of course, she says lots of things Esther would already know. I didn't solve the problem everywhere. Some scenes are ridiculous as letter. I didn't overcome that.

HANCOCK

I noticed the prose texture changed when Kate got to Athens and met Grace Hardwick. A whole different feeling. The clear, light air of the Mediterranean, perhaps?

RULE

No, that was a matter of her writing to Esther about things they didn't share so there isn't the tension of trying to create. When you're talking about a holiday you've spent together and you put in details simply to clue the reader, there's an awkwardness over and over again. The scenes that don't have Esther in them were technically a lot easier to do. And, of course, by the time you get to Greece, Esther's gone. The communication is a much more genuine one. I don't have the technical problems, so there is a release in that part of the novel. I was also probably feeling relieved I was nearing the end.

HANCOCK

How long did it take to write?

RULE

About a year and a half.

Do you think intellectual or religious experiences can be successfully transmitted in your fiction? Esther does have a religious experience of sorts. Religion is a common motif throughout the work.

RULE

Yes. Again, another technical problem about *This Is Not For You,* which I think is a valid one. It's not one that basically troubles me because it's Kate's perception I'm interested in. But you don't have any idea what Esther really experienced. Because one of the techniques for Kate to distance herself from that emotional requirement is to minimize Esther's experience. To make fun of it, to show Esther as much more childish than she is, much more naive than she is. Every now and then when you get a direct scene with Esther, you get a whiff — the scene with Esther and Kate's mother, for instance. You get a sense that, yes, there may be a kind of spontaneity and ease. But there's a kind of intelligence functioning up there that Kate won't grant her. If it's from Kate's point of view, and she's controlling the whole book, there's no way you could even write about what it was like for Esther. I mean a book written from Esther's point of view would be entirely different.

HANCOCK

In that sense too, were you discussing the role of the Church in people's relationships? It's something you deal with more seriously and in greater length in *Lesbian Images.* The role of the Church or the lack of a role. Was that something you intended to do in *This Is Not For You?*

RULE

Yes. Kate is more honest about that than she is about a lot of things, in that over and over again, her older sister says, "Why do you accept the Church, why do you let the Church impose these kinds of narrow doctrines?" Kate's answer is, "Because I want to. I'm a moral primitive," and she is a moral primitive.

HANCOCK

Are you hinting then, that there is perhaps the possibility of salvation for your characters? Or is it ironic, just a limited salvation?

RULE

You know, it isn't even ironic. I'm exploring what Kate thinks and feels. She is, after all, the child of a minister, and she has accepted a whole structure of being *right*. And Kate, of all my characters, has to be *right*. She has to cut off both feet and her nose and everything else. But she will be right. The Church gives a definition for right. I think she's pig-headed. But my own value structure has nothing to do with churchly judgement except that I'm interested in morality as a subject matter, as it feeds into people's lives and how it affects them.

HANCOCK

Against The Season has an entirely different tactic. You open up your explorations of point of view. Why did you change from a more "experimental" to a more "conventional" type of fiction?

RULE

I suppose for me it was the other way around. I was being very dutiful about all the laws of point of view in the other books. I was observing all those things that Henry James is supposed to have taught us, and creative-writing classes teach us about controlling a book through a particular sensibility.

And though I agree with you, *Against The Season* is a much more "conventional" book — the kind of book people write who haven't studied creative writing or Henry James and don't know you're not supposed to do that — for me it was a real breakthough. A real freedom to finally say the direction I want to go on in is a novel that is *not* controlled by one sensibility. A novel that does not have a central character. There is no main character in *Against The Season*. There is no main character in the new book.

I did a lot of perfectly ordinary technical things in *Against The Season* that I had never done before. It was brand new for me, it was very "experimental" for me, though recognizable in every Tom, Dick and Harry's novel.

I have gone on from there to a notion that, if I'm going to go on writing novels, I've got to develop the *way* to write about community that interests me and it will start with this very conventional exercise in shifting point of view to a statement about the way I think people live in the world.

Nobody is a main character. We are all parts of a whole structure. And the novel of one sensibility or two begins to feel to me a terrible ego-pressure. *This Is Not For You* was meant to be a stifling egotistic exercise. I mean you were so inside Kate's head, it's awful. And that's the point of this book. But I don't always want to live in the awfulness of one person's obsessions.

HANCOCK

And yet at the same time you do keep your characters' relationships at that distance. They are reaching out for each other and in some cases they do touch, if only briefly. Yet these personal commitments and permanent relationships don't seem to come easy to your characters. They have to fight for them, struggle for them.

Yet, I was quite impressed by the variety of relationships that you explored. I personally felt that *Against The Season* was one of the more perfect novels I've seen in revealing the number of relationships that are possible between characters and yet be all together in the social whole. I thought in a general way, it was something like the metaphor George Eliot used in *Middlemarch,* that society is a web in that you can't touch a single strand without disturbing all the others.

Yes, the sense of interrelationship is very important in that book. I think your sense that it's hard for all my characters to make any commitments is true. That is also true of our contemporary society. We now can choose whether or not to make commitments. The minute you introduce choice, where a woman doesn't *have* to marry to leave home and lead her own life, a man doesn't *have* to marry for him to have an economic unit that's viable for him to run the farm. Men and women don't *have* to have children, they don't *have* to take care of their parents — there's social security. We don't *have* to do anything.

The minute you take away that simply *expected* role in human relationships then stand with someone else, with other people and think — why, why are all of the questions of personal differences, of personal need which were minimal in a society that required relationship, why are these questions now our maximum concern? No wonder, not only my characters, but people we all know, live together rather than marry, put off having children, maybe decide not to; move two thousand to five thousand miles away from their parents; lose track of their brothers and sisters. Why care? My characters are always asking, why care? Nine times out of ten there's a real answer. But it's a hard answer and it means a lot of voluntary risk.

HANCOCK

Yet, there's also a great deal of humour in your work which most critics seem to miss. Why is that?

RULE

They probably don't think the same things are funny that I do. Often when people criticize my characters, male characters particularly — Cole, for instance is a funny, endearing character — but he's embarrassing for many male readers. Instead of thinking he's funny and dear, they think he's weak. So then there's no laughter and laughter at Cole is a blessing. An accepting of him instead of rejecting him.

A good deal of the humour in my work is an accepting humour. It's not a put-down, it's not satire. Unless you *feel* pretty open and pretty easy, that sort of humour is not pleasant and so you don't hear it. It's threatening to dignity and its concepts of right behaviour and strengths. A lot of my humour people just don't hear.

HANCOCK

Let me ask you about some specific scenes to get a feel for some of your working methods and ideas. For instance, in *Desert Of The Heart*, the scene where Evelyn first sees "the desert of the heart," "a valley of brilliant, burning sunlight, arched with rainbows, edged with lightning." How did this scene come about?

RULE

I actually drove through that scene. It was a visual scene I held in my head for a long time. The desert is a very dramatic place for vision and

41

when it came time to deal with Evelyn, who is such an understated character and who never melodramatizes her own emotions, who's inclined to intellectualize things, to put them in their place and be decorous, I needed some outside metaphor that she could see, that would dramatize what was going on inside her because she wouldn't. The storm was sitting there. I've seen a number of storms like that on the desert and it's wondrous. That whole passage, beginning at the lake, had been very visual. But Evelyn wouldn't say that in an interior, emotional state. She'd clamp it. So I had to project it outwards to let it be.

HANCOCK

In my copy of *Desert Of The Heart*, I noticed a word and I wondered if it was a typo or a pun. Aweful. A-w-e-f-u-l.

RULE

Oh, I had to fight the editors to leave the "e" in.

HANCOCK

It was meant then.

RULE

Yes. We've lost the old sense of "aweful". Now it means "terrible," instead of "full of awe." And I wanted that word. I don't think I'd fight for it now.

HANCOCK

In *Against The Season*, there's a scene in a Greek restaurant where Rosemary reaches out for Dina and "pulls her out of the space she's made for herself." The scene is described in almost mythic terms. In fact, the word myth appears in the passage. In addition, the walls of the restaurant are decorated with various Greek mythological characters, almost personified in the flesh, complete with flaws. A conscious tactic?

RULE

Yes. That, in a tiny way, is the same technique that's functioning with the diaries. Dina's past is Greece. Only she doesn't know it. Dina has a second language. She doesn't have a first. She speaks English. She's never spoken Greek, but she speaks English like a foreigner and that Greek restaurant, which is such a terrible parody with statues that are flesh-coloured, with shoulders and no arms, is the grotesque of the past.

But the present Dina has a kind of dignity that stands up against and draws from it. She is more authentically an expression of the culture than its garish setting. That's part of the theme.

Also, in that scene it's important to see Dina as one of the people that you really have to accept as locked into her own world. The only way you'll get to her is to go to her. Rosemary has always been the one pursued. The one loved, not the lover. It's very important, at that moment, that Rosemary will risk, as she's risked once before, being the fool. Only this time it's not the fool. It's a gentler gesture. But it's an affirmation of accepting that role, of saying she matters to me enough to stop being locked in role and to make a commitment.

"Literature thrives on taboos, just as art thrives on technical difficulties," says Anthony Burgess. Are there limits you think an author should observe in the language used to present "controversial subject matter," however that be defined? You never write explicitly about sex. Is that hedging?

RULE

It doesn't seem to me hedging at all. It may be in a sense an overcompensation for what people expect. People will say, "If you're going to write about relationships like this and you're not going to be erotic, what's the point?" Because we as a culture define these relationships as only erotic. Well, there is an erotic scene between Rosemary and Dina. The erotic scene is only used as an emphasis for the fact, and it's a very strong emphasis, that Dina is lover and will not be loved; that Rosemary will accept this for a while.

Again, it's like being fascinated with the physical description of a person. If it seems to me important to deal with sexual technicalities, fine. I do. But I'm much more interested in the whole dynamic of people moving together. Sexual scenes, like plot, tend to distract the reader from thinking about anything else. They tend to become utilitarian, erotic, pornographic and distract from the sense of what is actually going on between those two people. Now, when we can write sexual scenes that don't do that, they are magnificent. But sexuality in itself is something that people are still so prurient about, still so excited about, that it's a heavy weight inside any delicate framework. You introduce it and it's like a fist smashing against a face. You could say, "This is a gentle man who lost his temper." He smashes somebody in the face and that's all anybody will remember. You make a relationship and talk a great deal about its eroticism and nobody pays any attention to the structure around it. It gets to be an enormous noise inside a structure that is threatened by it.

HANCOCK

We talked a bit about landscape. How about weather and seasons acting as counterpoint to the emotions?

RULE

Very important to me. Just as I was saying about the scene in *Desert Of The Heart,* there are lots of things you can do with weather that work, that don't seem unnatural or forced, that are available to all of us in our experience. I live pretty much by the weather.

HANCOCK

In *Against The Season,* the title itself is a clue to understanding the book. The season we're against is spring. What exactly did you mean by that?

RULE

That also had to do with the seasons of life. I wanted to very gently break some of the clichés about old age, about youth, about middle age. Many of those characters are in situations that you usually associate with certain age groups. Old people don't propose to each other. Young people aren't reasonable and sensible. Cole and Agate do not have a love affair. They go to bed together, but they never get emotionally embroiled and involved. They are really more responsible than anybody else in the book in terms of what's going on and how it has to be coped with.

Take that poor librarian. She's going through a courtship you'd assign to a fourteen-year-old. Well, a lot of people do. The novel opens, "Against the season, which was spring, Amelia was in a burning mood." In a way, all the characters are against the season they're supposed to be in. They're in some other. The real season and the one they're in play against each other. It's one of the thematic patterns to the book.

HANCOCK

Very few of your characters are happily married men and women. Your characters, at least in my reading, tend towards "marriages of convenience." For example Peter and Harriet . . .

RULE

That's not a marriage of convenience.

HANCOCK

No?

RULE

No.

HANCOCK

Ok. But they tend to become spinsters, a nun, divorcees, unwed mothers, lesbians or homosexuals. How is a relationship made?

RULE

If you look at the range of fiction, I think you'll find very few happy heterosexual or homosexual relationships. The image of the happy relationship is the sort of thing you get in Shakespeare. The beautiful young couple assigned to the *ingenues,* who have nothing much to do but stand around and look pretty.

I don't think in my own fiction, there are fewer happy relationships. There may be fewer relationships. For instance Andrew and Monk in *This Is Not For You* have a relationship that's pretty sound. It has its ups and downs and its difficulties. But it's very requiring of them both and they grow inside it.

A great many relationships, because they are voluntary, break down, don't make sense, aren't worth being committed to. And given that as a comment about the world we live in — yes, there are happy heterosexual marriages in my fiction. Andrew and Monk. Or Peter and Harriet, given who they are. They're limited people, but they're very brave, given their own shynesses. I think you can have an ideal of how people get together, but it isn't convenient for either of them. It's embarrassing and threatening. There's Peter saying, "I finally would rather care when you come right down to it. I look at Carl and Ida and I can't bear the fact that I'm so fright-

44

ened of caring that I would rather not." It's a rather awkward proposal. But coming out of Peter, it's a real breakthrough.

When Harriet says, very shyly, "I read books. I'm a librarian and it says if people really like each other, they go to bed. Here on page 96." I mean, that's just *awful*. But that's Harriet. And that's as far as she gets. But convenient? No.

HANCOCK

Your characters often have a strong maternal sense. Many, in fact, work in orphanages, adopt foster children, run homes for unwed mothers, babysit for friends. Is this ironic?

RULE

Oh, heavens, no!

HANCOCK

I mention this because children are seen in a variety of ways. Cole has an image of an unborn child as a rather nightmarish fish . . .

RULE

He changes his mind at the end of the book.

HANCOCK

A woman dreams she gives birth to a light bulb . . .

RULE

That was a real dream. Somebody delivered it in a classroom. Extraordinary.

HANCOCK

And the narrator in "If There Is No Gate" feels the "terrible familiar vacancy in her passive womb." How do children fit into people's relationships?

RULE

(*Laughter.*) This is the universal question parents ask. Probably they don't. They're born to kill you. That's the generational fact.

Again, in *This Is Not For You,* the only place where I deal with this at all, with grown-up children and parents, Kate's relationship with her mother is an extremely important one. She goes home to tend that woman until she dies. The parent-child relation is a strong one.

In Andrew and Monk's relationship you see what the child does. It threatens the whole structure of what they think is proper. Monk is ineffectual and Andrew wants to hire a nurse. You see in minor scenes what any new, marvellous, amazing, difficult creature presents to any two people who have these solid notions of how their lives are going to go.

But I'm also interested in children by themselves. As in "My Father's House," you don't see the adults except in the huge projection of the parents' houses and churches, I really think of children as playing alone in the edifices their parents build around them with enormous inventiveness, pressure, fear. Children learn to live in the nightmares and dreams of their parents, and play out their destinies in those ways.

But children "fitting" into a relationship is simply not true. The relationship, the whole package changes. When a child is introduced into a relationship, the relationship becomes among three people. Some people *think* a child fits into an established relationship. That's the fantasy. But I don't think that any parent who pays attention to parenting says, "Where did our relationship go?" Looking around five years later. "It's gone. It doesn't exist any more."

HANCOCK

How important is understanding lesbianism to an understanding of your fiction? Or is it just one aspect among many?

RULE

I don't think there is such a thing as understanding lesbianism. I think there is such a thing as understanding a range of human experiences and being able to understand that one man could love another or one woman could love another or that they could be attracted to each other. I think a lot of people have difficulty in my fiction understanding how any of those people relate in the ways they do. I think it's as difficult for people to understand a Harriet and Peter or a Cole and Agate.

None of these people are carrying out a silverware-ad notion of what it is for one person to relate to another. I suppose the difficulty in understanding my fiction is, if you come to it with a number of clichés about how people relate to each other, you will be in a world that doesn't make any kind of sense at all. You will say over and over, "People don't do that, people don't feel that. . . ."

One of the reactions to *Against The Season* and the lesbian relationship was, "But Rosemary's good looking!" Well, that is not a matter of understanding lesbianism or not. That is a matter of having such a silly mindset that you can't imagine anyone good-looking being attracted to someone of his or her own sex. That's just a naivety that no book on lesbianism could help.

HANCOCK

Let's move to your short fiction. Do you like to write short stories or do you feel your talents are better suited to the expansiveness of the novel?

RULE

I really love to write short stories, but I don't think of myself as a short-story writer. When I'm writing short fiction, I'm teaching myself things in craft that I need to know about novels. The space of a novel is where I need to be. I need the space to teach people how to read me. And in the short story there's not enough space to do the necessary teaching.

Much of my short fiction I don't even think of as short stories. "Theme For Diverse Instruments" is a thirty-page novel with fifty-four characters. The "Outlander" is a twenty-seven page novel with very few characters in it. But it has an overview range which I don't think of in a short story.

HANCOCK

Have you written many stories? *Theme For Diverse Instruments* has only thirteen stories.

RULE

At least fifty. I have drawers full of them. But I send few of them out ever. Because they are my private explorations. Only sometimes do I think they might be interesting to share.

HANCOCK

I was both annoyed and amused at the both cautious and sometimes caustic reaction of critics when dealing with your work. Why is there such a blind spot? Is it the lesbian aspect of your prose?

RULE

I think that is the stop. Interestingly, the most hostile reviews were for *Against The Season* which is the gentlest of the three books and certainly doesn't deal with lesbians as a basic theme. Two characters in the book happen to be lesbians. They also happen to be a social worker and a furniture mender. I think the hostility to the book was that those people were included in an ordinary world. There is a moral offense that some people feel and want to respond to. Whatever else is in the book, there is also this red flag to a bull.

One critic said *Season* was a book about death. Well, that doesn't make sense at all. But he said it was a book about death because lesbians don't produce children. Never mind a kid is dropped on the last page.

But there's this terrible fear that if you allow this kind of relationship in the ordinary world, it's like pesticide. It's going to kill all fertility, wreck our world, threaten the patriarchal structure. The gentler it is, the more ordinary it is, apparently the more threatening it is.

The best reviews I've had were for *This Is Not For You.* This is because Kate decides she won't go to bed with her lover. So that's good. I think Kate's an absolute *idiot* in that respect. But that book is praised as humane, as perceptive, as on the side of the angels. Because what you're supposed to do, according to Freud and the Bible, is sublimate. And Kate surely does sublimate.

HANCOCK

Do you read all the reviews and criticism of your work?

RULE

Yes. All that are sent to me. I don't ferret them out.

HANCOCK

Do you care what they say?

RULE

It would be silly to say I don't because these reviews stand between me and my readers and when a reviewer so distorts a book that somebody reading the review can't tell what it's about, what its attitudes and tonalities are, then it's angering. And I have been angered by reviews.

47

But I've put up with it for so long that I've learned a kind of deep indifference and a kind of hope that people go to books not only through those channels.

HANCOCK

And how about more formal academic criticism?

RULE

I've never had any. People don't write M.A. theses on books like mine. Yet.

HANCOCK

Margins magazine said your best reviews were in Canada, not the U.S.A. Any reason for that?

RULE

In Canada there's a good deal of generosity in reviewing space for anybody who lives here. But one of the sad things is that, though a book can be widely reviewed, it's still not bought and read.

One review in the States will sell five hundred books. Twenty reviews in Canada will sell three. So Canadian writers are in a bewildering position of being given quite generous reviews in the press. I've had quite generous space in terms of the number of words that have been written, and in fact, most of the really hostile stuff comes out of the States and England. And the good reviews too.

HANCOCK

Why did you write *Lesbian Images*?

RULE

One answer is I was commissioned to write it and that is true. I don't think I would have voluntarily got into the place of deciding this was the thing I would do. I resisted writing it for a year or two with editors insisting why not try this or that.

Then, partly because this issue comes up over and over again in my work. It's not that I'm not interested in talking about lesbians and lesbian experience. Of course I am. But there's a lot that seems as important, or more important, in the work I do.

Still, people are very curious about this and I thought that perhaps I ought to sit down and really make what I think of as a statement. Also a great deal of nonsense is written. I felt it was time, now that the publishers were interested, to say something from a different point of view. It's my one public-service message to the world.

HANCOCK

It's not just propaganda, as Adele Wiseman claims? (*Books In Canada,* September 1975)

RULE

I think any fairminded statement about lesbian experience would have to be considered propaganda in a heterosexual world because there's so much homo-phobia in the world we live in. Anybody talking about it seriously and simply presenting it as a fact is thought of as a propagandist.

HANCOCK

Do your novels sell well?

RULE

No.

HANCOCK

I noticed the U.S. paperback edition of *Against The Season* promises in its lurid jacket, "lesbian smut," "pulp Sappho," in fact just pulp smut. Obviously you weren't consulted in the book's design.

RULE

(*Laughter.*) Obviously I wasn't.

HANCOCK

Should a writer be involved in "dressing the words"? In the design of a book?

RULE

Oh, it would be lovely. The one entirely happy moment for me in book publishing was bringing out *Theme For Diverse Instruments* with David Robinson (Talonbooks, Vancouver.) I was consulted at every turn about the design, the blurbs.

By now I am beginning to be consulted about design in the hardbacks. But when you get into pulp paperback, if you're publishing with a big firm in the States, you don't exist. The publisher signs the contract. It's gone from your hands entirely. You have a choice of not reaching the market, or shutting up about it and hoping people do not judge a book by its cover.

HANCOCK

What about distribution, paperback rights, remaindered copies?

RULE

Desert Of The Heart was only remaindered in hardback about two years ago and now it's out in a new hardback edition. (U.S.A.) It's never been in paperback. The paperback industry in the U.S. buys right for five years. They issue one edition for six weeks. For six weeks you could buy *Against The Season* anywhere. And after that it's not available unless a bookstore, knowing it will go out in six weeks, buys a whole packet of them.

If there's a push for a particular writer's work, the paperback company may issue it again for six weeks. Paperbacks are now marketed like cottage cheese in Safeway. Not good after six weeks.

This is the marketing circumstance. All the distributors get copies. If the books haven't sold in six weeks, there's a new shipment of another book coming in to take up the shelves. The bookseller is asked to tear off the covers of the books they haven't sold, ship those torn covers back to the publisher who will reimburse the bookseller. Then the books are destroyed. Any book that is not simply an entertainment for the airport is treated the same way. That's standard behaviour for all paperbacks. So if you want

Against The Season in the six weeks it's out, you can buy it anywhere in North America. Then it's gone.

HANCOCK

That happened to *This Is Not For You* as well. I remember the paperback was around and then it wasn't around.

RULE

Yes. But fortunately in Canada people are more used, particularly with Canadian fiction, to dealing with Canadian paperback firms who incline not to do the mass dumping. The paperback is actually in print a lot longer. But any American paperback is the same, with the exception of the classics and the ones that are reissued and reissued.

HANCOCK

Betty Friedan considered lesbians the greatest threat to the woman's movement. Has she changed her mind?

RULE

No, she's gotten more virulent.

HANCOCK

So the changing views of lesbian images, which is part of your thesis, hasn't really made much of an impression?

RULE

Oh yes. *Lesbian Images* wouldn't have been published five years ago. You couldn't possibly have published a book that made any kind of positive statement about lesbians. The only way you could say anything about lesbians was to confirm the negative views. Then the book would be accepted.

Interestingly, Betty Friedan is head of an organization, N.O.W., which endorses lesbian experience and she is outvoted and outnumbered in her own organization. I think she feels threatened. She's of a generation where any woman who did what she wanted was called a lesbian and that frightened her very badly. She wants to say that women can write books, run organizations, and be human beings and they aren't necessarily women who are lesbians. That's a terrible bugbear for her.

HANCOCK

Is there anything you'd like to say about your new novel, *The Young In One Another's Arms*?

RULE

Probably not. I'm glad the first chapter is going to be in this issue of the magazine so there will be a sense of "its beginning." But before a book is out and I've lived away from it for a long time, it's very hard to talk about it even though it's finished.

HANCOCK

One last question. Have you changed anybody's life with your fiction?

RULE

Mine.

JACK HODGINS

Jack Hodgins' two story collections — *Spit Delaney's Island* (1976) and *The Barclay Family Theatre* (1981) — and two novels — *The Invention of the World* (1977) and *The Resurrection of Joseph Bourne* (which won a Governor General's Award, 1980) — create a magnificent panorama of Vancouver Island life, from Spit Delaney who keeps a tape recording of an old locomotive, to a mayor who dresses in archaic naval costumes, to loggers who rip apart a wedding party with chainsaws while ghosts wander about. Yet all this inventiveness began simply, on the backs of English-class questionnaires from the high school where Jack taught for nearly twenty years.

He now teaches creative writing at the University of Victoria, but when I interviewed him in February 1978 he was living in Lantzville, B.C., about nine miles north of Nanaimo. At home, in a house he built himself — a reminder that he originally wanted to become an architect — Jack presented a perfect portrait of a school teacher with his wife Diane, three children, a dog, and two and a half acres of land that would have over-looked the Straits of Georgia except that he could not bear to cut down the arbutus trees blocking the view. The house had Danish modern furniture, a big grey brick fireplace, and shelves of books in alphabetical order with the dust-jacket photos of favourite authors, such as Alice Munro and Carlos Fuentes, turned facing out.

Jack picked me up at the ferry terminal and drove to his house along the same route Becker takes in the opening scenes of *The Invention of the World*. A sharp frost had fallen the night before and the mountains on the mainland were etched crystal clear across the glittering blue of the Straits, which Jack called "The Trench." This vivid scene prompted our opening remarks in the two-and-a-half-hour interview.

HANCOCK
I'd like to hear your comments on the B.C. Ferry as a starting point for fiction.

HODGINS
The B.C. Ferries are a constant reminder that this is, in fact, an insular society. Vancouver Island, despite the attempts to drag it closer to the mainland, is still very much an *island*. The ferry is a reminder of this — not that we need one — the fact you mailed a letter to me on Tuesday in Vancouver thirty miles away and it arrived only today, Saturday, is enough to keep me aware of the real distance represented by the Strait.

HANCOCK

You've called it "the Trench" in your stories.

HODGINS

Yes, it's a convenient image. And it has connotations that are appropriate. On either side of the Trench, people build their houses with their picture windows facing the water — on either side you've got people facing each other. What is the space between them?

HANCOCK

Is that the space you're trying to find as a writer?

HODGINS

I think so. I'm fascinated with the space that separates people, that keeps them from overlapping. But while I'm interested in what makes people on this side of the water different from people in other places, I'm much more concerned with finding out what makes people the same anywhere. I'm not particularly obsessed with "getting the region right" so much as I am in getting the people right. If I can get a person in Vancouver Island just right on paper, he's not too different from someone in Montreal or New York.

HANCOCK

Even though this seems to be rural Canada.

HODGINS

Someone on the CBC said not so long ago that the B.C. Ferries brought what was essentially a hillbilly society into mainstream civilization. (*Laughs.*) Well, I suppose I should resent the hillbilly reference, but I can certainly appreciate it. After all, Li'l Abner was my childhood hero, his comic strips the closest of my world I ever saw in literature.

This is very much a rural society; my own roots are rural; I have never felt entirely comfortable in any city.

HANCOCK

Two questions come out of that. What were your roots in boyhood on the "stump ranch" in the Comox Valley?

HODGINS

This was, I realize, very much an oral society. As a book lover, I felt very strongly that there must be something weird about me. I was the only person I knew who wanted to write. In fact, I was one of the very few people who read. People talked. I spent my whole childhood listening to other people's conversations. I resented being told to go and play. Whenever there were guests there were two groups to listen to: you could go in the kitchen and sit on the woodbox and listen to the women talk about other people. Or you could go outside to the garage or barn and listen to the men talk about machines and work. I listened to both. So the spoken word to me is very important. I feel compelled to get the way people talk exactly right in my fiction.

HANCOCK

Is that one of the things you liked about your recent trip to Cork, Ireland?

52

Listening to people talk? Yes, but coupled with that was here were people who read all the time. Everywhere you went people read books. Waiting for a bus they read books. Sitting in a doorway they read books. They talked about books. Bookstores were as crowded as supermarkets here. I'd never been anywhere where so many people thought books were *exciting* things, normal things, part of everyday life. Even at the University of British Columbia I'd met very few people who loved books.

HANCOCK

Why don't people read books on Vancouver Island?

HODGINS

Many do, of course. But books are viewed with a certain amount of suspicion. Particularly in British Columbia. We're not very far from the frontier after all. The job was to build your log cabin, shoot the bears, and dig your garden. Books are a gentlemen's frivolity. A lady's pastime.

HANCOCK

Is it also a suspiciousness of art?

HODGINS

There's a suspicion of anyone who isn't doing something productive. That includes teachers as well as writers. The product can't be measured, therefore we can't be doing anything worthwhile. Books are viewed not only with suspicion, but often with hostility. Consider the value our provincial government puts on culture. Compare that with Alberta where the Alberta government is aware that Alberta books are important — important enough to deserve government help in the millions of dollars.

Recently some teachers in this district (Nanaimo) did a survey after Christmas in a certain elementary school: how many children received books for Christmas? In a school population of 400, only four had been given books. Perhaps British Columbia hasn't yet discovered the power of the printed word to do anything more than sell used cars or real estate.

HANCOCK

Were you writing stories when you were at the University of British Columbia?

HODGINS

Yes. But I've written stories all my life. Even as a little kid, when I ran out of something to read, my mother would say, "Write your own." And I did.

But when I got to UBC I thought I'd take this more seriously and enrolled in Earle Birney's creative-writing class the first chance I got. This was before there was a writing faculty. About seven of us met every Thursday evening and ripped each other's work to shreds.

HANCOCK

Was Earle Birney a good influence?

HODGINS

I think so. If you ask me what did he teach me, it would be very hard for me to know at this distance. But he reinforced my determination to write. He somehow gave me the confidence that it wasn't a wasted dream. I'd gone through my childhood believing this was a fantasy that couldn't possibly come true. I hadn't seen it come true for anyone else. He treated our work with respect, even though now I can see some of it was very bad.

HANCOCK

What books were you reading at the time?

HODGINS

I was reading John Steinbeck, Ernest Hemingway, William Faulkner and company. I had discovered American Literature. I didn't know there was such a thing as Canadian Literature. I may have heard of Margaret Laurence who was just beginning. But no one else, not yet for awhile. I was busy reading every word by John Steinbeck. I *grovelled* at the feet of William Faulkner. I *wallowed* in Faulknerian prose. I nearly destroyed myself as a writer doing it. It took me a good ten years to get over the spell of that man's writing. In fact, I was well into my twenties before I decided I shouldn't read Faulkner any more, ever again in my life. His prose overwhelmed me so much that I couldn't write anything unless it sounded like his. And there's nothing worse than imitation Faulkner.

HANCOCK

I'm surprised you didn't fall under the spell of Roderick Haig-Brown. He lived just a few miles away.

HODGINS

It will be my regret forever that I didn't go knocking on his door. Only twenty miles away. It just didn't occur to me as a kid. For one thing, he was a magistrate, which made him a frightening creature right there.

I once saw my parents reading a paperback novel called *Timber* by Haig-Brown. But it had a half-dressed woman on the cover and seemed to disappear whenever someone wasn't reading it. I was never able to get my hands on that book, and to this day I haven't read it and can't find a copy of it. I'd still very much like to read it. And I also think it was one of my dreams to write the invisible story that hid between those covers.

HANCOCK

What was the first Canadian book you recall reading?

HODGINS

Margaret Laurence's *The Stone Angel,* I think. It staggered me. This woman was writing in a language different from anything else I had read. It's about *us*! It's the way *we* talk! I began reading Hugh MacLennan and Morley Callaghan about that time too, and Ethel Wilson — a magnificent writer.

HANCOCK

I saw a travel film a few weeks ago, put out by the British Columbia government. You've probably seen it — they recycle the footage year after year. But the narrator said something interesting. "This island is waiting to be discovered." It's 280 miles long, 80 miles wide at its widest point. It has mountains, lakes, ocean, surf, shipwrecks, caves with stalactites, Indian cultures, totem poles, sealions, bald eagles, gigantic ravens the size of German shepherd dogs. Do you agree that this island is waiting to be discovered?

HODGINS

While you were listing those things, I couldn't help but recall the numbers of people who have said to me, "Aren't you afraid that if you stay on Vancouver Island you'll run out of things to write about?" As if it's a tiny village, as if one book could exhaust its possibilities.

There is an immense area to be discovered. One of the things that writing is for me is discovering. Discovering place and the meaning of place. Discovering character and the mystery that's behind character.

HANCOCK

You needn't go anywhere else to get all the material you need.

HODGINS

As long as they keep making people, how can I possibly run out of material? I'm not writing about trees and flowers — as soon as I'd written about every tree and flower on Vancouver Island there'd be nothing more to say. I'm writing about human beings.

HANCOCK

So you'd agree with Robert Harlow that we all have enough material for 150 books. The problem is *how*?

HODGINS

Where do you start? What must be written first? And how much of it do you get into one book?

HANCOCK

How do you solve that problem? Where do you start?

HODGINS

One way I've approached that question is to decide that I've got to write every book as though it's the only book I'll ever write. I cannot see myself partitioning myself over a lifetime and thinking I'm going to write a little bit in this book and save something for another book. When I'm writing a book I have to treat it as though it's my only chance.

HANCOCK

You're certainly not like Irving Stone. He said, "I'm going to write ten books." He makes a list and puts it on the wall. Each year he writes one of them. He really does this.

HODGINS

I couldn't do that. For one thing I'd start stealing from my future books. Whenever I know what I'm going to do next I find myself reaching ahead and borrowing things, people, situations from other books and stories that I haven't written yet. So I don't dare plan ahead too definitely. It would have disappeared by the time I got there.

Did you discover any other Canadian writers?
Rudy Wiebe and Robert Kroetsch are among those whose work has excited me most. Also Roch Carrier.
Some reviewers and critics, including myself, often connect you with the South American writers. Would you care to comment on your discovery of cultures outside North America?

In the preparation for *The Invention of the World* I read a great number of Irish writers. This was before I went to Ireland. It wasn't intended to be a literary preparation so much as a geographical preparation. I got hooked on Frank O'Connor, Edna O'Brien, Flann O'Brien, several others. I had, of course, read contemporary writers from other places: Patrick White, Chinua Achebe, Alan Paton, and others. But this was a concentrated discovery of a nation's literary culture.

I first read Gabriel Garcia Marquez' *One Hundred Years of Solitude* about this same time. That book worked some kind of magic in me. I don't know what it is or was and I don't even want to analyze it in case it'll disappear. But it triggered off an excitement that led to the reading of other Latin American writers. Jorge Amado. Mario Vargas Llosa. Asturias. Puig.

What do they have that I respond to? *Energy!* There's an energy coming off the pages which I see so seldom coming off the pages in North American writing. Even more important than the energy is the sense of *enjoyment!* I have the feeling when I'm reading them that the writer is really having a good time. I think that's important. The writer should be having a good time. Otherwise how can he expect his reader to enjoy what he's done? I have got so used to the idea that the writing and reading of a novel was a painful experience. So I appreciated that energy, that love of what you're doing.

And one other thing, the same thing I had fallen in love with in William Faulkner, the *sense of community*. The whole world gets in on those Latin American novels just as the whole world got in on a William Faulkner novel. This is such a contrast to the many novels that tend to be about one person's problems that ultimately weren't of much importance or interest to anybody but himself.

You said you were "getting ready" to do *The Invention of the World* with all this reading. Why did you have to "get ready"?
I was "getting ready" to go to Ireland. I knew the beginnings of my novel existed somewhere over there. A deserted village. A prehistoric stone circle.

I didn't know exactly where, but I had to find out. I knew there was no sense in going to this place blind and I wanted to do as much preparation for the experience as possible. Not just the tourist stuff, but all of the books and poems. This came in very handy later on, as I would need to learn the rhythms of Irish speech.

HANCOCK

Did you also learn novelistic structure from writers like Mario Vargas Llosa?

HODGINS

I don't know if I learned so much *how*, as I gained courage to try, from reading Llosa's *The Green House*, Rudy Wiebe's *The Blue Mountains of China*, Ray Smith's *Lord Nelson's Tavern*, and Robert Harlow's *Scann*. All these books, and several others I can't recall, called themselves novels. Why? Why weren't they just fragments all thrown together in a box? Then I began to discover the relationships between the parts, that there is a way to build a novel to suit its own material. Not to suit what some critic decided should be the shape of all novels.

HANCOCK

Would these Latin American and Irish influences put you outside the Canadian tradition, whatever I mean by that?

HODGINS

I suppose if there is a Canadian tradition, you probably mean the Upper Canadian tradition. Probably. Writing that kind of novel is dangerous, full of pitfalls. But that doesn't worry me very much. A writer writes for other people who like to read what he likes to read.

HANCOCK

Does that put you in rarified isolation?

HODGINS

No. It should, I suppose, but strangely, for some reason or other the reaction to my first book, *Spit Delaney's Island*, has been enthusiastic and excited, especially in the east. Though they had never heard of me before, both Toronto papers managed to have extremely generous reviews on publication day. Nobody in B.C. noticed for quite a while. By the time *Invention* came out most reviews seemed prepared to be friendly and generous, though some were a bit worried about me, afraid I was about to fly off into space and lose contact with the things they'd valued in my first book. As if I were in danger of joining those writers who are interested in nothing but playing games with language. They needn't worry, of course. My interest is still in people above everything else.

HANCOCK

Does fiction in Canada begin at the regional level?

HODGINS

The minute anybody mentions regional writing to me my back is up. If somebody from Ontario says it they assume Ontario means Canada and the rest of us are the regions. If somebody from B.C. says it they probably mean you're only writing about your own little part of the world and the rest of it doesn't matter. I think all writing has to be regional to start with. It has to come from somewhere, it has to take place somewhere. But the important thing is, if the fiction is any good it rises above the place and talks to people anywhere. I have no sense of a typical Canadian readership. I think I'd be fooling myself if I thought there was one because Canada is a collection of regions with a collection of regional literatures.

HANCOCK

All linked together by telephone wires.

HODGINS

All linked together by invisible threads that tie souls to souls in every part of the universe.

HANCOCK

Is your Nanaimo somehow equivalent to Margaret Laurence's Manawaka, Alice Munro's Jubilee, or Sinclair Ross' Horizon? Or anybody else with a town?

HODGINS

When you put the question that way I have to back up and think about it. The whole Island is to me what Manawaka is to Margaret Laurence. Larger than a town but still a fixed place. With a movable population and characters who wander in and out of different stories. If that's what regionalism is, then I'm a regionalist. But if that's all I am, then I think I've written everything I need to write and I might as well quit. Surely no one calls Margaret Laurence a regional writer.

HANCOCK

Since you're a rural writer does that automatically mean you have to have that struggle between man and nature?

HODGINS

(*Laughs.*) No. I'm not conscious of a struggle between man and nature at all. Life is pretty comfortable here. At first this was one of the reasons why Canadian literature seemed so foreign to me. People were always getting lost in the snow and freezing to death or being starved out in droughts. All these strange things happening to them that never happened to anybody I ever met. In this part of the world the struggle between men and the elements is not very dramatic. The scenery is dramatic, but the struggle is not.

HANCOCK

Does this mean the idea of Canadian characters being victims of their environment, which has some popular currency, is wrong?

HODGINS

It doesn't relate to anything that is part of my experience, let's put it that way. Man on Vancouver Island is not the victim of anybody except his own politicians and his real-estate agent. In fact, that's a new version of man against nature. The real-estate developer versus the nature that belongs to us all.

Did you have a long, lonely apprenticeship?

It has to be lonely. Writing is a lonely activity. And I've never been one of those who get together with other writers to read, criticize, and congratulate one another. Long? Some people's apprenticeships are longer than others and I thought mine was going to go on forever. Since I began writing when I was in elementary school, I thought maybe I had a head start, so I was terribly disappointed when I got to be nineteen, still unpublished, and the whole world seemed to be full of overnight sensations, all the same age as I was. First novels. Best sellers. I thought I might as well forget the whole thing.

I didn't make my first sale until I was twenty-nine. In fact, I did not sell my first story until I stopped, looked around, and realized first, I had to stop writing like William Faulkner, and second, that I had to learn from scratch. I got out every book on creative writing that I could find anywhere, read them all, made notes, made a list of about seventy-five different ways you could develop a character and used nearly all of them in one story. That became the first story I ever sold, and gave me the encouragement I needed to carry on. If I could write a first story then maybe I could write a second one.

HANCOCK

Significantly, that story was not sold in Canada.

HODGINS

I have a whole bag of rejection slips from Canadian editors. That was sold to the *Northwest Review* in Oregon. Then I sold several other stories in the States. A story to an Australian magazine. I think my first Canadian sale was to *The Canadian Forum*.

HANCOCK

How much do the materials of your own life enter your fictions? Or are you an observer?

HODGINS

I've written very little out of personal experience. I'm not all that interested in doing it. My first motivation in writing is a *nosiness* about other people. I already know more than enough about myself. I like to take somebody who's *out there* and pull him up close and have a good look at him. Not only that but to get inside and find out what it's like to be him.

It also makes life more varied and interesting. How many people can go through life pretending to be other than themselves? Without being put in an institution?

HANCOCK

You said in the introduction to *The West Coast Experience* (Macmillan)

59

that western writers were "like Adams gone mad in Eden, naming every-thing in sight." That British Columbia was "unexplored territory, that writers were making maps." They go behind a concern with landscape description to a concern with its safety, even exchanging places with it, a common theme in western Canadian poetry. That landscape is somehow an extension of themselves. Is this a fair assessment of what you're doing as a writer, opening up the possibilities of fiction for western Canadian writers? I emphasize "western Canadian" deliberately.

HODGINS

Possibly. I hope I prefaced that statement with "sometimes it may seem on the surface that this is what B.C. writers are doing." But the landscape is ultimately only your setting.

Maybe I can illustrate it better than I can explain it. Often a story for me begins when I discover a place has a meaning. Either in the lives of the people who live there or in the lives of people who come to it. It can then take on some symbolic importance that touches everybody. That is the only importance landscape has to me in my fiction. The role it plays in human lives. Writers are more than mapmakers. We're not, I hope, *just* naming things.

HANCOCK

It seems to connect with your many British Columbia readers though. They seemed to feel you were documenting ourselves. They had no sense whatever that what you were doing was unusual. They thought only it was about time somebody went out and did it.

HODGINS

That's one reaction.

HANCOCK

There's an equally strong sense you are the only writer around.

HODGINS

That's a beautiful irony. I sat over here on this island feeling neglected, ignored, very much by myself all those years. Jealous of the writers over in Vancouver who were getting some attention. Feeling that if I was going to be noticed I'd have to scream louder than anybody else so I could be heard on the other side of those Vancouver writers, as far over as Toronto. Then, so soon, to find out that even those other writers that I was jealous of have not been given the attention they deserve.

HANCOCK

Would you care to name some of them?

HODGINS

Andy Schroeder, J. Michael Yates. I think everyone in the world should read Ethel Wilson. I think everyone in the world should read Robert Harlow's *Scann*. Those are the real writers on the west coast. I don't feel part of it at all.

So you felt you had to take greater risks in your writing.

That apprenticeship we talked about went on for so long that I decided to go for broke. All or nothing. I'm going to be read or fall flat on my face. It seemed as if I wasn't going to slip gradually into the picture. I'd have to scream and holler louder than anybody else.

Did you have many attempts at longer fiction?

Yes. I wrote two or three novels in my twenties. Very bad. But at the time I believed in them enough to finish them and send them out. Now I'm grateful they came back. But I needed to do them to learn. They were very timid and imitative; I was writing the novels I had already read somewhere. Then *The Invention of the World* began to grow in my head. So I took a leave of absence from teaching, went to Ireland in the summer, then wrote the first draft in the fall and winter of 1974-75.

I can't say I deliberately set about writing a novel that was different. As I said before, I was going to write it as if it was the only novel I'd ever write. I figured if it left me panting on the floor incapable of ever writing another word, then that would be just too bad. Being timid hasn't got me anywhere. And though writing it did leave me panting it did not exhaust me — in fact, it opened up new possibilities.

Is British Columbia really the edge of the world, the last frontier?

I've always taken it for granted that people everywhere else thought they were the centre of the world. It seems a natural point of view. Yet, people here on the island, and perhaps everywhere else in B.C., are aware that this is the edge of the continent. All of our country is to one side of us.

It's not the last frontier by any means. It's a *recent* frontier and perhaps we can fool ourselves into thinking the frontier experience is more important to us than it really is. There are other newer frontiers in this world.

As a writer, what's on the other side of those frontiers?

Reality.

With a capital "R"?

The Reality that exists beyond this imitation reality that we are too often contented with. The created rather than the invented world. I didn't call my novel *The Invention of the World* because it is an arresting title. It is a story about counterfeits.

HANCOCK

So the ocean is not a metaphor for you? Somewhat like Herman Melville and his approach to "reality"? There are possibilities beyond the surface.

HODGINS

What you and I call the ocean is to me only a metaphor. All those trees, for instance, are metaphors; the reality lies beyond them. The act of writing to me is an attempt to shine a light on that ocean and those trees so bright that we can see right through them to the reality that is constant.

HANCOCK

Do you drive around the island taking notes?

HODGINS

I drive around my life taking notes. I'm never very far from my notebook. Not in deliberate search for material, but knowing that my memory can't keep everything I need. At one time I thought I should dip only from the unconscious well and all that. But I'm afraid I need the notes too. Those little reminders. Sometimes just the act of writing something down helps embed it in the memory.

HANCOCK

When you talk about "the island," is that in italics or capitals?

HODGINS

In Capitals. People here speak of this as THE ISLAND. There aren't any other islands. While I was at UBC a friend and I were hitchhiking to class one day and were asked by this couple where we were from. We said, "THE ISLAND," assuming that was enough. They said, "Do you mean Prince Edward Island?" Both our jaws dropped in surprise. That's how self-centred we must have been. We even define the other side of the trench in relation to this Island as THE MAINLAND.

HANCOCK

For the benefit of American readers, Vancouver is not on Vancouver Island. Vancouver is on the Mainland.

HODGINS

I've had phone calls from people in New York connected with the American publication of the novel. They're embarrassed by it, but they have to ask, "Where is it?" I don't know how to answer them when they ask where I live. I don't know whether to say Nanaimo, or Vancouver Island, or the west coast of Canada. American reviewers have solved the problem by referring to the setting of *Invention* as Victoria Island.

HANCOCK

That leads to the next question. You were talking about "reality." Can your fiction be considered within some system of ideas in Canadian literature? Fiction in Canada seems to be a mimetic reality. Authors walk around and write down what they see in front of them, instead of creating an alternative reality. Your fiction doesn't seem to fit into the same world as Mordecai Richler, Alice Munro, Margaret Laurence, Sinclair Ross, Mavis Gallant, or some other major Canadian writers.

HODGINS

I don't know if this is a literary question so much as a philosophical one. Reality to me isn't the same thing as it is to some of the other people you mentioned. Each of us sees the world according to his own particular vision. What I write is to me "realistic," though not everyone thinks I'm describing "reality." I'm often considered weird or almost surrealistic though I never write about anything that I don't want people to believe quite literally.

HANCOCK

You have a reaction to life, rather than a distortion.

HODGINS

Yes. I'm not playing games with words. Important as rhythm, language, vocabulary and all those other things are when I'm writing, I'm not playing games. I'm not trying to trick my reader. Or manipulate my reader in any way. I'm using my language to describe the world as I see it.

HANCOCK

Is reality distorted when a fictional form is imposed on it?

HODGINS

Yes. That's why I tend to resist fictional forms which come from elsewhere. The forms of my stories have to grow out of the subject matter. The people I'm writing about tell me how to write their stories. When I was writing *The Invention of the World* I was aware that this was not the way novels are supposed to be shaped, but this is the way this novel had to be shaped. This is the way Maggie's story *had* to be.

HANCOCK

You don't have the political sense of the Latin American writers. That you're trying to improve society by removing certain masks and revealing certain realities. Your novels aren't instruments for social change.

HODGINS

We don't live in a climate where this is so important. Certainly in British Columbia we're living in a situation that could be much improved, but that's a temporary thing and we can go to the polls and do something about it if we want. That's very different from living in a society in South America where your neighbour is starving or being shot for saying the wrong thing.

But still a writer anywhere is political in another sense, I suppose in a moral sense. A fiction writer is creating myth and societies live by myths. The myths that are important to society create the way that people in it treat each other. Like John Gardner, I feel strongly that a writer has a responsibility to be aware of the moral implications of what he's doing.

Yes, in a way you are attempting to change the world. Though you cannot ask to change certain facts about the world, you can perhaps open up new ways of seeing it. Or just challenge old ways. Present modes of admirable behaviour. Suggest alternatives.

One of the things I sometimes do in a story is set somebody up who thinks he knows what life is all about. Then I pull the rug out from under his feet to find out how he functions when I challenge his values. In a way that's a way of challenging a reader's concept of reality too. Initiation occurs when a character encounters someone whose way of looking at the world is completely foreign to him.

HANCOCK

Does that account for all the failed Utopian colonies both on Vancouver Island and in your work?

HODGINS

Yes. People coming for the wrong reasons. People coming for a dream that is based on values that were doomed anywhere in the world and had no hope at all of surviving, here or anywhere else. It's a fact that Vancouver Island seems to have attracted romantic idealists from the beginning. They have been defeated, not because their dreams weren't worth going after, but because they brought with them their old values. The materialistic trappings and the selfish pursuits. You can't just change your location and expect the world to change. The people who come running here to set up a Utopian society could just as well have stayed at home and changed the way they thought and felt about things, about themselves.

HANCOCK

It's like the joke in the *National Lampoon*. The immigrants to this country came here seeking the worst aspects of the place they left behind. And found them. The Slavic peoples came to cold, bleak, windswept Manitoba and said, "This is it!"

HODGINS

They're at home. Here we have a large number of Prairie People who have dreamed all their lives of selling out and coming to the coast where it's nice and comfortable. Yet they often spend the rest of their lives complaining about the rain. As long as people search for their utopias in a physical geography they're bound to be disappointed.

HANCOCK

In your anthologies *The West Coast Experience* and *The Frontier Experience,* you included work by Andreas Schroeder, bill bisset, others you may care to name, who are often called "experimental" writers. Are you connected somehow with these experimental writers, here or elsewhere?

HODGINS

No. I can't say I've ever been connected with anybody, partly because of physical isolation. Before publishing my first book I had no association with other writers whatsoever, and being part of a group or a school of writing has never been attractive to me. Especially something that is labelled "experimental." I think all writing is experimental. Whenever a writer sits down he has to experiment in order to see whether what he wants to do can work. Even the most traditional writer is experimental in that sense.

HANCOCK

So you don't think like Robert Kroetsch when he talks about "foregrounding language," "layering meaning," and "deconstructing conventions." An academic approach to fiction and its possibilities. You find a different way to get your words to lift off the page.

HODGINS

I may discover years from now that what I'm doing is basically the same thing as Robert Kroetsch is talking about. What Robert Kroetsch has done with people of the prairies touches me in a way that's very important. His prose flies off the page, gets me all excited, makes me jealous, and makes me aware of how I can solve certain problems in stories I'm writing. But I can't intellectualize it. I can't turn it into literary talk.

While I was writing *The Invention of the World,* I was aware of the relationship between my novel and the conventional novel. I was aware of seven different levels that the story could be read on. I was aware of a single theme that controlled the imagery on every page and tied all these "layers" together. I had drawn strange charts and diagrams and written volumes of what could be considered literary criticism of the as-yet invisible novel — and yet, in the page-by-page writing of the novel, all of that had to be pushed aside in favour of the story-teller's *instincts* and *intuitions.* I discovered, when I'd completed the novel, all those high-toned intentions had found their way into my story in much the way I wanted but they've quite rightly become nearly invisible, even to me, and I certainly can't articulate them now in any way that would be helpful in, say, a university classroom. And when I read something as marvellously perceptive as David Jeffrey's piece on my work in *Book Forum* I know I'm right to stick to the writing of fiction and let others, who can see the patterns more objectively and therefore more clearly, do the intellectualizing and all the rest of it.

HANCOCK

Do you have a reader in mind?

HODGINS

I don't write for a specific person. It intimidates me to think of specific people some day reading what I'm working on.

HANCOCK

I'm waiting for an Anthony Burgess answer. "My ideal reader is five feet two, a lapsed Catholic, and wears an orange scarf."

HODGINS

I don't have an image of an ideal reader, but I try to write the stories I wish somebody else had written for me to read. So in a way I'm writing for someone who likes to read what I like to read. Whoever that may be.

Let's talk about your work habits and routines. Do you write with a pen, pencil, typewriter? What time of day do you prefer? Do you take your work through twenty-five or thirty drafts? Do you put chapter outlines on big pieces of cardboard on the wall? Do you prefer a wall or a window? Upstairs or down?

I've discovered I don't like to be downstairs. I went to all the trouble and expense of building myself a study in the basement, quite a nice one, and couldn't stand being in it. A basement is always a basement. It's too far from everything, not warm enough, lonely. I turned the room into a storage room. I definitely have to be upstairs.

I write with a pen. I need a pen in my hand before my head will start working. I cannot compose at the typewriter. I hate typing. I will rework handwritten manuscripts until they're unreadable. Only then I type them up.

When I'm free to work, I work all day. I get to work as soon as I can after breakfast and work until I collapse. If it's a good day, I'll come staggering out, in time for supper, shaking, sweating, in a daze. If it's a bad day I'll come out maybe an hour earlier, crabby and snarly. I work as long as I can every day because for so many years I had to steal time to write. I had only the weekends and holidays. So I had to learn how to use every minute.

I can't give you a set number of revisions. Some parts of *The Invention of the World* are little more than first draft. I felt if I touched certain parts I'd ruin them. "The Eden Swindle," the Irish legend for instance, is the way it came out of my head. Or my pen. Or wherever it came from. But some of Maggie's sections, because I was dealing with more detailed reality, had to be reworked and reworked many times.

You're still writing around a full-time job as a high-school teacher in Nanaimo.

Yes. Mind you, the first draft in that case was written while I was on a leave of absence. Just as *The Resurrection of Joseph Bourne* was done, or almost done, during a leave of absence. I found it's one thing to write short stories on long weekends and holidays, but to write a novel while teaching, as I did with those others in my twenties, takes so long that by the time I get to the end of it, I forgot what I was writing the novel about. Two years for a first draft is too long for a person like me. I change my interests. I'm jumping ahead to my next novel. The whole idea of a first draft for me is to nail it down before it disappears.

Aside from the inconvenience of a job and other duties, do you also get writer's blocks? If so, how do you deal with them?

HODGINS

I try to overcome a block by mental housecleaning, by recognizing the block is in me, it's not in the material, it's not in the, quote, inspiration. I've discovered that, almost without exception, a mental block is a warning that I'm going in the wrong direction. Days will go by when I sit down to write something and it's almost a physical revulsion that says, "Don't do it." I know what I want to write down but I can't make my hand write it. I can't care enough, I can't get excited enough. So I sit there and look at the paper. This feeling is telling me that I'm doing something wrong; back up, look at what you've got. Nearly always I'll find out that's not the way the story needed to go. Or that it's got stale.

For instance, when I sat down to write the second Spit Delaney story six months after I had completed the first one, I knew more about the man and I wanted to pick him up a year after the separation from his wife so we could see what was happening to him then. I knew the story I wanted to write. Yet I couldn't write more than a paragraph. And even it was blah. I wrote it again and again and again. Everything existed, but my hand, my body, didn't want to write the story. I knew I had to make myself excited enough to be able to do it. Maybe the problem is in the third person, I thought. I'd never used the first-person point of view. Why not try? The minute I put my pen down in the first person, that story poured out with no effort whatsoever. All I had to do was listen to it. The necessary excitement came from working with a *new* sort of literary problem for me.

HANCOCK

Do you always get inspired? Or do you get what John Fowles calls "an accident"? You forget about a fixed plan and follow the accident.

HODGINS

That's what inspiration is for me. Setting things down and letting them start. I don't like to begin a story until it's already alive, until the main character is so alive I just have to put him down on the paper and let him carry on with the story himself. Inspiration for me is listening to the directions that my story must take. "The accident" is the next step in the progression of my character.

HANCOCK

Does that accident give the story its shape, its structure, its form? Or do you bother with these patterns?

HODGINS

I know the general shape of a piece before I start. Otherwise I wouldn't know my speed, my pacing, how much detail I can afford to put in it. Beyond that the character has to decide whether I can follow that pattern or not.

HANCOCK

Your stories wouldn't then easily respond to the theme, symbol, image approach.

HODGINS

So far we've only talked about the first writing. At the end of it I can look back and say, "What is it I've written?" Then I can discover what I'm concerned with. Certain images recur that I hadn't noticed. My language tends to do certain things. I think, well, I can throw this part out and highlight this part if I want to give it theme or symbol, or support or expand theme or symbol.

HANCOCK

Did it take you awhile to find your voice? By voice I mean the sense of the creator behind the work so that we believe the story as it is being told.

HODGINS

I can't remember consciously searching for it. I guess that was the trouble I had with William Faulkner. His voice was louder than mine. I've always tried to let the character be the controlling factor. Even if I'm writing in the third person the language is the language that is appropriate to *him,* not me. I'd prefer the reader forget there is a narrator, unless I've invented one who is a part of the story.

HANCOCK

I think the voice of your stories though has to be a very confident one to keep some of the ideas and images from becoming silly. For example, a machine is invented which is supposed to be God. The wrong tone of voice would render the scene ludicrous.

HODGINS

This is where the whole task is to make the reader believe what you're saying. First, the reader has to believe that the person who is talking to him is real. And then he has to decide if he's going to believe what the person says.

HANCOCK

You don't talk shop with other writers.

HODGINS

Very seldom. Writing is such a delicate thing. It's like a dream. To talk about it shatters the dream. If I'm in the middle of writing something and I listen to another writer talk about his work I can come home quite shaken. I feel I can't finish that story because I'm not doing it the way he does. Or suddenly the whole thing has begun to look impossible or ridiculous. The story must be safely finished, out of danger, before I can risk talking about it with anyone else and by that time I'm not particularly interested in talking about it — I'm on to something else.

HANCOCK

Do you find reasons not to write?

HODGINS

Oh, yes. I love to read. It's so much easier to read than to write. Somebody else has done all the work for you. The world is full of reasons not to write. Those invitations to do readings, do workshops — it would be possible never to write another word. Yet I'm not happy when I'm not writing something, preferably every day.

HANCOCK

What advice do you give your writing students?

HODGINS

Perhaps the most important thing for young people who want to be writers is to learn to see. If I can't help my students to get anything else, it's important that I help them to get that. Learn to see the other things people don't notice, to train themselves to be so sensitive to all they see and hear that they can begin to find out what it's like to be people other than themselves.

HANCOCK

Are you aware of the changes in voice as you deal with different characters and their method of having their story told?

HODGINS

Oh yes! I'm probably more aware of that than I am of anything else. I have to hear these people talking before they have any reality for me. Until I can get the rhythms of their speech I don't have any right to put their stories down on paper. I was aware when I was writing *The Invention of the World,* for instance, that there were many different voices and that I couldn't write any of the novel down until I knew what all the voices were.

One of the easiest parts to write was "The Scrapbook" section. I had no responsibility to do anything except listen. I walked into my room, sat down, and said, "Who will I interview today? I'll interview a college instructor. I haven't interviewed one of those yet." I turned him on and listened. I don't think I changed a word of the first draft of the whole scrapbook.

HANCOCK

How does a short story start? Let's take "Spit Delaney's Island," parts one and two.

HODGINS

It began with an anecdote told by someone about a member of my family who went through an experience I found interesting. Having run a steam locomotive in a pulp mill for forty years and enormously attached to it, he went to work one day and found it sold out from under him to a museum in Ottawa. He hung a painting of the locomotive on his wall, he made a tape recording to play whenever he got lonely for his machine, he hung the big number 1 in his home. I realized I'd like to do something with this situation, so I wrote a little story about Spit Delaney suffering this blow and then took him on a trip to Europe while he tries to adjust and his marriage began to fall apart. Brought him back home. I looked at what I'd done and realized it wasn't a short story at all. It was just an anecdote. I put it aside for a year. During that year certain things happened. For one thing my wife and I noticed nearly all our friends were splitting up. Divorces, separations right and left. It was a time when we looked at each other and wondered if we were going to be the only married couple left in the world.

Sometime during that winter I read an article in a magazine about the mystical associations of the west coast in Indian mythology. "The Place of Transformation" it was called. Some mythical beast came roaring up out of the water and changed people into fish and fish into people. It made me aware of the line between water and land as a kind of separation between one kind of reality and another.

I realized at some moment that everything that I had been concerned with that year had something in common. They all involved one kind of separation or another. Separation of man from job; man from family; man from beast; man from his beginnings. It opened up this whole idea of the difference between the temporary and the lasting. Then I sat down and wrote the story.

HANCOCK

Do you set up the character's strengths and weaknesses first? Then move them through the various patterns of defeat characteristic of a traditional short story?

HODGINS

Setting them up is the right expression. Though I can say that only when I look back on a story. Set him up so we can understand him. And then introduce him to something that challenges his way of looking at himself. Capture him at a moment when his life is turning a corner.

HANCOCK

So you'd agree with Bernard Bergonzi's assessment that life's experience is filtered down by form to the prime elements of defeat and alienation.

HODGINS

Frank O'Connor said something very similar about the short story. The submerged population he calls them, the outsiders. However, I'm not interested in recording defeats only. Towards the end of *Spit Delaney's Island* some of the people have a hope of succeeding. I think the ending of *The Invention of the World* is positive whether anybody notices it or not. It's not a story of defeat. It's a story of triumph. People who triumph or succeed even in small ways must be recorded in fiction too, though this is contrary to the tradition of modern serious fiction.

HANCOCK

Is the Kafka mode of fiction a direction you might take?

HODGINS

No. That particular way of looking at the world doesn't appeal to me very much. I don't have much patience with the notion of man as victim. Or man as helpless victim. I look around and I don't see all that many tortured victims. I see a lot of people who are making decent lives for themselves despite their problems. I'm as interested in people whose dreams come true. Even though that's very unfashionable. It's much easier to write a convincing story with a horrible defeated ending. I think that says a lot about the world we're living in. People will automatically and unquestioningly accept a story that ends with people being defeated and smashed and bleeding and committing suicide. That's real life they say; that's realistic fiction. Yet they'll raise an eyebrow and challenge a story which has a person triumph.

Perhaps this is why I admire the courage of John Fowles. Do you remember Daniel Martin's search for a true ending to the novel he was writing? "To hell with cultural fashion," he declared. "To hell with the imagined which does not say the truth." And the truth, for him too, included hope and good fortune.

HANCOCK

At what point do you know what a story is going to be about? Before, during, or after revisions are taking place?

HODGINS

I know *who* it's going to be about in the beginning. I know *what* it's going to be about sometime during the writing of it. I begin to see where a story is taking me. What it is I'm going to be concerned with. The story is usually clear to me by the time I get to the end of the first draft. And if it isn't I'm in trouble! Otherwise what would I look for when I go back to revise?

HANCOCK

I immortalized myself for a few minutes in the late *Weekend Magazine* by calling you "a magic realist." Are you really a magic realist? Mixing the real and improbable in your prose? Or is it just a label? Are we suffering "hardening of the categories" here?

HODGINS

It's dangerous to start throwing labels around, but I can't deny this particular one has appeal to me. I was quite excited about it when I first read it in your introduction to *CFM* 24/25. It had never occurred to me before. Then I started to think about who I like to read and what paintings I like to see and yes, I do very much like the magic realists.

Obviously I'm impressed by the Latin American novelists. I didn't know they were called "magic realists." But I can't say that I sit down and say, "Now I'm a magic realist and I'm going to do it this way." The label may describe what I've already done but who knows what I'm yet going to do?

Each story or each book has its own reality. I don't know what it's going to be. Slap your labels on me a hundred years from now when I'm beginning to grow tired of trying new things!

HANCOCK

Robert Kroetsch calls this "nipping at the heels of realism and making the old cow dance."

HODGINS

That appeals to me. But let's not forget what I said before. What may appeal like "magic" realism to someone else is just "pure" realism to me. I believe in my own fictions.

HANCOCK

Douglas Barbour, in a review, said your stories were an exploration of the search that people on the edge of society engage in. Is he right?

HODGINS

If he says so. I certainly wouldn't want to contradict such a nice review as that one was. But these people are not peculiar. I'm not aware of them as having special problems. They're just people.

HANCOCK

That's why I was so surprised to read the jacket notes on *Spit Delaney's Island.* Margaret Laurence, Margaret Atwood, Alice Munro described the stories as "chilling," "eerie," and so on. Is that perhaps the Ontario view of the world reacting to the exoticism of B.C. even though these particular writers are from various parts of Canada?

HODGINS

Their reaction may be to what you call the "exoticism" of B.C., but I think it might be this other thing that you want to label magic realism. It's not the realism of the tree. It's this other thing, the reality beyond the tree. That can be a little scary. Even people who live here on this island have told me some of my stories scare them.

That doesn't bother me. Maybe that's what I'm doing. Challenging not only my characters' comfortable view of things, but also my reader's. I think good writing *should* sometimes scare the reader a little, the way a bolt of lightening does — it startles, frightens, but it also illuminates for a moment, perhaps even shows us our way in the dark.

HANCOCK

If you moved to Toronto, would that affect your roots as a writer?

HODGINS

Probably not. One of the reasons I had to go to Ireland was to see Vancouver Island from another point of view. I saw it from there as I'd never seen it before. I was able to get the distance you can't get when you're sitting right on it. Moving to Toronto or Halifax or Ottawa (where I spent six months as writer-in-residence in 1979) would do the same thing. If I didn't get too involved in playing tourist.

HANCOCK

One question about form. I noticed *Spit Delaney's Island* and *The Invention of the World* are both enclosed in an envelope so to speak. The books come full circle and close off very nicely. What does that say about your sense of resolution?

HODGINS

I suppose I wanted to do more than just raise a few questions and leave people squirming in the blood. Things *do* resolve. Problems *do* get resolved, even if only temporarily. At university I majored in mathematics. I like things to have shapes. I love patterns.

72

The idea of the book-ends in *Spit Delaney's Island* came after the book was accepted for publication. I wrote both Spit stories later than the others and saw that they could enclose the book nicely.

HANCOCK

Your characters have large personalities. You also like large narrators muscling about in your fiction. Your characters take on lives of their own. Do they dominate you or haunt you? I'm sure people have commented that Richard Starbuck or Maggie and Wade can come strolling down the road, like Don Quixote, or Captain Ahab, or Hamlet.

HODGINS

That's a very flattering comparison. One of my dreams is to create a character so appealing and real and gigantic that he or she will take on a life beyond the book. Someday. I haven't managed it yet. I'm humble enough to recognize that. To create someone who can belong to the world and not to me.

Before I can begin to write, my characters have to have enough depth and life to them to keep me interested. When I'm writing about them I don't think of them as large personalities or overwhelming people. If I thought of them that way I'd be frightened of them. To me they are quite ordinary.

HANCOCK

But you're still saying all our lives are extraordinary if looked at in the right way.

HODGINS

But they only become extraordinary when I get so close to them I can feel their bones. When I get to that point they take over. They run the story. They can run my life temporarily. And they can come back later and demand to be written about again. This happened with Mrs. Wright of "Three Women of the Country" until I told her where to get off. There was no way I could stand that woman's company through another story.

HANCOCK

Is Strabo Becker an obsessed character? With his tapes and his notebook he reminded me a little bit of Jeremy Sadness in Kroetsch's *Gone Indian*. It seems that a character who wants to be God must be an obsessed character. And then goes about to invent a world to prove he is a God-like character.

HODGINS

My relationship with Becker is not quite clear to me. He began as a funny little character who rustled about in the pages. Then he took on other proportions. I hadn't anticipated this. It wasn't until I had finished the first draft (of *Invention*) and probably other drafts that I saw Becker was indeed the artist. The inventor. But originally he was just a funny little guy who conveniently kept a scrapbook and conveniently knew the story of Donal Kenneally. The rest grew out of his personality, the needs of the story, and my own preoccupation with a certain theme.

73

HANCOCK

He's a good example of your point about reality. His account is "true" in the novel. It's a completely accurate transcription of events as they occurred in his imagination.

HODGINS

Of course. Not only that, but all the way through the novel he is dropping hints to the other characters that there is another way for them to perceive things. Not necessarily the story of Donal Kenneally, but their own realities. Becker is to me the one who pulls the novel together, the one who knows what the others are seeking and could tell them where to look if they'd only listen.

HANCOCK

But so few reviews picked up on that. Canadian reviewers aren't used to reading the so called "unreliable narrator."

HODGINS

I know. I was a bit disturbed by that reaction only because I hadn't anticipated it. I was more afraid that I was being too obvious.

HANCOCK

Do you try to balance opposites of character? For dramatic purposes?

HODGINS

In a story like "Three Women of the Country" it is quite deliberate. Often, if there is a contrast in character it's something I discover as I move through to highlight or rewrite. But I don't usually sit down and say now that I have this kind of person I need another kind.

In the case of Maggie Kyle and Donal Kenneally, I knew that his story took a certain direction, and that her story took the opposite direction. They had to be opposites in every way that I could think of.

HANCOCK

Almost like the X shape of Tolstoy's *Anna Karenina*.

HODGINS

Yes! There was a great X in my mind all the time I was writing. Kenneally's story is a downhill slide, inevitable from the moment it begins. He moves from the top of a mountain to a hole in the ground. Hers begins under a cabin, a shack, and rises gradually through the whole novel.

HANCOCK

Are names a clue to character? How do you keep your characters from becoming types or symbols? Details?

HODGINS

I don't know a character until I know his or her name. And I'm very careful about finding the name.

There isn't too much danger of them becoming types or symbols if you don't start writing about them until you know them. If they have individual personalities then they can't possibly be types. I just don't worry about that.

74

HANCOCK

I've noticed so many reviewers missed what you were doing.

HODGINS

That's one of the frustrations of writing. You must sit back and watch other people do things with your baby. A writer doesn't have the right to stand up and say, "But what I meant was. . . ." Once you've written the book, you've had your say and it's up to other people. One of the problems I had in reaction to *The Invention of the World* was that reviewers tend to pick up one minor concern and decide early in the novel that is the main theme of the novel. What it's like to live on an island, or, the transplanting of Irish myth to North America. Then they'll get to the end and have a sense of dissatisfaction. Obviously, many things in the novel don't fit into that pattern.

I was aware as I was writing that this was a novel about the island mentality, about utopias, about history, about half a dozen concerns. But none of those was the whole novel. One other concern for which these were metaphor only includes and supercedes all of them and is present on every page. All of them came together, culminated in the journey to the top of the mountain in Ireland. I felt I planted several signposts on the way. I did everything short of putting a neon sign at the top of the mountain to explain what this thing was all about. I didn't always feel that's what reviewers got from the novel.

HANCOCK

People seem to approach them with their own sets of conventions.

HODGINS

As one reviewer said, he doesn't read a novel to puzzle out things. I can appreciate that. A reader has a perfect right not to dig out the meaning or look for signposts. It doesn't bother me at all if a reader doesn't take the time to notice all the things I wanted to do in that novel. But it does matter to me that he have a sense of the richness that's beneath the surface. Personally, I like to read a book where I have the feeling that there's lots more here. That in a lifetime of study I would never get it all. It's the richness beneath the surface that's important. Perhaps a reviewer who doesn't think it's *fun* to read a novel that requires a little work ought to review only cookbooks or catalogues.

HANCOCK

You're right. It has to be a reading experience first. Then a literary experience. Then an intellectual experience.

HODGINS

But all those things are of no importance until the reading experience has happened. The people and the story have to be interesting enough to keep you reading to the end.

HANCOCK

Would you comment a bit on the germination of *The Invention of the World*?

It's a very complex germination. It began when I toyed with the idea of writing a novel about the infamous Brother Twelve and his colony of religious followers. It's a bit of local history. Just south of Nanaimo. Brother Twelve was an unusual character who did fantastic things, including fraud, scandals, and murder. I discovered very early in my attempt at research that people didn't want to talk about it. So I couldn't get very far if I wanted to be faithful to fact. And then, while I was making these attempts, some other story began to tell itself in my head, much more interesting to me. I abandoned Brother Twelve very early and got on with the job of the Donal Kenneally story.

I wasn't interested in writing a novel with him as the central character, however. Maggie Kyle had begun to grow. I could see the relationship between the two of them and the story began to form. I guess it was the gradual revelation of the character of Maggie Kyle as opposed to the character of Donal Kenneally. That, and my fascination with a pattern that began to grow involving various types of counterfeits — maps, fake historical sites, alter egos, idols, imitation Edens, as well as images of second growth.

And Becker?

He was a convenient bridge between the two characters and between the past and the present. Especially since my protagonist and antagonist did not live at the same time. They needed a bridge. Also he could be my spokesman in the story. And he was interesting, this little guy.

Would you like to say more about Maggie Kyle?

She's a type of woman I've been familiar with all my life. I've known many Maggie Kyles. To me they embody energy, life, optimism, determination, joy, excitement, all the positive qualities. I loved her as I wrote her and I love her still.

George Woodcock and other reviewers felt that some of the images you used were "an excess of the diabolic." A juxtaposition of true myth with fabricated myth. Would you care to elaborate on this? Is myth a safety net beneath plot?

It's difficult to talk about myth since the book itself becomes a myth by the time you finish it.

What do you mean by myth?

Lies that tell the truth, someone has said. A story we can look at to help us answer an unanswerable question. A story that we feel must have been true even before someone made it up.

HANCOCK

Myth is not just a self indulgence of the artist?

HODGINS

No! To me myth is closer to reality than history. While history is a collection of the facts, myth is the soul that surrounds those facts.

The "excess of the diabolic" doesn't make any sense to me either. That is ignoring the whole balance between Maggie Kyle and Donal Kenneally, the whole essence of the novel. It's Maggie Kyle who triumphs. Donal Kenneally is buried in the ground. I'm not revelling in the diabolical at all. I'm seeing it as counterfeit and therefore destroying it.

HANCOCK

This is more than a literary convention. It's something basic to your view of life.

HODGINS

Oh yes. I'm writing allegories I suppose.

HANCOCK

In the penultimate chapter of *The Invention of the World* do I detect faint echoes of Garcia Marquez' "Big Momma's Funeral"?

HODGINS

No question about it. The last chapter was intended to be an epilogue, and I neglected until too late to label it such, something I regret now. When I was about three-quarters through the first draft I suddenly knew how the thing had to end and I recalled having read "Big Momma's Funeral" with its notion of everybody coming to the funeral. It sounded like a Vancouver Island wedding. And, of course, it was the logical, appropriate after-ending for this story.

A more definite influence, though, was Pope's "The Rape of the Lock." That last chapter is a mock epic, just as "The Eden Swindle" is a mock myth.

HANCOCK

What technical problems did the novel present? Each chapter is devoted to a different character. You have problems of interaction between the characters, especially between the dead and the living, or characters who live in different epochs. That's a lot of balls to juggle in the air.

HODGINS

Yes, and if I remember correctly, I decided not to worry about it in the first draft. To relax and know that when I got to the end pieces were going to fall into place.

I was more concerned with each section to make sure I got the voice and the point of view right. During revisions I could concern myself with balance and interaction, with creating a sense that the unseen story is still going on in the background while the novel is primarily concerned with just one thread.

77

Would you care to say anything about your second novel, *The Resurrection of Joseph Bourne?*

Strange, but I don't feel the need to talk about this novel at all, as I did with *Invention*. If I do, it's only to recall some of the episodes I think are particularly funny. I have no urge to explain it, no need to talk about its origins, no compulsion to "sell" it to anyone.

I know it's more conventional in structure than *Invention* — a continuous narrative — but I also know it's a more ambitious novel. I know that it'll be an easier novel to read than *Invention* for those people who want to be entertained only, and more rewarding for people who like to notice things. I know that the book in its early drafts nearly drove me crazy. I used to wake up in the night sometimes washed over with cold fear absolutely sure I'd never be able to pull it off, and once went several weeks unable to write, overwhelmed by the task I'd set myself until the tremendous relief I felt upon deciding to burn the whole thing, forget it, made me so relaxed and happy that I was immediately flooded with a huge vision of the novel I'd been searching for and went back to work like a madman.

And yet the final impression the book has left me with is one of total enjoyment. I loved those people, I did a lot of laughing in their company, and I was really very sorry to have to let them go at the end.

MAVIS GALLANT

At the time of this interview, in 1977, few of Mavis' works had been published in Canada. Since then nearly everything, with the exception of a few *New Yorker* stories, has been collected. Titles now available include *The Other Paris* (1956), *Green Water, Green Sky* (1959), *My Heart Is Broken* (1964), *A Fairly Good Time* (1970), *The End of the World and Other Stories* (1973), *The Pegnitz Junction* (1973) *From the Fifteenth District* (1979), *Home Truths* (1981), *Overhead in a Balloon* (1985), and *Paris Notebooks* (1986).

The interview was recorded in two sessions on the sunny afternoons of October 23 and 25. The first took place in her airy, elegant apartment in the fashionable Faubourg St. Germain area of Paris. But a jackhammer is a jackhammer even on the left bank, and because of street construction noise the second session, which began with my question "You're not Peter Handke...", was held in a neighbouring apartment overlooking a leafy courtyard.

The neighbour's apartment, as Mavis had warned me, was a "typical" French middle-class home, with a loud red door that resembled the entrance to either a French bordello or a Chinese restaurant. Or perhaps a Chinese bordello. By contrast, Mavis did not have mismatched brown velvet chairs and rococo lamps; her chairs and sofas were light-coloured and comfortable, the coffee table was wrought iron inlaid with painted tiles, and on the walls were favourite paintings and prints, including a Picasso etching of Stravinsky, and a rare copy of the newspaper *L'Aurore* with Emile Zola's famous "J'accuse" headline — a gift from a friend. The fine antique sideboards held Persian tiles and heavy plates with rooster designs, and guests could choose their own wineglasses. Bach, *Der Rosenkavalier*, or even Charles Mingus might be playing on the turntable.

Books filled an alcove from floor to ceiling, and naturally, when we played the "what books have you read?" game, Mavis held her own. Among many others, we talked about Paul Theroux, Edna O'Brien, Alejo Carpenter, Maurice Pons, Mikhail Bulgakov, Peter Handke, Peter Mathiessen, John Updike, Donald Barthelme, Philip Roth, and Joseph Wechsberg. Nor was Mavis out of touch with Canadian writers. Her comments on Robertson Davies, Anne Hébert, Morley Callaghan, Rudy Wiebe, Marian Engel, Kent Thompson, Irving Layton, Margaret Atwood, Graeme Gibson, Sheila Watson, Clark Blaise, Bharati Mukherjee, and Ian Maclachlan ranged from praise to damnation. But since she didn't live in Canada, she laughed, she didn't want to seem impertinent: "If I don't like a book, I'll just say it's ahead of its time."

Mavis wouldn't normally talk about her writing or her private life, and certainly not for nearly three hours. She would rather discuss politics, the latest art shows, current German cinema, especially Herzog and Fassbinder, or even lovers' triangles and marital breakups. But once she warmed up to the idea of doing an interview, she responded at generous good length. She sketched out a fifteen-page response to the initial questions, which allowed me to rework the shape of the interview. The original transcript was then revised for style or clarity of meaning, especially places she considered "garbled, incomprehensible, meaningless, barely literate, or libellous." In other words, she filled in the gaps between spoken and written English. Some passages, such as the segment on "the super-Canadians," were substantially expanded. I personally miss her untaped and hilarious account of how a Canadian story usually began: "God, it was cold." Or, "They had been quarrelling again. Harriet and Jim walked silently to the station. The wind blew through the trees." At which point a Canadian critic would query: "What does it *mean*? This wind blowing through the trees."

Naturally, Mavis would not waste time with frivolous or prying questions. If a question came up she didn't like, such as an inquiry into her private life, or her opinion on certain writers, she would smile graciously, shake her head, and wave the question off. She developed her answers carefully and kept asking if it was alright, if it was what I wanted. Though she thought the final transcript "a bit testy at times, but why not?", I should add that in places we were laughing so hard we had to sort ourselves out before we could continue. The tape is filled with gusts of laughter, the popping of wine corks, and the clink of ice cubes in large glasses of white wine.

HANCOCK

What attracts you to Paris? Is it the light? The sense of assertiveness and security Parisians have?

GALLANT

No. When I left Canada I was looking for a place where I could live on my own terms. That may sound very pompous, but it's true. If it had turned out to be Madrid, I'd have stayed in Madrid. I found Paris the most open city, the one that leaves you alone most, the one where you can live exactly as you like. It's very malleable. London is too large. Rome in the 1950s was provincial.

HANCOCK

Did you always intend to have a career as a writer?

GALLANT

Oh, I never intended anything else. I was going to be a poet. I wrote nothing but poetry until I was about eighteen or nineteen.

80

HANCOCK

Which writers were you reading at the time?

GALLANT

I read everything I could get my hands on. Then I began reading in waves. There was a long wave of Russian writers, in English translation, of course. Chekhov, Gogol, Turgenev, Dostoevsky. That was followed by a wave of French — Stendhal, Flaubert, Proust. Proust was and remains my favourite writer, if there is any such thing.

HANCOCK

What attracted you to them?

GALLANT

You are attracted to the writers who reflect what is going through your head and your life at the time. I read more at eighteen and nineteen than I do now. The writers you read when young seem not only close to you, but prophetic. After a certain age, they tally or don't tally with life as you know it.

HANCOCK

You've also met a fair number of writers in Europe. Have they influenced you in any way? I'm thinking of people like Samuel Beckett and Jean-Paul Sartre.

GALLANT

How would they influence one?

HANCOCK

A different sense of looking at the world perhaps?

GALLANT

The writers who help you look at the world are those you read when young. I don't think that after a certain age anyone can change your way of looking. Do you?

HANCOCK

I don't think so. What did you learn from the Russians?

GALLANT

I don't know. I can't tell you why I was drawn to a certain group of writers any more than I can explain why I'm attracted to German cinema now, why I see every German film that comes along.

HANCOCK

Which writers in Europe do you like currently? Say, in France.

GALLANT

Robert Pinget, for one. If you like Proust, you'll like him. I can't think of names off hand. Siegfried Lenz, in Germany, who wrote *The German Lesson*. Beautiful. Have you read it?

HANCOCK

No.

GALLANT

A beautiful novel. I don't like Heinrich Böll very much. But I like Günter Grass.

And Nabokov?

Oh, yes! I read Nabokov in Canada, long before I came to Europe. I read *The Real Life of Sebastian Knight*, in Canada, soon after it was published. When I came to Europe I found no one had heard of it. He was unknown until the mid-fifties when *Lolita* appeared. Just as no one had heard of Webern. Or Schoenberg. Paris seemed very provincial to me in some respects. The French knew nothing at all about modern music. When you said "Webern" they thought you meant *Weber*. Their idea of modern music had stopped with Ravel. More went on in Canada than even Canadians knew. The best Sartre I have ever seen on the stage was in Montreal in the late 1940s, a Rideau Vert production of *Huis Clos*.

HANCOCK
So coming to Europe was a learning experience in reverse?

GALLANT
I certainly didn't find any writers here that I hadn't heard of in Canada. Unless Canada has greatly changed, there's no reason why you can't read absolutely everything. It's a matter of finding the right bookshop.

HANCOCK
Would you care to comment on your contemporaries in Canada?

GALLANT
No. It would very impertinent of me. I don't live there.

HANCOCK
Let's talk about your Montreal background. Do you think the many schools you went to, being in that halfway point between French and English Canada, helped shape you as a writer?

GALLANT
I don't know about *that*. I don't know what shapes people as a writer. I think you come into the world as a writer.

HANCOCK
This ties in with a comment you said earlier, that talent is beside oneself.

GALLANT
Yes. It alights. Harold Ross, who was the first editor of *The New Yorker*, said talent doesn't care which branch it sits on. It just alights. Like a bird.

HANCOCK
You learned French very early.

GALLANT
Yes. I was bilingual as a child.

HANCOCK
Perhaps that's a reason you ended up in France.

82

GALLANT

No. Obviously the fact I could speak to people helped, but had I liked Munich better, I'd have learned better German and gone there. I lived in Spain two years. I pick up languages very easily. And forget them easily. When I left Spain I spoke Spanish with a Madrid accent. People sometimes thought I *was* Spanish. Now I can hardly put a Spanish sentence together, though I can still read it.

HANCOCK

Were any of your family writers?

GALLANT

Oh no.

HANCOCK

Your parents died when you were young.

GALLANT

My father did. My mother later. I have no sisters or brothers.

HANCOCK

Going to seventeen schools in Canada and the United States must have been very influential in helping you develop a strong independence of mind.

GALLANT

It has a different effect on different people, doesn't it. If I had children, I would not have put my child through that. I imagine some children could take it, but it would absolutely break another kind of child. But it did something positive for me—there's no milieu I don't feel comfortable in, that I don't immediately understand.

HANCOCK

That same sense of milieu applies to your fictional world. As I've been reading it, your fictional world is pervaded by a sense of family, especially a family that doesn't communicate.

GALLANT

Some people are quiet and some people never shut up. Communication is quite other. In that sense all families are the same.

HANCOCK

Here's a critical question. The central characters of many of your stories are trying to get out of a family situation . . .

GALLANT

Most people are, you know. Most people are, unless they're neurotic. Oh, I don't mean that it's normal for people not to like their families. But most people are trying to get out of the coop, aren't they?

HANCOCK

. . . yet at the same time your characters find comfort and a false sense of security within the family. Escape doesn't work so your characters dominate, betray, or withdraw from each other.

GALLANT

You would know more about that than I do because I don't reread my work and I've never read it as something with a pattern. I can't help you there. I don't begin with a theory. If I did, I'd be lost. I wouldn't know what to do.

HANCOCK

But in your own words, the family experience is "a dialogue of the deaf" between people who know too much about each other because they are so close.

GALLANT

I think most of the trouble in life comes from people who think they know too much about each other. (*Laughs.*) People simply don't leave each other alone enough.

HANCOCK

Love is often equated with resentment because people don't leave each other alone. Would you comment on that?

GALLANT

I'm stuck there. People want such different things. I'd have to think about it.

HANCOCK

Does fiction have to have conflict?

GALLANT

Well, it has to have something that interests you.

HANCOCK

But not necessarily conflict?

GALLANT

I suppose it is really. I'd have to think about it. I'm sorry to keep repeating that, but I don't think about writing in those terms. Something interests me or it doesn't. It's as simple as that.

For example, the writer I reread most is Proust. What draws me, why, I don't know.

HANCOCK

If I was an academic critic and asked you if the wind in one of your stories was such and such a symbol . . .

GALLANT

I'd burst out laughing.

HANCOCK

You don't agree with people like Baudelaire, for example, who believe literature is a forest of symbols.

GALLANT

Well, probably it is. But he was a poet wasn't he. And he was a poet of that particular period. Did Auden ever say literature was a forest of symbols? I don't think so.

HANCOCK

But your work suggests someone who is searching for broader meanings to experience.

GALLANT

That's part of age.

HANCOCK

You think so?

GALLANT

Yes, absolutely. Otherwise you're a pretty poor thing. There's no point in going on living.

HANCOCK

What about the Montreal of your childhood, the war years, that uniquely Canadian preoccupation between French and English?

GALLANT

I've never lived in a city exactly as Montreal was then. It was unique, unclassifiable. All those small worlds of race and language and religion and class, all shut away from one another. A series of airtight compartments. But a handsome city, the most attractive imaginable. It's ruined now. People didn't know what they had.

HANCOCK

Have you been back there recently?

GALLANT

I was there last year. (*1976, and Christmas 1977*)

HANCOCK

Do you think the search for a place is a unique Canadian theme?

GALLANT

I've never noticed any single Canadian theme. But there perhaps is one which I mentioned to you. That is the role of the father in fiction. That has struck me. The father seems to be more important to us in fiction than the mother.

HANCOCK

Margaret Atwood in . . .

GALLANT

Surfacing is about the search for a father.

HANCOCK

Margaret Atwood has noted in *Survival* that the strong characters in Canadian fiction are old women.

GALLANT

She's read more about it than I have.

HANCOCK

She mentions your story "The Legacy" as part of her thesis that . . .

GALLANT

There's no old woman in that.

HANCOCK

Actually she was referring to the whole family as a trap, not just the dead parents.

GALLANT

I haven't read that story for twenty years. The reason I remember it and can still see it is because it was based on something that was told to me. I was working on a newspaper story when I came across a family like the one in "The Legacy." I sat in someone's kitchen in the east end of Montreal while a young woman standing at an ironing board told me the story of her life. An unhappy life. She told me how she tried to get away from home, and about her delinquent brother, the one so dumb that the police caught him running away from a foiled holdup, still hanging onto a gun. I didn't invent any of that.

HANCOCK

You're still a Canadian citizen.

GALLANT

Good God, yes! Why would I be anything else?

HANCOCK

You've not thought of taking out French citizenship?

GALLANT

I could have become an American citizen at one time, but I chose to remain Canadian. I mean, that the choice was open to me. That was a long time ago. Being Canadian is one of the facts of my life. I would be a Canadian even if Canada ceased to exist, because it is a part of being myself. I have no identity problem concerning Canada, if that's what you're looking for. In fact, I don't believe anyone has. It's something people like to imagine about themselves because it sounds tense and stormy and romantic.

HANCOCK

Have you ever written in French?

GALLANT

No, and I wouldn't. First of all, I prefer writing in English . . .

HANCOCK

What attracts you to English?

GALLANT

Oh, it's an absolutely fabulous language. It's so misused, so underused. For writing there's no comparison between English and French. When Beckett chose French, deliberately, it was because he wanted a tighter, smaller framework. I can't imagine anyone wanting that.

At the same time, I much prefer French for conversation. We English speakers are not taught how to speak. English-speaking children are used most often to be told to shut up. Conversation is apt to remain on the level of anecdotes. I had the experience in Edmonton two years ago of talking to a small group of English-speaking students and then a class of French-speaking students on the same day. In English I could not elicit more than "um," "er," "I mean," "well," "like," "er," and so on. In French, the conversation sailed, the questions were pertinent and interesting, the students had opinions. It had everything to do with the way they had been taught to use their language as children.

As for writing in French, because I live in France I avoid doing that at all. I speak French all day. All my friends, with the exception of about two, are French-speaking. Even if they are Poles or Spanish or Germans we speak French. I have the feeling that if I begin writing anything in French I would lose my feeling for written English. I don't even write letters in French if my correspondent can understand English — except for one or two Quebec friends and I do that as a courtesy. It is a courtesy that was not often extended to French-Canadians in the past.

HANCOCK

You're writing a series of Montreal stories that are dated from approximately the 1920s . . .

GALLANT

They go from the 1920s to the end of the war and stop. One very very long story is about the war and that's the end of the series.

HANCOCK

Could you tell me a bit about that series?

GALLANT

Well what do you mean? What do you want me to tell you? You've read them.

HANCOCK

Why are you writing this series of stories?

GALLANT

Oh come on! You're not going to ask me why I'm writing something. An intelligent man like you! (*Laughs.*)

HANCOCK

It seems important that you document this particular period of vanished time.

GALLANT

It seems important to me. For one thing, an earlier Montreal is intact in my mind. I wasn't there to watch the gradual changes taking place. When I see the Sherbrooke Street of today I see it without remembering it. When I come back to Paris I remember only that other, older, much handsomer street. Then, my having been sent to a French school, where I was the only English-speaking child and the only Protestant — the only one in the entire history of the school, for that matter — gave me, or has left me with, a *total* Montreal, not only a racial fragment. That particular experience might seem commonplace today, when so many parents prefer Catholic schools for their children, for a number of reasons. But then, before the war, it was unheard of.

I had never intended to write anything of that kind until I began working on a book about the Dreyfus case. Reconstructing the Paris of the eighteen-nineties I began in some other way to reconstruct that other, lost city. The stories began entirely on their own, as if they had been there waiting. I simply got up one morning and wrote most of the first one, and in a day or so the notes for the rest of them.

HANCOCK

You have a very good memory. You can easily reach backwards.

GALLANT

Yes, but once something is written, I forget its source. Once you have put reality through the filter and turned it into that other reality called fiction, the original ingredient ceases to exist. Ceases to exist in memory, that is.

HANCOCK

Are you finding these stories easy to write?

GALLANT

No easier than anything else. But the people in the stories are not identical with people I knew in my life. The stories are really the reconstruction of a city which no longer exists. The girl (Linnet Muir) is obviously close to me. She isn't *myself*, but a kind of summary of some of the things I once was. In real life I was far more violent and much more impulsive and not nearly so reasonable. Straight autobiography would be boring. It would bore me. It would bore the reader. The stories are a kind of reality *necessarily* transformed. The people are completely other, and some characters two or three different persons all at the same time.

HANCOCK

What kind of child were you?

GALLANT

Some people remembered me as a little girl with perfect manners and some remembered me as a brat. So I must have been both. The kind of child I was undoubtedly changed with the changes in my life, which were often unexpected and violent. I have been told that I was docile and easily managed until I was sent to school. Then I became stubborn, obstinate, what adults call difficult. At the age of four, I was sent as a boarder to an extremely severe Jansenist kind of convent school, a kind that no longer exists in any country. I was lifted onto a chair in the *parloir*, the convent parlour, which contained some uncompromising very hard chairs, and I was told, "Sit there and wait, like a good girl, and I shall be right back." How the nuns got me off the chair and out of that room I can't imagine.

I could read then—I can't remember when I couldn't. So that from the age of four, I was half in life and half in books. I got on well with other children, but mistrusted adults. I was not afraid of them, but had the curious idea that they were incompetent. My one desire from the age of about ten was to grow up and become independent and not have anyone try and tell me what to do. All writers have something of the failed delinquent about them. Even the most respectable-seeming writer is always a bit *voyou*, a bit rapscallion. Go through his life with a fine-toothed comb and you will always find that at one point he was walking with a foot off the curb. In childhood, in adolescence, or just in his own head.

HANCOCK

You went to seventeen boarding schools.

GALLANT

Not just boarding schools. I went to every kind of school you can imagine. Some people have been to more. Clark Blaise has been to seven times as many, I think.

HANCOCK

At age twenty-eight you left Canada.

GALLANT

That's right.

HANCOCK

And you came to Paris. Did you say you nearly went to Vienna?

GALLANT

No. I nearly went to London, then came to Paris. I went to Vienna much later. Well, one year later. For three years I moved around all the time. Sicily, Spain, southern France.

HANCOCK

This would be in 1950.

GALLANT

Yes. Don't forget I left a job with a newspaper. I gave it up without prospects. I didn't have anyone behind me. I didn't have a penny behind me. I gave myself two years to see if I could live on writing.

HANCOCK

What prompted the move to Europe?

GALLANT

I was twenty-seven when I quit my job. I was getting too old. You can't hang on until when? Until you're forty? I knew I had to do it before I was thirty.

HANCOCK

You couldn't have a writing career in Canada?

GALLANT

Are you joking? You're thinking of a different Canada. You're much younger than I am. You're thinking of a Canada with Canada Council grants, and nouveau-riche prosperity where art is taken to be ornamentation.

HANCOCK
Why didn't you go to New York?

GALLANT

I had already lived in New York. I knew all about it, and wanted something different. Going to live in New York would have meant going backwards. There were people living there then who still considered me a child. I would not have felt free, even at twenty-eight. I went first to London. London in 1950 was not welcoming or open. I found it ugly, heavy, very remote from my idea of it, which had been purely literary. The Canadians I met there were often pretending to be something else—British usually. I wonder if you are aware of the number of Canadians abroad who pretend not to be Canadian? It is the only nationality I know of where this happens. I mean English-Canadians. French-Canadians always identify themselves at once.

HANCOCK

A small point: did you come by boat?

GALLANT

No. By plane. I came by plane. Air Canada made me a present of the flight. That is, their public-relations man gave me the flight as a going-away present. May I roast in hell for having forgotten his name. He was a pal, a *copain*.

Only two things were given me. That, which was nice. A free flight was a big thing in those days. It was a long long flight. I think sixteen hours.

And the man who owned the paper, *The Standard*—John McConnell, who is dead now—gave me a personal present of five hundred dollars. Which was kind. He didn't have to. Once, when I was collecting money for the strikers during a Dominion Textile strike, I started with him. He gave me five dollars, and told me not to mention it. This is the first time I have ever spoken of it. McConnell and the man at Air Canada. Everyone else, or nearly, said, "You'll be back with your ears drooping."

HANCOCK

You also worked briefly for the National Film Board.

GALLANT

Oh, God!

HANCOCK

What did you do there?

GALLANT

Ha! I worked in the negative cutting room for which I was about as fit as I am for piloting a submarine. I was absolutely unsuited for the place, for the work, for the atmosphere, for anything. The only thing that could come out of the Film Board thing is a satirical novel. That I'm sure will still come.

HANCOCK

From there you went to work for the Montreal *Standard*.

GALLANT

Yes.

HANCOCK

You did a lot of work for them as a reporter.

GALLANT

For the *Standard*? I was there six years. I adored it.

HANCOCK

You wrote feature articles . . .

GALLANT

From the beginning. Soon after I started to work I suggested a story I could do with a photographer. It was a young paper, almost everyone working there was young. You could try almost anything you suggested. I wanted to follow a city kid around the streets and see what his tracks were — his pattern, his routine. (I was amused that not long ago a very solemn book was published on this subject.) I choose a little boy aged about five by the name of Johnny. The photographer was so good — he took some marvellous pictures of the child. The photographer was called Hi Frankel. We followed the kid for days. There really *was* a pattern. When he sat on the sidewalk with his feet in the gutter it was always in the same block, in the same place. Fascinating. That was my first by-line.

HANCOCK

You were writing fiction all this time?

GALLANT

All the time, yes.

HANCOCK

"The Events in May: A Paris Notebook" suggests you keep many notebooks.

GALLANT

Yes, I keep many notebooks. It's a habit now.

HANCOCK

Do you ever tamper with the distortions of memory?

GALLANT

No. I think that's a great mistake. For example in the Montreal stories, I never check anything. If I remember a street wrong, it has to stay wrong.

HANCOCK

About this time you started selling stories to *The New Yorker* . . .

GALLANT

No. What happened was . . . Do you really want to know this?

HANCOCK

Yes.

Does it really interest you? Well . . . I had decided to quit my job and come to Europe. I had never published anything except for two very short stories in a literary journal, not a proper magazine. It was mimeographed, I believe, and called *Preview*. The editor was Frank Scott, or perhaps he was one of a committee. I have forgotten. One of the very few persons to whom I'd shown anything was Kit Shaw, the librarian at the *Standard*. She showed these two stories to Frank Scott without telling me, and they were printed. I never saw them again for about thirty years, when someone sent me copies. It was like reading someone else's work, someone young, who had been reading Russian stories. I was up to there in Chekhov then. They were stories about a refugee. I was fascinated by the war refugees in Montreal. I used to try to write from their point of view; that is, seeing something familiar to me the way someone from an entirely different culture might see it.

I had never sent any of my work anywhere, not to a magazine or a publisher. In the spring of 1950 I gave notice that I would be leaving in the fall. I must tell you something here. Even when people like you, they just slightly hope you might fail. Even when they love you. It is an unconscious hope. If your bid for freedom — because that is what it amounted to — should fail, then it justifies the risks they've never taken. The failure of a woman reassures men just as men. It reassures the women who have hung onto safe jobs, boring husbands. One's defeat will reassure. I felt very strongly that my failure was desired more than my success. There were only a few persons with whom I didn't feel that.

A reporter I worked with pointed out that I hadn't published anything, which was sensible enough. He said, "You're like an architect who says he's an architect without ever having passed an exam." Do you really want to hear this? It's a long boring story.

Yes, certainly.

I had a picnic hamper full of manuscripts. Novels, poems, plays, stories. I wrote more than I've ever done since. I think. All this in longhand. I think I wrote faster then. Now, I'm very slow. After the remark about the architect and the exam I thought perhaps he was right. I took a story out of the hamper and typed it and mailed it to *The New Yorker*. I had an answer saying something like, "This is too specifically Canadian for us, but have you written anything else." I got out another story, which was set in the United States, in Connecticut, where I had lived for a time, and that story was accepted. And that is exactly what happened with *The New Yorker*.

I did not, as people mistakenly imagine, "sell a story and throw up my job." My leaving was not an impulsive gesture. I had been thinking of it for over a year. I was twenty-seven when I quit, a few months short of twenty-eight. I saw thirty as a deadline, a trench across one's life.

As for the Canadian story, I gave it to John Sutherland who published it in *Northern Review*. As for *The New Yorker*, I didn't know a soul there, and no one there knew anything about me.

HANCOCK

Tied in with this hope of success, did you also have the feeling that you wanted to write for the best magazine in the world? Which I think *The New Yorker* was.

GALLANT

It was then. Yes. I was very happy to be published there. I carried my letter of acceptance around and showed it to people. It amazes me now to think I could ever have done this. I had a letter not long ago from one of the editors of the paper I used to work for. The Canadian stories have drawn letters from Canadians I haven't heard from in twenty-five years. Canadians take Canadian fiction very literally. If you say the wind was blowing from the east, they'll write saying it must have been blowing from the west. In the letter this editor said that I had once told him I did not want to be a writer, but a *New Yorker* writer. His memory is wrong. I never said a thing like that. Because one of my worries about *The New Yorker* was that it would be too strong for me — that it would put a kind of hand on me.

HANCOCK

What does "kind of hand" mean?

GALLANT

I was afraid that there would be so much editing that my work would cease to be mine.

HANCOCK

But they never have?

GALLANT

It was my work, always. But it was a kind of editing that consisted of queries. I once had fourteen on a single page. Everyone has his own favourite story about them. My own is being asked if Angus Muir was a French-Canadian or English-Canadian name. My own feeling about fiction is that it does not matter if something is mixed up or muddled or if the author forgets which colour dress the heroine was wearing. For example, what if a careful staff of checkers had gone over *War and Peace*? Tolstoy gets everyone's age wrong. When they should be sixty they're forty. When they should be twenty they're suddenly thirty-eight. What does it matter? In the last volume of Proust the characters' ages are cuckoo. Not nearly enough time has gone by for them to be as old as he makes them. Although the early volumes have the Dreyfus case as their background, as their frame, in a way, everything

93

historical is out of sequence, in the wrong season, at the wrong time. That doesn't stop *Remembrance of Things Past* from being the most important and accurate thing ever written about the Dreyfus case, or the greatest novel ever written about anything, for that matter.

HANCOCK

Are you interested in politics?

GALLANT

Something I found hilarious in Robert Weaver's introduction to that collection of stories (*The End of the World*, New Canadian Library) was his saying I'm obviously not interested in politics. Everyone I showed that to howled with laughter. I'm *extremely* interested in politics. My writing is permeated with politics. I read I don't know how many newspapers a day.

HANCOCK

The left or the right?

GALLANT

Those words haven't the meaning they had then. Don't forget the war was "Fascism or else!" The situation has so changed now that we'd be hours talking about it.

HANCOCK

Did the war affect your political opinions?

GALLANT

I was passionately anti-Fascist. I wasn't anti-German. I was anti-Fascist, anti-Nazi.

HANCOCK

Moving up to date, you're also well informed on current Canadian political affairs.

GALLANT

As much as I can be, yes.

HANCOCK

You go to the *Centre Culturel Canadien* which is not too far from your home.

GALLANT

I go occasionally and have a bash through the papers. The French press gets everything wrong. And the *International Herald Tribune*! I've never seen an American who could write properly about Canada and I don't know why that is.

HANCOCK

You've never written directly about the war. Only its effects.

GALLANT

I wasn't a storm trooper, you know.

HANCOCK

You wrote me that you took part in the D-Day landings with the Queen's Own Rifles and were then transferred to the Black Watch, where you were rapidly promoted Colonel and decorated under fire. That only modesty keeps you from writing directly about the war.

GALLANT

Oh, that was a joke! You mean you took that seriously? Oh, poor you! (*Laughs.*) You really took it seriously!

HANCOCK

I'm from the coast. I didn't know about the Queen's Own Rifles.

GALLANT

That's a Toronto regiment.

HANCOCK

I take Canadian fiction literally.

GALLANT

(*Laughing.*) You poor thing. Forgive me. Did you really expect me to write about the Battle of the Bulge? Did you think I was there? Do you think we had girl partisans? How funny! God, imagine. I'm going to have another drink on that.

HANCOCK

Are you religious? Are you a practising Anglican?

GALLANT

I'm not a practising anything.

HANCOCK

You said you were "teetering".

GALLANT

No, I'm not a practising anything. Practising means going to church. But I can't completely — and this is nobody's business — take seriously a philosophy that excludes the possibility of Divine Intervention. On the other hand, I find it hard to believe we're in a world where God walked. Don't you? Do you think God Incarnate walked here and left us? Look at us. Awful. Dreadful. Get in the Métro and look at people.

HANCOCK

Does it matter where you write?

GALLANT

No. All I need is nobody bothering me. Hotel rooms are divine.

HANCOCK

Do you need a window or a wall?

GALLANT

Oh, a window or a wall. As long as I have a good light and it's not too hot or stuffy. The usual things. Noise, that is people, bother me.

HANCOCK

You don't have to be in Europe to write?

GALLANT

I've never written anywhere else. At least not for years. But I suppose I could.

HANCOCK

What makes Europe so attractive to writers?

GALLANT

The context I should think.

HANCOCK

I find it odd that so few Canadian writers come here to share part of that context.

GALLANT

Who else lives here? Anne Hébert is the only one I can think of.

HANCOCK

But what happened to that Henry James sense, that Hemingway or F. Scott Fitzgerald sense of coming to Europe to write?

GALLANT

The American writer who lived in Paris and wrote out of Paris was Gertrude Stein. Hemingway — if you look at his life — was in and out of Paris. As for Fitzgerald, he was scarcely here at all. He spent less time here than the average exchange professor does today. He never learned a word of French. I've known people who met him then. No one could communicate with him, partly because he was always drunk, partly because of the language difficulty. People are apt to think of Hemingway and Fitzgerald in connection with Paris because of a cliché image of the nineteen twenties. Edith Wharton was much more closely tied to Paris. She lived easily in two, actually three languages, and she could write in French as easily as English.

HANCOCK

You started to write *The Other Paris* as soon as you arrived, in the autumn of 1950. On this, your first trip to Europe, you must have seen Paris with fresh eyes.

GALLANT

Every idea I'd had about Paris turned out to be wrong. You must remember this was soon after the war. I was politically naïve about France. I had imagined nearly everyone in the Resistance. The Resistance turned out to be a few thousand out of a population of nearly fifty million. The Occupation was no joke, but it was nothing compared to what the Dutch or the Greeks went through, not to speak of the Poles. The schools and universities were never closed in France. Restaurants, theatres and the opera continued to function, and so did the nightclubs. The upper classes sailed through without much more than inconvenience. The poor, the honest, the conscientious bore the brunt. I hadn't been in Paris a week before I heard the phrase I would hear often: "The Germans were very *correct*," meaning they were well mannered, they weren't drunk in the streets. Now, no one would dare say it except as a joke. Then, it was an enormous shock to me. I couldn't believe it.

In Canada of 1950 was it difficult to prove yourself as a writer of talent? In your story "In Youth Is Pleasure" you write "In those days there was no such thing as a Canadian."

GALLANT

I'm not sure of the date, but I believe there was no such thing as a Canadian until about 1935. You were whatever your father was. If he was the thirteenth generation of Norwegians in Canada you were considered Norwegian.

HANCOCK

You suggested I ask Sinclair Ross what it was like being in Canada then. I wrote to him and he replied he thought he was too isolated to be representative. He even went so far as to say he did not consider himself as an author working in a bank, but a bank clerk trying to do a little writing on the side. Did you know him then?

GALLANT

I can't remember when I first met Jimmy Ross. It may have been in the forties. It is not up to me to comment on him, and I'm not at all sure that he'd thank me for it. I look on him as a writer whose gifts had to be sacrificed to financial need — the need of holding down a dull job, the incomprehension of the milieu he lived in. However, he is almost the only person of whom I think this. I have absolutely no patience with the people who say they would write if they had time. It might be worth pointing out that this is said only to writers. No one ever says, "I'd design the new city hall if only I had time."

HANCOCK

Do you agree with the New York publisher who said that Canada is the boondocks?

GALLANT

I was very offended at that. Someone wrote to me, thinking I would agree, that the whole country is like a second-rate university in the boondocks. Even if I thought such a thing I wouldn't say it — of another country, I mean. I certainly didn't think it of Canada.

HANCOCK

But it means your recent books are very difficult to find in Canada.

GALLANT

That's the publisher's problem, not mine.

HANCOCK

But it is a problem for readers.

GALLANT

It's up to them. When I want a book, I find it.

HANCOCK

I've found from talking to people that if the book isn't around, few will take the trouble to look for it.

GALLANT

Then the hell with it.

HANCOCK

In your case, there's the additional fact that many of your stories are uncollected. This means a great deal of scrounging around, of getting a bibliography, or back lists, then writing to *The New Yorker* with the titles and the dates . . .

GALLANT

Are they good about sending them?

HANCOCK

Very good. Prompt. But as the issues get older the back-copy price increases.

GALLANT

Oh, I'm sorry. I only have one copy and not even of everything.

HANCOCK

Are there any plans to have a complete collection?

GALLANT

None that I know of. The German stories were collected in *The Pegnitz Junction*, all but one, which I finished too late, "The Late-homecomer", which might have been the best. This is the favourite of my books, and the title story, the novella, is the favourite of all my writing.

HANCOCK

These stories connect very closely with something I find in all your writing: people in exile.

GALLANT

I wrote the German stories because I was trying to explain something to myself. They were a kind of personal research. Can I tell you an anecdote?

One thing you truly cannot imagine was what the first concentration camp pictures were for someone my age. That's something you can't imagine because you've seen them all your life. You were born after the war, which means that this knowledge is part of your culture. When the first pictures arrived in Canada I was twenty-two, working on a newspaper. The pictures I saw had been taken by British and American army photographers. The art director called me into his office. He had all this stuff. You couldn't believe it. You can't imagine the first time seeing them. I kept saying, "We're dreaming. This isn't real. We're in a nightmare." You couldn't believe it. *The Standard* had decided to put out a special issue. I was to write what went under the pictures, and a little information of 750 words. I did this at home. I can see those pictures to this day, spread on my table.

Some were the concentration-camp pictures of the dying it was too late to save. I showed one picture to a Montreal doctor who said, "Oh, that's just tuberculosis." There were also pictures to do with slave labour, as we called it then. That is one aspect of deportation people seem to have forgotten. Polish, Lithuanian, Russian, Belgian, Dutch—they've been forgotten. But among those first pictures, about half were slave labour dead. Buried in shallow graves, dug up for the photographer. A number of them had been burned alive with blow torches because when the Germans were retreating they lost their heads. I prefer to say the Nazis instead of the Germans.

Now, imagine being twenty-two, being the intensely left-wing political romantic I was, passionately anti-Fascist, having believed that a new kind of civilization was going to grow out of the ruins of the war —out of victory over fascism—and having to write *the explanation* of something I did not myself understand. I thought, "There must be no descriptive words in this, no adjectives. Nothing like 'horror,' 'horrifying' because what the pictures are saying is stronger and louder. It must be kept simple." I remember what I wrote because I kept a copy of it for more than twenty years. I tore it up when I saw that the concentration-camp experience, its lesson, its warning, had become kitsch. Kitsch SS, kitsch Gestapo, kitsch prisoners. Even worse, it has been turned into sexual fantasy. Particularly in films. Young people must come away from those films imagining that the camp scene was pretty good sex.

What I wrote and thought at twenty-two I think and believe now. I wrote, then, that the victims, the survivors that is, would probably not be able to tell us anything, except for the description of life at point zero. If we wanted to find out how and why this happened it was the Germans we had to question. There was hardly a culture or a civilization I would have placed as high as the German.

But what the pictures said was that neither culture nor civilization nor art nor Christianity had been a retaining wall. Why not? What had happened? What had happened to the people who produced Bach and Goethe, who had been singing "A Mighty Fortress is Our God" since the Renaissance? How could a nation like that one drop to zero so quickly and easily?

We had no way of knowing then or for a long time that there had ever been any German resistance. If the Resistance in other countries has sometimes been inflated out of all historical reality, the German resistance has been played down. If you want to learn anything about it you have to take trouble, search out the books—very few—and try to find witnesses, first-hand accounts. Ask people in Canada, today, if they have ever heard of Sophie Scholl, decapitated at nineteen for distributing anti-Nazi tracts at the university in Munich. Her brother, aged twenty-one, was beheaded too. Of course, we didn't know that. Even today no one knows, except those who have taken the time and trouble to find out. All that I knew, or felt, looking at those pictures was that we had to find out, from the Germans themselves, what had gone wrong. I'm putting this very crudely now; don't misunderstand me. The victims, the survivors that is, could tell us what had happened *to* them, but not *why*. The *why* was desperately important to people like myself who were twenty-two and had to live with this shambles.

What I wrote, I need hardly tell you, wasn't run. Nothing was said to me — I wasn't asked to rewrite it. When I read the special issue all I could see were the adverbs and adjectives smothering the real issue, and the covering article, which was short, was a prototype for all the clichés we've been bludgeoned with ever since. I must tell you that I was very spoiled and not used to having my copy tampered with, let alone thrown out. I did ask what had happened. I was told that I was obviously completely crazy and the editors had never read such crap in their lives. Which may have been true. One man said to me, "Culture! Our readers never went to high school and you're talking about culture? All the Germans are bastards and that's that." But that wasn't that and it still isn't. I went home and wrote in my journal, "That is how it is going to be."

I never lost interest in what had happened, the *why* of it, I mean. Nothing I ever read satisfied me. Yet I didn't go to Germany for a long time. In a story called "Virus X" there is a Canadian girl, a young woman, who goes as far as the Rhine and only a few yards further. That was a part of myself. It wasn't until the early sixties that I began going there, with a purpose. The colonial wars of the fifties and sixties proved that civilization was no barrier anywhere. I had the feeling that in everyday living I would find the origin of the worm — the worm that had destroyed the structure. The stories in *Pegnitz Junction* are, to me, intensely political for that reason. It is not a book about Fascism, but a book about where Fascism came from. That is why I like it better than anything else. Because I finally answered my own question. Not the historical causes of Fascism — just its small possibilities in people.

HANCOCK

To go back a little bit. Do you want to say anything about John Sutherland?

GALLANT

John Sutherland was a fine dedicated man who has never been thanked enough. He lived for *Northern Review*. He had no money. Copies must exist somewhere, surely?

HANCOCK

Bound in university libraries.

GALLANT

He was an odd man. He had absolutely no sense of humour.

100

Absolutely none. That's very rare. You've heard of "the honest Scot"? Well, he was it.

HANCOCK

And the people that were associated with him? Ethel Wilson, P. K. Page, Irving Layton, Louis Dudek, Anne Marriot?

GALLANT

I never met any of them, though I met Layton years later. Of the writers you mention the only one I laid eyes on in the forties was P. K. Page. She was a stunning beauty. We did not exchange two words and I would be surprised if she recalled the meeting.

HANCOCK

So it goes without saying that you never received suggestions or words of encouragement.

GALLANT

I seldom showed my work to anyone.

HANCOCK

Were there any writers of the period you liked? You liked Paul Hiebert, I think.

GALLANT

Paul Hiebert! *Sarah Binks*! I wrote about that in *The Standard*. I had a lovely letter from him. How old is he now?

HANCOCK

Eighty-four.

GALLANT

I wrote the piece on Sarah Binks as if she had really existed. Readers took it seriously. You can't write ironically. Anyway, not in a newspaper. You have to be very careful. Well, look at you with the war and my being in the Black Watch. You thought I meant it. Sarah Binks, Sweet Songstress of Saskatchewan. Hiebert was so funny. I can still remember Sarah Binks' translation of "Du bist wie eine Blume" — you are like one flower. Or the Lorelei, which Sarah Binks rendered as "The laurel's egg." Sarah had a German friend who "spoke German only in the home." That was the standard expression people used when their parents spoke a foreign language. Sarah finally made it to Regina, I remember, with its stupendous freight cars.

Do you think one could still find a copy of *Sarah Binks*?

HANCOCK

The book has been republished in the McClelland and Stewart New Canadian Library Series. It's been reissuing and reprinting a great many important, and not so important works, often with incredibly tawdry editing. Leaving out entire chapters and so on.

GALLANT

I remember Paul Hiebert wrote me a nice letter.

HANCOCK

So you don't feel you belonged to a literary movement in Canada.

GALLANT

There wasn't one, was there? I'm not aware of it.

In fact, the most stifling genteelism prevailed in what might have been considered literary circles. People would say things like, "Constance is thinking of writing a novel about good and evil." "Oh, poor dear," would be the answer. Then you would meet the author and *she* would say, "I'm writing a novel about good and evil." This said while holding a tea cup. One's only desire was to escape.

But anyone deciding on a writing career had to want it more than anything else. The economic risk was abysmal.

HANCOCK

Obviously, you're not associated with a literary movement in Europe. You missed the Dadaists and Surrealists . . .

GALLANT

They were rather before my time.

HANCOCK

The existentialists?

GALLANT

That was also before my time. I was still in Canada. It was dying when I came.

HANCOCK

Later there was Robbe-Grillet, Michel Butor, *le nouveau roman* . . .

GALLANT

I don't care for that. The only writer I like in that group is Robert Pinget. I find Robbe-Grillet very boring, don't you?

HANCOCK

I find his theories more interesting than his work.

GALLANT

You *can't* write out of a theory.

HANCOCK

I attended a lecture Robbe-Grillet gave at the University of Vienna around 1971. Too political for me.

GALLANT

I don't like his films either . . . What's the best film you ever saw?

HANCOCK

The best film I ever saw? The one that affected me so much that I was literally shaking when I left the theatre was Mikhail Tarkovsky's *Andrei Rublev*, especially that segment entitled "The Bell-Maker."

GALLANT

Andrei Rublev? That's a beautiful film. My favourite is still Fellini's *8½*. It's a man's life. Perhaps because it's so literary. I don't know what I'd think of it now. But it's remained in my mind as my favourite film.

HANCOCK

Do you go to many films?

102

GALLANT

As many as I can. I always have.

HANCOCK

What did you like about 8½?

GALLANT

That it was a man's life, as life was in Europe exactly then. The mixture of dream and fact. You know the scene where he imagines his wife and his mistress waltzing off together? Isn't that what men long for? Oh, God wouldn't it be wonderful if those two creatures would stop talking and just waltz!

HANCOCK

Do you know anything about, or care anything about, the literary climate in Canada now?

GALLANT

Yes, I do know, but I'm not there. I can't comment on that. It's something outside me. I would advise any young writer to keep out of it. To go his own way.

HANCOCK

What do you think about statements like this? Mordecai Richler considers you Canada's most compelling short-story writer since Morley Callaghan. Do statements like that flatter you, annoy you, or are you indifferent?

GALLANT

No, they don't annoy me.

HANCOCK

You met Edmund Wilson while he was here compiling his book *O Canada: American Notes on Canadian Culture*.

GALLANT

Edmund Wilson thought I was an Irish writer when he met me. I think he had me mixed up with someone who has a similar Christian name. He was in Paris writing the book about Canada. I didn't like the book. I don't think it was helpful or needed. Canada didn't need it, and I doubt if Americans were the least interested. It was a completely eccentric book. He had a funny idea about Canada, and he simply tailored everything in his mind to fit the image. It contained some howlers. For instance, that Queen Victoria had sent her father, the Duke of Kent, out to Canada as punishment for his scrapes. I wonder how many Canadians noticed that? Jean-Paul Lemieux took the trouble to write pointing out that if the Duke of Kent had been alive, Victoria would not have been Queen.

Wilson kept asking me, "How do you know so much about Canada?" I'd say, "I'm from Canada. I'm a Canadian." And he would say, "No, you're not. You're Irish." As it happens, I've been taken for Irish in Ireland, but I don't think Wilson knew that much about Ireland either. It was a fixed idea of his. It happened that he had not heard my name in Canada, and had never made that connection. He thought I was an Irish writer, living in Paris, published in the United States. He wrote a sentence or two about me and put it in the book finally. We both thought it was funny.

HANCOCK

Does it bother you that you're not as well known in Canada as you should be?

GALLANT

No. Quite truthfully. My life and work did not depend on Canadian reaction. Luckily for me. I have often, more than often, been treated with discourtesy and that bothers me more.

HANCOCK

You had an interesting comment to make on voices. My voice, which I describe to myself as "lazy" is because I speak from the larynx instead of the diaphragm. You said your voice was a particular Canadian kind of voice.

GALLANT

I think it is a voice specifically from Montreal, of my generation. It's a pre-television voice. The television voice came from America in the 1950s. Now *you* have a voice which I can identify on the telephone as Canadian. The way you say "O-u-t" for one thing. I like the Canadian accent.

At one time Canadians didn't sound like Americans. All through the 1950s I could tell who was Canadian. But I can't any more. The young talk American now. They pronounce *t*s as *d*s. Coddage for cottage. TV did that.

HANCOCK

When you write of characters from Hamilton, or Victoria, or Calgary, or Montreal, do you ever feel nostalgic for Canada?

GALLANT

No, but it has nothing to do with Canada. Nostalgia is not something I am inclined to feel consciously. Probably it is experienced in some indirect way and turned into writing. My feeling about Canada is something else. I don't allow foreigners to criticize Canada, especially when they don't know what they're talking about — which is most of the time. I'm very firm about that. Canadians getting together abroad are apt to be gloom and doom, and I'm as bad as the rest of them. But that's a private matter. Canadians talking to one another about Canada talk in circles. You have probably noticed it.

HANCOCK

Do images in film bring back anything?

GALLANT

No. The cities have so changed I don't recognize anything.

HANCOCK

If you ever come back to Canada, is there any place you'd like to live? Do you know western or Maritime Canada?

GALLANT

I know both slightly. I like both, particularly the Maritimes.

HANCOCK

There's not much sense in asking you what your stories are about. You're not Peter Handke so there's no great mystery . . .

GALLANT

There's no mystery and there's no pattern that I'm aware of. You'd be more aware of it than I would.

HANCOCK

But as I read the stories a number of questions occurred to me. I'd be interested in your response. From the beginning I've sensed you've chosen to write about exile, world refugees, crises of faith, if I may put it that way, ordinary people who are alone, families who don't communicate, people like the latehomecomer, who is also called "Pedestrian-traffic residue" . . .

GALLANT

Those are the people who fall one minute behind when the light changes.

HANCOCK

Do I detect a philosophical sense here as well?

GALLANT

It wouldn't be deliberate. I wouldn't choose a theme and write about it. A story usually begins, for me, with people seen in a situation, like that. (*Locks fingers together*.) The knot either relaxes or becomes locked in another way. Why that should be I can't tell you. But that's what occurs to me. The situation has a beginning and as much ending as any situation has in life. The story builds around its centre, rather like a snail.

HANCOCK

I've noticed that in your stories. They have a spiral to them, not a straight linear sense until recently.

GALLANT

I've been told that.

HANCOCK

Do you think it's true?

GALLANT

I've been told that for better and for worse. William Maxwell, who was my wonderful editor at *The New Yorker* for twenty-five years, until he retired, wrote to me after ten years to say, "You've finally stopped going around and around." But he had never said to me, "Don't go round and round." I had no idea I was doing it.

HANCOCK

Do you think that exile is the world condition in your stories? If you did have a theme?

GALLANT

I'm not aware of it, but I am sure you are right. It is what I often feel about people when I meet them.

HANCOCK

Do you think that everybody is a refugee?

GALLANT

It would be too easy to say yes. Yet if you move from one social class to another you're a refugee, aren't you? Isn't a religious convert a refugee? Or someone who loses faith in ideas and people? If you move from one province to another you are a refugee of a kind. There is always something left behind.

HANCOCK

Is that what attracts you to the characters you write about?

GALLANT

I don't know what attracts me to them. I really couldn't tell you. They occur to me. Characters arrive with their own faces, voices, and names. I change the name when it happens to be close to the name of someone I know, who might believe he or she was the model. But I have to keep the original name until the story is finished. Otherwise, I lose the character.

HANCOCK

You've written about servant girls, war orphans, Walter, the poor unmarried man having his summer on the Riviera . . .

GALLANT

That was a situation I had observed. The ambiguous master-servant relationship was common at one time on the Riviera. Not so much now. The "masters" have gone to live in Morocco and Tunisia, where "servants" are poorer, therefore cheaper.

HANCOCK

You also observe, almost like Akira Kurosawa, your minor characters very closely. They're not just there, as say, furniture. They all have a purpose, and in many cases, they almost seem to dominate the main characters.

GALLANT

If you were saying that one used them as "furniture" I would be inclined to say they were the principal characters. Not the minor ones at all. If you *were* to say that, and you haven't said it, but I would almost accept it.

HANCOCK

Do you know the end before you begin?

GALLANT

It occurs on its own. It springs to life. But, and I've often wondered this myself, it's a scene. I see it. I see where it is. I'm writing a story now which is very very long. What I *saw* was a family getting down from a train. In France. A father, mother, three children, a lot of luggage.

That's how it began. And the descent from the train doesn't even come into the story. It won't even be mentioned.

HANCOCK

Do you hear the characters?

GALLANT

Oh, *yes*.

HANCOCK

You also take the images of a romantic life abroad and break it down to a flat reality . . .

GALLANT

That's what this story is.

HANCOCK

It happens over and over in your stories.

GALLANT

It's unconscious.

HANCOCK

Sarah in "In the Tunnel" sees the Alps as "shabby," the Reeves in the same story never look at the Mediterranean — it has no tides, it's not interesting. Annabel in "New Year's Eve" is "too old for sightseeing" and besides, "the museums were all closed." Yet there seems to be the sense, at least in one of your characters, Irina, that the world has a further meaning. She looks for symbols. She thinks that "the shape of the table holds some further meaning." Do you think that accounts for that closely observant style of yours?

GALLANT

I don't know. Irina was a character very close to me. I realized that when I read the proofs. That there was a great deal of myself in it. Not the circumstances. I was never married to an old writer and God forbid didn't have a lot of grandchildren. I would have absolutely hated it.

HANCOCK

Irina says, "If children are numbers, then children are zero."

If you look back on your work, which you don't, but if you did, is there anything you'd be completely happy with?

GALLANT

Completely? No. When it's done, it's done. You can't change it. I find it very hard to reread. I don't like rereading my own work. I get a sick feeling.

HANCOCK

What don't you like about it?

GALLANT

I don't know. It is physically unpleasant to read my own work once it is in print. I can read it in proof, but after? No. I think it is because I read so much while I'm writing it. I read over and over. Page by page, to the point of obsession. There is an obsessional quality to the way I

107

work. But when it is finished, it is finished forever. I don't want to hear about it anymore.

HANCOCK

Does that help you develop your work? When you find things you're dissatisfied with, say the way dialogue is treated?

GALLANT

I read to make sure the meaning is clear, and try to cut out the rubbish.

HANCOCK

We've talked about the narrative through line. As we just said, it has a tendency to work in circles, it eddies about. You obviously don't hold the traditional view of the short story, that it rises and falls, has a dramatic resolution or a plot.

GALLANT

Well, I don't think the story should be a fragment. A short story is not just something snatched out of a larger fiction, or something you don't know what to do with, that you turn into a story because it's not good for anything else. That's the French view and I don't agree with it at all.

HANCOCK

I've noticed you seem to prefer the implications of an incident, carefully and precisely observed details, the arrangement of the details, a sharp contrast of scenes, life below the surface. Almost in a subtextual way.

GALLANT

Perhaps. You would notice that more than I.

HANCOCK

You said that a story has to be "interesting." What makes it interesting?

GALLANT

I don't know. I can't read anything boring.

HANCOCK

What makes a story boring?

GALLANT

Dullness, flatness, insincerity, where you have the feeling of a boring person behind it. A boring way of telling it. A flat, droning voice.

On the rare occasions when I have shown anything to anyone before it was published I have usually asked, "Is it interesting or is it boring?" Because that is all I want to know. But that is something no one will tell you. The person you show your work to never thinks it is enough. He wants to make a literary statement. A literary statement is no use to anyone. I have only one friend, a man, who is in that sense a competent reader. His comment will amount to a sentence or two, with perhaps an afterthought the next day.

I myself dislike being asked to comment on or to read unpublished work. It's the job of an editor. I always warn the writer that I shall say I like it whether I do or not. It is criminal to hurt the feelings of the young, while an older writer is obviously looking for reassurance because he is in a bad patch of some kind. If you can't give it, he's sunk. And so no one gives it. It isn't criticism — it is psychotherapy.

HANCOCK

When you're reworking your stories, and I know you rework them a lot, you actually cut the pages apart with scissors, rearrange sections . . .

GALLANT

Some stories have been cut down almost from novel length. "Potter" was nearly a novel. Most of my work is cutting.

HANCOCK

Obviously you don't bother with outlines.

GALLANT

Good God, no. It's in my head. I can't imagine anyone bothering with that. Do you suppose that's what they teach the poor kids to do in those lunatic creative-writing courses?

HANCOCK

Are you like William Faulkner, running behind your characters with a pen and paper, writing down what they do and say?

GALLANT

No. Some authors work that way. I have a friend who does. It's the funniest thing. She was going to write about a painter and she went to a painter's studio. She wrote down everything that was in it. East wall, west wall, and so on. But, of course, her character wasn't a real painter to me. You can't just put a character in a set.

HANCOCK

Do you consider yourself a tragic or a comic writer?

GALLANT

I can't take that question seriously, which must make me comic.

HANCOCK

Where do your characters come from?

GALLANT

I don't know.

HANCOCK

Let's take Mrs. Castle in *A Fairly Good Time*. She's a character that pops in from Saskatoon.

GALLANT

Oh, yes. Physically she was based on a woman I saw once in my life — a Canadian woman — travelling in England. A mutual friend invited us to tea in a village. I've forgotten where. The thing about Scottish pancakes was real. This woman really said, "Do you have Scotch pancakes?" And the waitress said, "No." The woman went on, "Well, I've just been in Scotland and there I had Scotch pancakes." Then she told the waitress, belligerently, that we were all Canadians, as if that was going to bring the Scotch pancakes on. I thought, Oh God, I'm going to kill her. I'm going to put her head in the teapot. What am I going to do with this woman? The attitude of Mrs. Castle towards a younger woman is something else again. It's a certain kind of Canadian woman of that generation, the generation of my parents.

But I can usually see where the characters come from later on, when I'm reading the proofs. Usually someone I knew only slightly or saw once or twice.

HANCOCK

You look at your characters' actions very closely. I like that elegant description of the Reeves in "In The Tunnel," putting the jam on their toast, feeding the chockie bits to the dogs, and so on. Do you use your notebooks when you're compiling a character this way?

GALLANT

No. Memory and imagination do the work.

HANCOCK

You have a good ear for dialogue. You're developing it more. I think from *A Fairly Good Time* there's been a change.

GALLANT

I don't know.

HANCOCK

You also like telling a story from many different points of view. You don't stick to third person limited, or anything like that. You jump around, sometimes first person, sometimes an objective narrator.

GALLANT

Perhaps. I don't know.

HANCOCK

Do you like the sound of character's voices?

GALLANT

Voices are important. The language, the tone, the pitch, even the accent.

HANCOCK

Do you use them in a musical sense? As texture, as counterpoint?

GALLANT

I don't know. I can hear them.

HANCOCK

All your stories have a firm foundation in actual experience.

GALLANT

Essentially. All work, unless it is Surrealist or Dadaist or Gothic, is inevitably founded on experience.

HANCOCK

You've written about the Surrealists. An essay on André Thirion, a

110

minor and largely forgotten Surrealist. Are you interested in the Surrealists?

GALLANT

The Surrealists were interesting as a political movement. It was a revolution that never came off. Surrealist painting is much older than that particular movement, as I don't have to tell you. And still goes on. There is a group of young artists, engravers, working in Berlin now. The curious thing about Surrealists, whatever the decade, is that they all seem to be having the same dream at the same time. The dream being dreamed by the Berlin group—they are all under thirty, I believe —is a mixture of childhood, nostalgia, dream cities, empty planets. The first impact is of charm, the second of escape and fear.

HANCOCK

Here's a question you're absolutely going to hate. It's a critical question. There are a number of elements, which I shall call technical rather than critical, in your stories. Your characters are trying to comprehend the present with a misunderstood, or forgotten knowledge of their past. I'm thinking of a character like the Latehomecomer who is displaced. His files were misplaced. Officially he doesn't exist anymore.

GALLANT

That's right.

HANCOCK

He was in the Hitler Youth and he's trying to forget "Old Adolf" because that's all he meant to him. This happens in all the German stories.

GALLANT

Try to put yourself in the place of an adolescent who had sworn personal allegiance to Hitler. The German drama, the drama of that generation, was of inner displacement. You can't tear up your personality and begin again, any more than you can tear up the history of your country. The lucky people are the thoughtless ones. They just slip through. As for guilt—who can assume guilt for a government? People are more apt to remember what was done to them rather than what was done in their name to others. To wrench your life and beliefs in a new direction you have to be a saint or a schizophrenic.

HANCOCK

A number of people have commented to me that an irony seems to be at work in your tone of voice . . .

GALLANT

Perhaps.

HANCOCK

. . . and the reader has to pick it up if the story is to have a meaning. I'm asking this from a writer's point of view because what is involved is the author-narrator-character relationship.

111

GALLANT

I think it is just simply a way of looking at things.

HANCOCK

But my sense about your tone is right?

GALLANT

It's not laid on. It is the way I am, probably. People sometimes take seriously things I mean as a joke.

HANCOCK

That's what I mean. If you miss the irony . . .

GALLANT

Look at you with the army thing.

HANCOCK

Exactly. Perhaps we have to learn to read again. In many cases we're totally illiterate as readers. We read too seriously.

GALLANT

Canadians are very literal readers, especially when they read something about Canada. It's curious. They seem to think the writer has been accused of a crime and that his work is part of the evidence against him. He is on trial. He will be caught out and found guilty, simply by having some of his own work read back to him. Guilty of what? Probably of having written anything in the first place. Instead of spending time in some better and more useful manner. The writer on trial will be asked, "This is what you wrote. What have you got to say about it?" What on earth is he to answer except, "You can read what I've said." But it never ends there. I have been asked, for instance, "Did you mean it?" Another question will be, "Did it really happen?" That is where the feeling of being on trial comes in. I think there still exists a suspicion about art, about that part of the creative personality that cannot be classified or dissected or controlled. It is a feeling of suspicion about the person who doesn't seem to be working normally — who doesn't go to an office every day. The cultural attaché at the Canadian embassy in Paris a few years ago said to me, "A lot of people think they can write, but what do you really *do*?" In Canada this attitude hasn't changed for fifty years.

HANCOCK

Do you find a gap of several years between the seeds that start a story growing and the completion of the story?

GALLANT

Yes.

HANCOCK

Let's take a story like "The Four Seasons."

GALLANT

I started that in the sixties and then put it away.

112

HANCOCK

I got the feeling it was carefully crafted over a long period of time. It was much different from some of your other works.

GALLANT

The story of the little servant girl had been told to me by the girl herself, by then a woman. She had been employed when she was eleven or twelve by an English family in the south of France. I set the story in Italy, for a number of reasons. The child was Italian. She had something the matter with one hip and one shoulder all her life, as the result of carrying the children of this couple around when she herself was still quite small. They paid her very little at first, and then nothing at all. When the war broke out the family went back to England. They told her they had no money and would pay her after the war. She told me about how she had cried, and how her mother had beaten her because she did not believe this story. The family came back to their villa after the war and paid the girl in pre-war francs. Do you know what that meant? A few cents. And there they sat, in their charming villa, comfortable, respected. I used to look at them and think, "You bloody hypocrites."

HANCOCK

In a lot of your stories the major threat for many of your characters, whether it's hinted at, or directly expressed, is that they will die unloved.

GALLANT

Is that so!

HANCOCK

I can almost pick a story at random. "His Mother," "The Latehome-comer," "An Alien Flower," "Irina," "The Accident," almost at random. It comes up over and over again.

GALLANT

That's interesting. I've not thought of that, but it's interesting.

HANCOCK

Yes, it appears over and over. It's added on to the fact that your characters are sometimes living in another language, in a foreign land, getting old, living almost in a bubble and the emotional communication between the people that they are closely associated with is not complete. Would you say that's an accurate reading?

GALLANT

Many people seem to have children as insurance against being unloved. North American parents seem to be particularly afraid of that—that their children won't love them. It makes them do quite foolish things.

HANCOCK

Would it be fair to connect it with a comment you said the other day about living in Europe as a foreigner, needing a residence permit, and not being able to vote?

GALLANT

Any person living in a foreign country needs a residence permit. What I said to you earlier was that for someone who is not a refugee, and who is a citizen of a perfectly good democracy — Canada — there is something not quite normal about needing permission just to live. Canadians abroad can't vote. That also makes one feel abnormal. There is something abnormal about everywhere. The Canadian winter is abnormal, for that matter. (*Laughs.*)

HANCOCK

It's worse than Gothic. At least the Gothics had the sense to try and reach for light. Anyways . . . you're not deliberate in matters of technique. Edmund Wilson had an interesting comment. He thought your stories were slices of larger fictions . .

GALLANT

I think that's a lot of baloney.

HANCOCK

But a story like "The Accident" . . .

GALLANT

That came from a novel.

HANCOCK

And it fit so nicely into the novel, yet is so often anthologized that Wilson's comment seems applicable.

GALLANT

Edmund Wilson had not read that story, which had not yet been published. In fact, he probably never read it later, either. He told me — not as a confidence, there were other people present, which is why I can repeat it — that he did not like fiction and seldom read it. That was one of the reasons why the Canadian book seemed so eccentric to me. I felt he did not understand or care for Canada either. Why pick a country that just simply doesn't interest you, for which you have no feeling? He understood the French-English situation in Montreal so little — the *nuances* and shadings of one's relationships, that is — that he had me meet a friend of his, a French-Canadian student, actually expecting me to argue and quarrel with him. He obviously didn't understand what it meant to be *from* Montreal. For, of course, I had more in common with the young man than either of us could have had with Wilson himself. Wilson said to me, "You must admit you haven't been kind to them." He meant the collective "you," but even there I felt he was dead wrong about most things.

As for the personal "you," I have spoken French and been closely involved with French-Canadians one way and another all my life. I don't know why non-Canadians get everything so muddled. Probably

114

because the country seems so open and simple. Canada seems to encourage people to get hold of the wrong end of the stick and then bash one over the head with it.

Wilson had decided that the only interesting thing about Canada was the Scottish-Canadians of Montreal. I'm not persuaded that this is the most interesting thing. You're part Scot and so am I, and so we can say it. They brought, along with their excellent qualities, which we all know about, that iron-clad Presbyterian hypocrisy too. And we're still suffering from it, don't you think?

HANCOCK

Yes. Do you ever get stumped writing a story?

GALLANT

Every time. Every time. (*Laughs.*) It's not a technical problem. It's a feeling of . . . do you really want to hear this?

HANCOCK

Yes.

GALLANT

My first feeling is of enormous exhilaration. I write by hand. It simply flows. When I begin to type, it seems cretinous, stupid. The typed page becomes criss-crossed with corrections, additions, deletions, and so on. As I type all that I have a new low. "No one will ever make sense of this. Even I can't make sense of it." Then there is a kind of upswing. I'm not sure how to describe it. It is not that the story seems all right, but that it seems inevitable.

HANCOCK

So critical comments like Wilson's aren't of much help?

GALLANT

I don't see how they can be.

HANCOCK

Sometimes your stories are ironically set during New Year's Eve, or Christmas, as a device to force your characters together . . .

GALLANT

I don't know why. If there is one thing I disapprove of, it's the novel set during Holy Week in Seville, with the climax coming on Good Friday.

HANCOCK

Your stories have to be visual, don't they?

GALLANT

They are to me.

HANCOCK

They are to me too. I thought you might liked to have been a painter at one time.

GALLANT

I often think something like, "If I were a painter, I would do this and

115

that." Once in Yugoslavia I sat for a painter. While he painted me I looked out the window and thought that if I were a painter I would not be painting me, but the harbour.

HANCOCK

But you also like your prose to be—shall I be colloquial here?—lean and clean and mean. You don't like pulpy centres to your sentences.

GALLANT

Who does? No writer does.

HANCOCK

Could you tell me a bit about the origins of *A Fairly Good Time*? That seems to signal a major change in your approach to fiction.

GALLANT

What I saw was a girl on the Métro. It was so long ago, and so much writing in between, that I can't tell you now if I *saw* her or if she was part of my ideas about the novel. I've lost the origin. It was in the early sixties. Did I see her or was it one of those flashes in the mind? Anyway, a girl going home one morning, having been out all night. She was wearing a dreadful-looking raincoat and had her hair cut in some funny way and she was reading a letter from Canada. That's how it began. At first, oddly enough, my sympathies were with the husband. I was more like him than the girl, in a sense. My way of getting out of a hopeless situation was like his—to disappear. I had, when I was young, that same absolutely cold-blooded and probably cowardly way of getting out of things. I would just disappear. I would take a train and go somewhere—to Vienna. Helsinki, once. And come back when the situation had more or less arranged itself. When I read the proofs I realized how much of Philippe was in me.

HANCOCK

Yet "The Accident" was written some years previously wasn't it? Did you always plan it as a chapter of *A Fairly Good Time*?

GALLANT

It was part of the novel. I had put the novel away because I wasn't sure I liked it. After a time I read it again. That part seemed to stand on its own as a story. That was all. Another story called "In Transit" was part of it too, but I didn't want it and rewrote it as a story. That is, I rewrote the whole novel and it didn't belong any more.

HANCOCK

Did the novel flow easily for you?

GALLANT

In a way. It was easier to write than any story.

HANCOCK

There's a question that has to be asked and that's the influence of *The New Yorker*. Since this is an important question, I shall be rude and partially answer it myself. The only influence that I can discover is

116

based on E. B. White's comment on commas, "that they fall with the precision of knives in a circus act, outlining the victim."

I write almost without commas. They're all put in.

That means E. B. White is correct then.

All editors and publishers are mad on commas. Some are also semi-colon addicts.

I'm not so sure *The New Yorker* could influence a writer otherwise.

This thing about *The New Yorker* publishing writers who write alike is so absurd that I'm surprised it still has currency. Take any four consecutive issues and try to find the link. Usually those things are said by people who never read it, or haven't since their last Christmas gift subscription ran out in 1964.

Do you need to know your audience? Do you have an ideal reader?

No, no ideal reader. But when letters come from readers one is bound to think about them. The people who write to me tend to be young, under thirty. Usually coming across something for the first time. I had a letter not long ago from a student, it must have been, saying "I have now read two stories, don't be discouraged, do go on writing." Young men are apt to write. Sometimes they think "Mavis" is the name of a man.

Both Canadians and Americans?

Oh, not Canadians. Canadians rarely write.

You said you never show work in progress to friends.

Hardly ever. You forget that I live in a language that is not the language I write in. A great many of my friends in Europe do not read any English. Most have never heard of *The New Yorker* and would not understand that kind of a publication, which has no equivalent here. For years this situation has given me the most marvellous peace and quiet.

I think people began to understand what I was doing after the Russier book, because some of the information was obtained from people I knew. For example, a friend at Radio Luxembourg gave me tapes of all the interviews they'd done. That sort of thing. Then when I began to work on the Dreyfus book everyone knew I was doing it because I went to people for advice and information and help in meeting other people. But of the dozens and dozens of people I have been to see over the last four years in connection with this book, only two happened to have read American fiction and to imagine that I must be such and such a person. I have always lived as a writer and have made no secret that I was writing. But I was never forthcoming and the French are not inquisitive.

HANCOCK

How do you react to criticism?

GALLANT

It would only affect me from someone I respected. When I published my first book, my editor at *The New Yorker*, William Maxwell, advised me not to read any reviews except one or two in certain publications. Critics do not read carefully enough for their reviews to be interesting. I do read the Canadian reviews which people sometimes send me. They were for a long time merely spiteful. If I were not Canadian I wouldn't read them. But then if I weren't Canadian they wouldn't be so small-minded either. I have more and more the impression of a society where everyone hates everyone else. Class to class, race to race, province to province. But I don't know what you call criticism.

HANCOCK

Here's a few I ran across. Someone—a Canadian—said there was a brittle, puzzle-like cleverness . . .

GALLANT

That's what he thought.

HANCOCK

Someone else said there was a lack of emotional substance, that the works were too arty for their own sake.

GALLANT

I would shut the book or paper on anyone who uses the word "arty." Right then. So that's the end of that.

HANCOCK

To go back to the tone of voice. Someone felt they were overworked because the "author withheld judgement" or was too detached . . .

GALLANT

I've been told that.

HANCOCK

. . . or forced the reader into the story as a participant.

GALLANT

That is a good example of the meaningless remark.

HANCOCK

Do you think critics are of any use to the writer?

No. I think critics are of use to the public. When I write book reviews, I don't write them with the author in mind. I write them for the people who are going to pay thirteen dollars and fifty cents for something so they know what they're paying for. That's all.

Would you call yourself a Canadian writer? Or an international writer?

I'm a writer in the English language. Was Katherine Mansfield a New Zealand writer to you?

No.

No, she wrote in the English language.

Do you like the term "expatriate"?

It has a specific meaning. I don't think of myself as that and have never used that term in regard to myself. It has too definite a sound. I certainly never came away thinking I was going to be an expatriate. I would apply it to refugees, people who couldn't go home.

You know there are different reasons for living outside your own country. If you work for the multinationals, that is one reason. You can live without mingling with the local population, except for waiters, and what is called "locally engaged staff." Then there are the political refugees. The two refugee currents flowing into Paris now, in the seventies, are those running away from Communism in eastern Europe or Fascism in South America. It isn't a matter of choice for such persons — they go where they can. France at least doesn't humiliate them by forcing them in interviews to keep saying they are happy. That was the North American attitude after the war . . . interviewing refugees and forcing them to praise one's country. As a reporter I was guilty of that too. I didn't know any better. I took it for granted it was their duty to say that Canada was better than anything, once they were in it. Very few people ever move without a strong political or a strong career motive. I've met very few in my life who have. For one thing, you have to maintain yourself economically. And the very rich, Americans for instance, can live much more comfortably in the States.

You will often meet Canadians abroad who will not want to say they are Canadian. I've come across them more often than you would want to believe. Or, despise other Canadians and don't want to meet them. When I arrived in London, for the first time, in 1950, I went to see the CBC incumbent there — I had an introduction. He brushed me off in the rudest coldest way you could imagine. About three years after that I met him at a party, again in London. This time he was more than anxious to be friendly. I told him that our first meeting had been disagreeable and I saw no reason why any other meeting would be any better. He said, "Oh, but you see, you looked so dreadfully Canadian. So frightfully Canadian. Everything about you was so Canadian." *He* was Canadian, but I suppose, like others I've met in Europe, he saw himself as a super-Canadian.

Perhaps some uninhabited island could be turned over to the super-Canadians. They could all talk to each other in divine accents and hold their wineglasses up to the light or toast Princess Margaret or whatever it is super-Canadians do when no one is looking. They could play out their super-Canadian fantasies, and develop their super-Canadian vices.

What, exactly, *is* a Canadian expatriate? What about the families based in England whose money springs, still, from a good old Canadian source? They don't need tax havens — they constitute tax havens just in themselves. Usually an ancestor of theirs went to Canada and made the dough, working the Irish to death, or the Chinese coolies. You know how it was done. The income exists, but it is spent abroad. Now, they consider themselves Canadians, though one has to see the passport to believe it. Oddly enough, Canadians never seem to think of themselves as expatriates, but as a natural product.

HANCOCK

Have you found that being a woman, a Canadian, and a writer living abroad creates special problems for you?

GALLANT

No, it does not create problems. But who is to say that all women react in the same way? I *am* a Canadian *and* a writer *and* a woman. If the basic facts of my existence created problems for me, I would not be myself but a character in someone else's fiction.

Once, in Switzerland, when I woke up after a long operation I had the temporary amnesia you sometimes have from anaesthetic. I did not know my name, my age, why I was in pain, or which country I was in. But I knew that I was a writer, from the province of Quebec, and that English was my first language. As for being a woman, there was not a second's doubt. One's identity — the real one — is never a problem. I don't see how it can be.

HANCOCK

Let's talk about your work habits. You're not like Katherine Anne Porter, starting a story at seven a.m. and putting it in the mailbox at midnight.

GALLANT

No. I envy that.

120

HANCOCK

You tend to work on your stories in the morning, and the Dreyfus book in the afternoon.

GALLANT

It's a bit like that, yes. That's why I've been taking so long with the Dreyfus book, I suppose.

HANCOCK

But you must have a regular discipline. You're extremely busy. Two novels, the collection of short stories, the Dreyfus book, two other non-fiction books . . . How do you break up your day? Like a train schedule? At ten a.m. you'll be at such a station?

GALLANT

Oh, no. I've arranged matters so that I would be free to write. It's what I like doing. I wouldn't call it discipline.

HANCOCK

Longhand first, and then typewriter?

GALLANT

Yes.

HANCOCK

And each page had to be perfect, seamless, flawless, before you go on to the next?

GALLANT

Pretty well. Especially in the last stage.

HANCOCK

Do you consider yourself a story-teller or a novelist?

GALLANT

I don't know what that means. Isn't a novelist a story-teller?

HANCOCK

I counted eighty-eight stories. With the Montreal stories that will push the total to close to a hundred.

GALLANT

That is amazing. Good God.

HANCOCK

You don't bother with the technical difference in time and tone and point of view and keeping things moving between the characters in a story, a novella, or a novel?

GALLANT

No. Each subject has its own length. I didn't think I was going to write a novel about Shirley Perrigny. The girl in the Métro had her own story, which was a very long one. I couldn't dismiss it. I couldn't condense it. There was too much in it. It couldn't be done any other way.

HANCOCK

And a variation on that is Linnet Muir's interlocking stories which form the Montreal collection. I'm going on at some length about this because the novella is very much a European form.

GALLANT

Wouldn't you call some of Eudora Welty's long stories novellas? Some of them are ninety pages long. She's a writer I like very much.

HANCOCK

Several of your stories, like "The Four Seasons," "In The Tunnel," "An Alien Flower," if not actually novella-length, are what I would consider novella-structured.

Anyway, to change the topic, how do you avoid the distractions of Paris when you're writing?

GALLANT

I don't try. They're not distractions, but a part of life.

HANCOCK

Which ones do you prefer?

GALLANT

You name some. I like the city itself. I'm in it a lot.

HANCOCK

Art galleries?

GALLANT

Yes. Restaurants, cafés, theatres . . .

HANCOCK

Shopping?

GALLANT

Just what I need. I'm not much of a shopper.

HANCOCK

Racetrack?

GALLANT

Mmmmm! But I've sworn off until I finish the Dreyfus book.

HANCOCK

You like the ponies?

GALLANT

The whole atmosphere. My idea of sport is to go to the racetrack, put some money on the horses, sit back with a drink and watch them run. Do you have a good racetrack in Vancouver?

HANCOCK

I don't know anything about horses. Do you like other sports?

GALLANT

I was always the one who said, "Let's sit down. I'm tired."

HANCOCK

Are the titles of stories important?

GALLANT

Yes, the title is the envelope.

122

HANCOCK

I'd like to talk a little bit more about "The Pegnitz Junction," the story itself. Why do you think it is your best work?

GALLANT

Because for once I brought off something I was trying to do. Brought it off to my own satisfaction, I mean. At least up to a point. It is always only up to a point. "Pegnitz" was a story Europeans liked and that I think North Americans did not like much. I think it bored them. But Europeans liked it, and that rather worried me. I would not want to seem remote to people who read in English. All the references in "Pegnitz" are to German history, German literature. Europeans are apt to see them at once. Look: (*Pointing out window.*) Isn't it lovely down there, that girl with the long hair. Like something out of Chekhov. It looks Russian.

HANCOCK

I thought that the suggestion of a train that hasn't arrived at the junction to take its passengers home was an especially apt metaphor for Germany. But it was also a good summation of your own writing up to that point.

GALLANT

I was interested in Germany, as I said to you.

HANCOCK

It was like *Waiting for Godot* on a train.

GALLANT

Oh, I don't know if I can talk about it. You see, a great deal of conversation in it is cut off, short circuited. When the young woman hears the older woman thinking about her life in America, she really does hear her thinking. She is not inventing or making up stories. Everything that the young woman sees when she looks out the train window, she really does see. A kind of magic, if you like. To my mind, a short circuit. She really does know all these stories. She really does know what has happened to everyone. Someone wondered if she was schizophrenic. No. There is a German expression, "I can hear him thinking." I've always liked that. I could hear him thinking. Because one does very often.

HANCOCK

Let's talk about your non-fiction. Do you plan to do more work in the essay form?

GALLANT

Yes.

HANCOCK

You've also done several satirical studies of French life and literature . . . .

Oh, yes. But just for fun.

Like your essay on the Prix Goncourt, in the *New York Times* Book Review.

Do you know that was taken seriously? An agent in New York wrote to a photographer in Paris and said, "I've never heard of these people. Could you find out who they are?"

What attracts you to Dreyfus?

I was asked by publisher if I wanted to write a book about Dreyfus. That was all. I knew about Dreyfus mostly through reading Proust. In fact, I began my research by rereading *Remembrance of Things Past*. I never dreamed, when I began, that I would spend four years doing research alone. I am not a trained historian, but when I read what there was to read—the historical accounts that is—I found too much missing, so I began from scratch, as if no one in the world had ever heard of Alfred Dreyfus.

You said there was sixty thousand documents . . . .

Sixty thousand documents connected with the trials alone . . . the two courts martial, the court of cassation investigation, and the rehabilitation. Obviously I did not read sixty thousand documents, but I had to read enough to know which ones were essential. The Dreyfus story is so dense, so dramatic, that while I was investigating it, contemporary French life seemed pale by comparison.

And you've uncovered much new material.

A surprising amount of new material. Call it beginner's luck. As I've told you, I had no training for this. I found that historians are very edgy about someone treading on their territory. And a woman at that. The Dreyfus historians here are all men. When I asked to see the army archives I was asked—perfectly politely—why a woman wanted to bother writing about Dreyfus. There are a certain number of letters connected with the case—love letters, and homosexual love letters. The army wondered if I should see them because I was a woman. I hasten to say that the homosexual was not Captain Dreyfus.

I was lucky about finding people who had been close to the story—the daughter of Captain Dreyfus, for instance, who is still alive and who helped me enormously. I found the children of Labori, of General

Boisdeffre. When I say "children" I mean quite elderly people, of course. No one ever refused to see me or to help me or to show me what they had still in the family in the way of letters and papers except for one eccentric old lady who told me she never received Protestants. That is so unusual in France, as behaviour, that I could only admire her for her eccentricity. Most of the people I saw, and I mean *most*, told me that they had never been approached before. With all the books that have been written about the Dreyfus case — so many that no living person can possibly have read them all — you would think that the families of the actors in that fantastic drama would have been investigated to the ground. On the contrary. I suppose that historians go to documents, while writers, and especially ex-reporters, go to people. It must be as simple as that.

HANCOCK

Would having begun your career as a Canadian newspaper reporter have been useful?

GALLANT

What I loved about newspaper work was the life. It was a very free life. I went all over Quebec and I met Canadians I would not normally have met. When something interested me — perhaps, unconsciously, as a writer — I would think of some way of doing a story about it. I was in convents and in construction camps, in slums and in the bush. It was a weekly paper, only features. Since I spoke French I wrote a great many stories on purely Quebec topics. Once I said to one of the editors, "Jean-Paul Sartre is in Montreal, and so is Paul Hindemith. I would like to interview both." He answered, "I'm sick and tired of these French-Canadians of yours."

The problem with writing for a newspaper that there comes a point where you are doing a different version of the same story all over again. I noticed that after about five years. A cycle starting all over. I thought, I can't do at twenty-six what I was doing at twenty-one. At that point you have to make up your mind to get out.

HANCOCK

You also mentioned you wanted to write a book on Martin Luther.

GALLANT

That's what I'm going to do with my old age.

HANCOCK

Are there any books you'd like to write and won't?

GALLANT

I would have written *Death in Venice* but an elderly German gent got there first.

HANCOCK

One last question — how shall I word this? Do you recognize your limits? Have you checked your ambitions?

ROBERT KROETSCH

In February 1977 I interviewed Robert Kroetsch at his rented house eight miles south of Winnipeg, in a nicely wooded area on the banks of the Red River. A heavy snow had just fallen and the temperature was a cold 19 below zero Celsius. But the skies were sunny, the light was mellow, and the snow drifts, sculpted by the wind and marked with long blue shadows from the trees, were dazzling. The visit was uncanny in one respect. Kroetsch and I found we had been reading the same authors over the past few years: Julio Cortazar, Italo Calvino, Roland Barthes, Edward Dorn, Pablo Neruda, and especially John Hawkes. These and other imaginative and artistically original poets and fiction writers sparked a rewarding and exhilarating weekend-long conversation between two people who suddenly know one another.

Kroetsch is an extremely orderly housekeeper. Nothing was out of place, he sang while poaching eggs, and the dishes were washed up immediately. He is a tall man, of imposing physical appearance, and very Canadian, from his figures of speech ("It that right, eh?") to his concerns with fiction ("Canadian fiction has a greater sense of story and landscape than American fiction, less violent intellectual factions, and less tendency to pursue dead ends, unlike, say, Donald Barthelme, whose stories can only be written once.")

Kroetsch was born in 1927 in Heisler, Alberta, worked as a labourer on the Mackenzie River boats, studied at McGill University, and then, like many Canadian writers (including Rudy Wiebe, Robert Harlow, Dave Godfrey, and Clark Blaise), attended the Iowa Writer's Workshop. His PhD thesis was a novel, "Coulee Hill," which became the prototype for the Notikeewin trilogy: *The Words of My Roaring* (1966), *The Studhorse Man* (for which he received a Governor General's Award, 1969), and *Gone Indian* (1973). His other novels include *But We Are Exiles* (1965), *Badlands* (1975), *What the Crow Said* (1978), and *Alibi* (1983). He has also published a travel book, *Alberta* (1966) and several collections of poetry: *The Stone Hammer Poems* (1975), *The Ledger* (1975, 1979), *The Criminal Intensities of Love as Paradise* (1981), *Field Notes* (1981), *Advice to My Friends* (1985), and *Excerpts from the Real World* (1986). His prose appears in *The Crow Journals* (1980) and a special issue of *Open Letter* (1983). A book-length interview was published as *Labyrinths of Voice* (1982). For nearly twenty years, he taught English at the State University of New York at Binghampton. He is now professor of English at the University of Manitoba.

Kroetsch is very much a man of the prairies. He responded to the light in the air, to the skate tracks in the snow leading up to the skating rink, to the kids playing hockey. He was also a fast driver, charging the amber lights and always on the edge of fishtailing.

He was eager to get the interview out of the way so we could talk about the trip I had recently taken to Peru and Brazil. He is very much a private person, and his natural style was to turn questions around, as if he were interviewing me.

HANCOCK

Has success discovered you?

KROETSCH

Well, in a certain way. I sort of like to stay in twilight zones, Geoff.

HANCOCK

Your books are very hard to find in Vancouver. Is non-success a problem or dilemma for the Canadian novelist?

KROETSCH

My books will all be in print by the end of the summer. Three of the novels are being reissued in paperback. Both books of poetry are being reissued. Everything will be in print... The problem of finding books has something to do with the methods of distribution. Publishers hit a market and get out of it.

HANCOCK

What's wrong with the distribution methods?

KROETSCH

Well, publishers hesitate to keep a book in print the way they used to. It costs so much to warehouse a book that a publisher would rather sell as many as he can in a short time and remainder the rest, I suppose.

HANCOCK

I find that quite alarming with a writer of your stature.

KROETSCH

I'm coming back into print, partly because of the academic market, fifteen years after I started writing seriously. That's not too bad.

HANCOCK

Are you happy here in Winnipeg as a writer-in-residence?

KROETSCH

Yes, I find this a congenial place. A combination of literary excitement and quiet. It's a nice location. I like winter. I like Kafka's *Castle,* where summer lasts only a few days, and sometimes it snows then too.

HANCOCK

What do you mean by "literary excitement"?

128

There are lots of people doing interesting things in publishing, editing and writing. David Arnason (co-editor of the *Journal of Canadian Fiction*) has sparked a great interest in Canadian writing. Joan Parr is running Queenston House. There are fine critics at work: Evelyn Hinz, Dennis Cooley, Ken Hughes. David Williams is at work on a new novel. Bob Enright is editing a new magazine, *Manitoba Arts*. Turnstone Press comes out of St. John's College. George Amabile edits *Northern Light*. The Four Humours Press.

HANCOCK

Could you ever imagine not writing?

KROETSCH

Sometimes I promise myself I can quit if I finish one more book. But then I wonder what I'd do after and I'm stuck.

HANCOCK

How do you keep your prairie roots? You've lived in New York State and taught at the State University at Binghampton for several years. Wouldn't you be influenced incredibly by the proximity of the most important American writers? People like the "super-fictionists" as Joe David Bellamy calls John Barth, Donald Barthelme, William Gass, Robert Coover, Thomas Pynchon, those people.

KROETSCH

William Gass is the writer I find most attractive in that lot — especially his book of short stories, *In the Heart of the Heart of the Country*. I suppose the bigger influence in New York State is the intellectual life. Which shouldn't be separated from the creative life — but sometimes is. I'm both a writer and a professor, and the combination turns me on. I need it.

HANCOCK

How do you make the division when you start writing?

KROETSCH

The world that I write about is non-intellectual — in the sense that it's terribly rural. The intellectual stuff in my head seems to work well in relationship to that.

HANCOCK

Let's talk about that rural world. What were the source materials as a boy growing up in Heisler, Alberta? Which is slightly to the south and east of Edmonton.

KROETSCH

That's right. About a hundred miles from Edmonton. Beyond the last tourist... First of all there was the actual experience of a landscape in which people were farming, or coal-mining, or ranching — along the Battle River. And part of it was the way we survived through the oral tradition. Women cooking and canning together, visiting. Men working together, drinking together. I grew up in what you'd call an extended family. I'm told I was spoiled rotten from the day of my birth; I had many aunts, cousins—

HANCOCK

You dedicated *The Studhorse Man* to your Dad, who told you stories...

KROETSCH

Yes, my father was quite a famous story-teller. I could never compete in his presence—maybe that's why I went upstairs and wrote. And I had a lot of uncles who liked to make speeches—especially on politics—at the slightest provocation.

HANCOCK

And Indian legends?

KROETSCH

The Indian legends... I was aware of the Indians as a presence. They came to our farm to cut brush when I was a kid. And they showed up at stampedes. That sort of thing. Rattlesnake, from the Hobbema Reserve, was a famous baseball pitcher—the first time I batted against him he threw the ball straight at my head. But I picked up the legends later. In libraries. That's one of the ironies.

HANCOCK

So life experience very largely informs your fiction?

KROETSCH

I often start from so-called real situations. I worked on barges on the Mackenzie River before writing *Exiles*. I knew a number of studhorse men—men who showed up at our farm travelling stallions—long before I wrote *The Studhorse Man*.

HANCOCK

I think you called it Genuine Experience.

KROETSCH

Jesus, did I... The word "experience" makes me uneasy. I mean, isn't reading a book an experience?

HANCOCK

Did you have a large library in your family?

KROETSCH

We had three or four books.

HANCOCK

What were they?

KROETSCH

One of them was on looking after horses, since we had a lot of horses. It was full of quotes from Ben Franklin... Or maybe that was another book. I can't remember.... One was on wild flowers. My mother could name lots of flowers and birds. One was on threshing machines.

HANCOCK

When you write a book — for example, *Badlands* — how much actual exploring do you do? Taking a boat down a river.

KROETSCH

Three of us spent ten days floating down the river, just to get a sense of what it felt like. Floating, camping, looking for bones. Drunk much of the time — until we ran out of booze. We used to go ashore and prospect. But before that I went to Ottawa and spent time in the Archives, looking at the records that were kept by bone-hunters, looking at pictures and field notes. So it's a matter of putting the two together.

HANCOCK

The Alberta Badlands, I believe, were the richest source in North America for reticulated skeletons, complete fossils.

KROETSCH

The American Museum of Natural History is now the richest source — about one-third of the specimens come from the Red Deer.

HANCOCK

What are the possibilities for a story-teller in Canada? Why stay here? You're in a position where you could go almost anywhere.

KROETSCH

Some days I like the idea that we're finally telling our own story. Some days I just like the company.

HANCOCK

Did you have a problem with loneliness when you were beginning?

KROETSCH

I certainly did, yes. Almost anybody who wants to write spends years being alone. It was very hard to find the community, and I suppose one is pretty shy as a young writer. That goddamned secret dream that's trying to kill your liver before the beer does it... I teach in the summer, in the Qu'Appelle Valley, down off the Saskatchewan wheat plains, and I like that.

HANCOCK

So you find teaching has a positive effect on your writing?

KROETSCH

Yes.

HANCOCK

Are you still interested in ice hockey?

KROETSCH

I'd like once more — or maybe even just once — to come sweeping down centre ice, take the goalie out with a beautiful fake, and score a

131

winning goal. Failing that, I'd like to be admired by the girls for staying on a bronco at a rodeo. Failing both, I go on writing novels.

HANCOCK

What twentieth-century writers, or any other century, for that matter, have influenced your work?

KROETSCH

I suppose Joseph Conrad was a strong influence on me. Perhaps he, in a strange way, turned me into a comic writer.... I admire the way Hardy and Faulkner deal with a rural world. I admire Samuel Beckett. John Hawkes. Ed Dorn.

HANCOCK

Which writers do you admire, not necessarily as influences?

KROETSCH

Italo Calvino comes to mind first. I try to read Francis Ponge and Roland Barthes, and some days I almost succeed. I like the way Octavio Paz's criticism leads me into Gabriel Garcia Marquez' work.

HANCOCK

What does Garcia Marquez teach you?

KROETSCH

He nips at the heels of realism and makes the old cow dance.

HANCOCK

Which Canadian writers?

KROETSCH

bp Nichol in *The Martyrology*. Michael Ondaatje in *Coming Through Slaughter*. That fascinating book by Frye — *The Secular Scripture*... I guess I admire Margaret Laurence for daring to invent a kingdom, because I'd like to do that; and all the while I have this skepticism that works against the ideas of both community and self: reality resisting design...

HANCOCK

Do you think that puts a narrative voice between you and the story?

KROETSCH

I hadn't thought of it that way. Hey, that's pretty good.

HANCOCK

Someone commented that the surfaces of your stories draw attention to themselves because they're so dependent on style.

KROETSCH

What intrigues me is the idea of "foregrounding" as they say. Foregrounding the language itself. Writers like Eli Mandel and Frank Davey think about language in an interesting way. Too many Canadian writers treat it like a heap of fresh bear shit.

HANCOCK

Would people like Nabokov and Faulkner have an influence in that way?

KROETSCH

Faulkner, yes. And that Nabokov novel with the poem inside...*Pale Fire*. I remember reading that with a great deal of excitement.

HANCOCK

Are there any good story-tellers around now? Good B.S.ers?

KROETSCH

Go to any kitchen table at which there are more than three people assembled — people tell stories and in that sense use narrative to construct a reality. I mean — stories about Aunt Millie, about a guy in the office, about driving through the traffic...

HANCOCK

How do they do it? It's so different from people who are dealing with pen and paper?

KROETSCH

Of course, they work in a very short form. The oral story-teller probably has less impulse to "deconstruct" his inherited conventions.

HANCOCK

Could you elaborate a bit more? Deconstruction?

KROETSCH

You take a given set of conventions and play with them in a certain way. I think some of the conventions of fiction control too much our way of seeing the world. It starts to get interesting when you take those conventions and both use them and work against them.

HANCOCK

Could you give me an example from your own work of how you've done that?

KROETSCH

Well, I suppose the biographer in *The Studhorse Man* slowly usurping the subject of his biography is unwillingly deconstructing the notion of a hero. He starts to see himself as the hero as he sits in the bathtub writing the book.

HANCOCK

When you're writing a book, do you have any sins that interfere with your writing? Do you smoke or drink too much? Bad work habits?

KROETSCH

I don't smoke. Probably drink too much. I generally like to sin. Next question.

HANCOCK

What are your necessary routines and disciplines?

KROETSCH

Well, I like to get up in the morning and write. I like to wake up and go to work. Early, seven o'clock, around there. I wake up with a high level of energy right out of sleep and I guess I trust that dream

133

condition that one comes out of. I'm always mystified by people who can work at night, like you. I'm totally exhausted by night.

HANCOCK

What would your ideal writing circumstances be?

KROETSCH

If the world would leave me alone for four hours in the morning, I'd sell my soul at the going rate in the afternoon.

HANCOCK

Academic criticism, and parodies of it, is very evident in your fiction. What does that say about you as an academic?

KROETSCH

I'm always looking for sub-literary texts that tell us how to be literary, if you want to use those terms. Like using the ledger. (Kroetsch's long poem, *The Ledger*). Critical method is interesting to me. So in a novel like *Gone Indian* I take the idea of the critical act and treat it as a way to write a fiction. In that sense I have a great deal of respect for the critical act. Ultimately, I think a good piece of criticism is an extension of the test, so why not recognize that in the primary text.

HANCOCK

Do titles come easily?

KROETSCH

Not always, no. Something like *The Studhorse Man* was a natural title. Some of my earlier titles were too literary, I suppose. Too hard to remember. *The Words Of My Roaring,* for example.

HANCOCK

Do you keep a notebook when you're writing a novel?

KROETSCH

I make a lot of notes before writing a novel. It's nothing so orderly as a notebook. Piles of pieces of paper.

HANCOCK

How do you organize them? Numbers in the corners, that sort of thing?

KROETSCH

No, I just reread them every so often. Not too often. And let my head discover whatever shapes might be lurking in the heap.

HANCOCK

Speaking of shapes, what's your mysterious process of character creation? First, how do the names of characters come to you? Some of the names are very suggestive. Obvious ones are Roger Dorck, Miss Kundt. But there's Grizzly, Tune, Mud...

KROETSCH

The naming is part of the whole question, isn't it? Like *Badlands* beginning with the woman saying, "I am Anna Dawe." She states the whole problem there, in a curious way. That tautology, "I am myself, I am Anna Dawe." Then there's the sense in which we control the world by naming it and lose it by naming it. Because the name starts to replace the whatever else... The way answers do.

HANCOCK

Are you using these names as a primary characteristic of character, as in the commedia del'arte, for example? Is the name the character, possibly?

KROETSCH

Yes, as long as you say "possibly." The possible is what haunts us.

HANCOCK

These characters are new types in Canadian fiction. There is something much different about them. What is wrong with traditional Canadian realism?

KROETSCH

I wouldn't say there is anything wrong with it. I just wonder about the nature of self, first of all. Second, the old notion of character is an example of a convention that has gone dead, it seems to me. There isn't a great deal of correspondence between that convention and the demands of fiction. If you know what I mean.

HANCOCK

Some of your characters, for example, the Prophet in *Words Of My Roaring,* Grimlich who lives in a coal mine and refuses to come out, in *Badlands*, Anna Yellowbird and her house of bones, the horses running loose in Woodward's Department Store, all these are different types of reality. It is "real" within the fictional world, but much different from the mimetic, naturalistic world.

KROETSCH

Yes, I'm interested in sharing with the reader the fact that I'm making a fiction. One of the assumptions of old-style realism is that the novel isn't a fiction. Verisimilitude, the textbooks demand. And I'm no longer interested in that. I want the reader to be engaged with me in fiction making. I work a reader pretty hard, I guess, in that I want him to enter into the process with me. Some writers fill in all the spaces, or they use all the conventions. They give all the details. I like that sense of process being fluid and open so that the reader...

HANCOCK

Like Anna Yellowbird and her house of bones.

KROETSCH

Sure, that's a good example.

HANCOCK

When you're working on a manuscript, do you type or write longhand?

KROETSCH

I tend to work on a typewriter.

HANCOCK

Foolscap?

KROETSCH

Just any kind of blank paper that's available. As long as it's terrifying in its blankness.

HANCOCK

How much revising do you do?

KROETSCH

I rewrite a great deal. That's where I discover what it's all about.

HANCOCK

Would you consider yourself a fast or a slow writer?

KROETSCH

A very slow writer.

HANCOCK

A page a day? Two or three pages?

KROETSCH

I'm satisfied with two or three pages.

HANCOCK

Do you ever discuss work in progress with friends or other writers?

KROETSCH

Not very much. I never talk about it until it's close to being a complete draft. Then I have a few friends I talk to. Jim Bacque in Toronto, for example.

HANCOCK

How does a novel begin for you? Do you set out a goal for your characters, does it begin with a character, a scene?

KROETSCH

It's pretty hard to remember. It seems where a character and a story intersect is the point where a novel begins. A lot of people will tell you about a character and they don't realize he's not a story.

HANCOCK

What is a story to you?

KROETSCH

That's a tough question isn't it?

HANCOCK

Is it in the E.M. Forster sense of the "and then, and then, and then," of events which create a dramatic action? Or is it in the plot sense where you arrange the "and then, and then," into the best possible order? Or is it an extraordinary character in an extraordinary situation?

KROETSCH

Sometimes I use conjunctions so that the "and then, and then, and then," is left open to the reader without subordination. I seem to like that a great deal, especially in my first novel and in *Badlands*. But sometimes I resist, almost violently, the tyranny of narrative. Even the necessary fiction of the idea of history... In one sense, every character in *Badlands* is trying to figure out what history is. Whether it's Dawe trying to deal with seventy million years of time, or Web trying to deal with it by burning down his father's shack, and maybe his father too.

HANCOCK

When you're working on a novel, do you perceive an overall structure first, or do events occur as they happen?

KROETSCH

I perceive shapes—literally charts, maps, outlines on my study walls—then I resist them with words.

HANCOCK

In that structuring do you work in levels, or symbolic actions? For example, *The Studhorse Man* has Homeric parallels based on *The Odyssey,* I believe. *But We Are Exiles* has the four levels of exile worked in.

KROETSCH

I'm intrigued by the way in which the world hints of meaning. That's exactly where my imagination encounters and counters both experience and language. Where there is a *hint* of meaning. If there was a genuinely apparent meaning, then you'd simply elaborate it, I suppose. If there was no meaning, maybe you'd be able to quit. But the fiction writer has a nagging suspicion that there might, or might not, be a meaning. That's exactly where I'm at. That's why I have to go back, so compulsively, and check details, Geoff. Not only do I go down the Red Deer River; I go outside and feel the sun on my neck—and in either case the darkness is there with a counter-proposal. I resist the traditional realistic novel because experience is always pestering me with this insinuation of meaning.

HANCOCK

How did you connect each of the books in the Notikeewin trilogy? Each book has a different meaning. It seemed to me a trilogy more in language than in time.

KROETSCH

Okay. That's right. I wasn't interested in connecting narrative. My questioning of narrative itself was of more interest to me. Except that I like a good yarn along the way.

HANCOCK

In fact, the only clear point of connection was Johnnie Backstrom.

KROETSCH

In that trilogy there are different versions, different attempts at dealing with possibilities of meaning...

137

HANCOCK

Did you have to learn how to control your own narrative voice? Or did you write it naturally? Do you like unreliable narrators?

KROETSCH

I might take the extreme position that there are no "correct" accounts. My narrators are simply like people in life—each one is of necessity an unreliable narrator. I—and the reader—have to hear something of the nature of that unreliability.

HANCOCK

Does that take a bit of tinkering? Walking around the block?

KROETSCH

Yes... Especially if there's a pub on the corner.

HANCOCK

The through line of your stories was something like Bob Harlow's sense of novella. You put your canoe on the river and you send it down stream. The action takes place on each side of the canoe...

KROETSCH

Yes...

HANCOCK

And the action doesn't concern itself with what's happening in the world.

KROETSCH

Yes, I certainly admire *Scann*. There's a brilliant story-teller right inside the novel itself, and I still think story is basic. Now...if I could figure out what story is...

HANCOCK

There's a very objective sense to your stories. They never occur in a subjective world. It's a real world with externally observed characters.

KROETSCH

Anything else I say would be unreliable.

HANCOCK

To go back to the image of the canoe on the river. A great many drownings occur in your works. Every novel, without exception, has a drowning.

KROETSCH

That question—if it's a question, Geoff—is too complicated.

HANCOCK

How complex would your perfect novel be? Like Julio Cortazar's *Hopscotch,* a novel with a hundred possible endings? You work with simpler structures now.

KROETSCH

Yes. I guess I'd like to think that the perfect novel would be simpler than that, in a strange way. I sometimes envy F. Scott Fitzgerald his *The Great Gatsby.* It's a simple story, but it resonates endlessly. The possibilities... But I also admire Lowry's wild attempt at one final, total book—

HANCOCK

Do you write short stories?

KROETSCH

I haven't written a short story in years. I'm just not on top of the form.

HANCOCK

What was the origin of *Badlands*? What was the starting point?

KROETSCH

I think it started when I was writing that travel book, *Alberta*. I stopped in Drumheller and discovered to my surprise that there had been this bone-rush at the beginning of the century into the Red Deer River Valley. I'd never heard about it before. Again, it was one of those hidden dimensions of our past. Initially I thought it would make a great parody of the male quest. And it still is in a certain sense a parody. But as I worked on the material I became rather sympathetic to some of the folly involved in such a quest.

HANCOCK

Was it a difficult book to write?

KROETSCH

I don't recall it was that difficult. It seems to me it went fairly fast.

HANCOCK

I felt as I read it that it might be a transitional book to a book you haven't written yet. What shall we call it? Magic realism?

KROETSCH

Yes?

HANCOCK

Super-realism? There was less pastiche, less literary parody...

KROETSCH

That might be a fairly prophetic observation. I'm working on a novel that owes a debt to your "magic realism."

HANCOCK

What do you mean by "magic realism"?

KROETSCH

I mean (the painter) Alex Colville. Come to think of it, there's a horse on a railway track—Good grief.

HANCOCK

Are you trying to call less attention to the surface of your books? Is good writing supposed to be invisible?

KROETSCH

How do you mean that, Geoff?

HANCOCK

Well, I had a writing lesson once. I was told that "good writing is invisible." In this day and age of the film, writers must think in scenes, and not call attention to the prose. *Badlands* did that in a very vivid sense. It would make a good movie script. It's written as a movie script. The scenes are there, the characters are there, the stage directions and even camera directions are nearly there.

KROETSCH

Well, that's interesting, because I am at the moment very aware of writing "chapters," which I suppose in a sense are "scenes," though I think a scene is too narrow a word at this point. I am intrigued by that larger unit. You're quite right.

HANCOCK

How do you conceive a chapter as a unit? Or the paragraph, as Robert Coover and Donald Barthelme would use it?

KROETSCH

Well, I'm interested in the chapter because it had become such a convention... In a way it dictated content.

HANCOCK

A convention for the reader or for the writer?

KROETSCH

For both. Life doesn't come in chapters, after all. This was a convention that almost everybody accepted without thinking. And I was already beginning to examine it in *Badlands,* where the chapters might become photographs or whatever. In the sense that there is a photographer making up a show. The chapter is another version of naming.

HANCOCK

Is the photographer in *Badlands* an author-surrogate?

KROETSCH

I was aware that he might be a sort of one-eyed novelist.

HANCOCK

What is the function of humor in your fiction? Is it satire? Parody? Do you have affinities with any Canadian humorists? Stephen Leacock. Eric Nicol perhaps? Good dirty-joke tellers?

KROETSCH

The professor at the University of Alberta — was his name Tracy? — who introduced me to Chaucer — It would be no exaggeration to say he changed my life. Chaucer is the pure master of narrative. Perhaps I'm interested in the narrative function of humour.

HANCOCK

Is Canadian humour different from American humour?

KROETSCH

It seems to be. If you take Leacock as your model.

HANCOCK

Why is that? Because the Canadians make themselves the butt of

140

their jokes, while the Americans makes somebody else the butt of theirs?

KROETSCH

American writers have commented to me on the self-mockery in my work. They see it as self-mockery — before Canadians do. Perhaps the posture is so natural to Canadians, they're slow to recognize it... I don't know that I believe what I just said.

HANCOCK

You are very concerned as well with the sound of words, with the resonance of words. A book like *Badlands* is a real treat to read aloud. Would this be the effect of poetry on your work, the oral tradition, what?

KROETSCH

A lot of my material is *profane*. But the telling of the story about that material, the language itself, changes it in some way to what I call sacred. Another writer might take what we call sacred material and treat it profanely and get his tension that way.

HANCOCK

Very much like Marlon Brando in *Last Tango in Paris*. That the dialogue is working at odds with the scene.

KROETSCH

I like that.

HANCOCK

What is the point where words change and fiction becomes better than reality? Can that be pin-pointed by you as a novelist? I believe you called it "un-naming to invent."

KROETSCH

When language begins to conceal its object — When Beckett's character repeats the word "pot" to himself and can no longer connect it with a pot — One of the functions of honest writing is to make language reveal again... Perhaps I should strike the word "honest"... No, keep it in.

HANCOCK

Do you do that through images? Fire, ice, bones, water, horses, are some of your images...

KROETSCH

By repeating, by establishing images —

HANCOCK

Do we abuse the old Canadian myths? Would Grey Owl be an example of man abusing myths?

KROETSCH

No. Grey Owl's story will go on being retold. Even the attempts at debunking will become part of the total story. His life is somehow a paradigm of our experience.

141

HANCOCK

Do you think this is good?

KROETSCH

In this case I think it's great.

HANCOCK

Would that be an example of how we "un-invented old mythologies and invented new ones"? That people like Grey Owl invented a myth that may not even have been there.

KROETSCH

That English boy became a Canadian by going Indian. You see, he uninvents in order to invent. He does in a spectacular way what we have to do in lesser ways.

HANCOCK

Would that be a fair assessment of what you're doing as a novelist?

KROETSCH

Grey Owl as a paradigm for the artist? Maybe. Yuh. I don't know... I keep returning to the figure of Grey Owl. Conservationist? Murderer?

HANCOCK

You always place your fiction on the edge of frontiers. Could you write in a different setting? Or must you always remain on the bald open prairie?

KROETSCH

Only if you take our skin as a version of the bald, open prairie.

HANCOCK

All your characters are partially crippled men. They almost have to deliver themselves into the landscape, plunge into the landscape to redeem themselves from failure. How important is this quest in the landscape? In your work and to yourself? What does a journey in a landscape teach you and them? Do your characters need mighty antagonists?

KROETSCH

How would you answer? The journey in a landscape. Maybe our landscape, finally, is our labyrinth. What is a journey in a landscape?

HANCOCK

It might even be tied up with why do people go anywhere?

KROETSCH

I like that. You're a compulsive traveller, Geoff—all over the world. Why do you do it?

HANCOCK

I can't answer that simply.

KROETSCH

Motion is certainly natural, isn't it? You ever think about a tree? Imagine! It can't go anywhere. Gets a little bigger. That's the only way it goes anywhere.

HANCOCK

Actually, natural motion, according to my friends, is to stay put.

KROETSCH

That's one hell of a good question. In one sense you narrate your life. You are free of words. You narrate your life by motion, by movement. That would be one of my answers.

HANCOCK

W.H. Auden considered that your ego was looking for its alternative in another hemisphere, trying to find its match in another latitude.

KROETSCH

Yes, I can understand that. Trying to rejoin the world. Stitching the parts together... It's human loneliness. Travelling the world back together. It's a double thing. There's an immense satisfaction in loneliness, a kind of sinful pride in it; and along with that an appalling sense of how inadequate—how, at whatever the cost, you have to seek a way to be free of that same loneliness.

HANCOCK

Coupled with that, the men and women in your novels have a strong urge, in fact an animal urge, to use your own metaphors, to combat that loneliness.

KROETSCH

Coupling—an interesting word... There's a kind of incredible loneliness sometimes in sex. Yet it's the ultimate attempt to deny the loneliness, to join the world and have consequences. Like writing.

HANCOCK

Tied in with that is your animal imagery. How close are men and animals?

KROETSCH

Close.

HANCOCK

The Studhorse Man says it in the name itself. Jeremy Sadness thought he was a buffalo in his other life.

KROETSCH

I look so much like a buffalo that some mornings I have an identity crisis myself... I think the connection has to be back to the world. The metaphor of upwards is everywhere in our thinking. I feel the connection is back to the earth.

HANCOCK

Your books are built on layers of action. Are structures perhaps a way of controlling what often appears to be a journey without maps for your characters?

KROETSCH

Sometimes structures might even be a way to stand still.

HANCOCK

Tell me something about your sense of resolution in your fictions. Do fictions end?

KROETSCH

I'm suspicious of endings that get us off the hook. Even Aristotle, as much as I admire the old cuss...I want to put an end to such endings.

HANCOCK

Your heroines seem to be getting more complex. From Carolyn Hornyak to Martha Proudfoot to Anna Dawe, there seems to be a steady intellectual growth.

KROETSCH

More and more, intelligence turns me on sexually. Maybe it's that simple.

HANCOCK

How would you deal with a feminist critic who didn't care for your treatment of female characters? Very often these ladies are idealized, or treated as furniture.

KROETSCH

I don't particularly care for the way some of my male characters treat women either. But this is often a male chauvinist society, particularly in the west, where men have a lot of exciting things to do, and women are left holding the fort — to go back to the garrison-bush metaphor. It isn't the way I live personally. For some reason, a lot of readers can't distinguish between a narrator and an author.

HANCOCK

Your satire — is that the right word? — is often very rough on Eastern muckymucks.

KROETSCH

That's part of Western folklore — we root our evil in the East. On top of that I'm a prairie democrat, ferociously egalitarian, and I don't like muckymucks of any sort. I prefer beer parlours to cocktail lounges.

HANCOCK

How do you feel about book reviewers? Critics?

KROETSCH

Criticism, as I mentioned, is an extension of the text. In a sense we create a culture by elaborating texts — consider the Bible and Shakespeare in our cultural development. I wish reviewers would take themselves as seriously as I take them.

HANCOCK

Let's talk, then, about some specific scenes in your books so I can get some idea as to your working methods. For example, the climactic scene in *Badlands,* where Anna Dawe and Anna Yellowbird, carrying gin and Labatt's Blue, are hiking in the woods up the side of the Rocky

Mountains and along comes a helicopter with a grizzly bear in a sling.

KROETSCH

You can't go to that without looking at the previous ending. The ending of the male story, so to speak, when the bone-hunting expedition gets to the ferry and begins to land the specimens. Here's the great adventure. They've got their bones and they're all standing there. What do we do now? I'm sort of mocking the form a bit. Dawe ends up standing there with a stick in one hand and a dead rattlesnake in the other. That is counterpointed against the experience you mention — the two women watching the bear pass overhead, under the helicopter.

HANCOCK

And how about the conclusion of *Gone Indian*? Where the snowmobile collides with the train and everybody goes over the trestle.

KROETSCH

If you want to believe the couple went over the trestle, through the ice, and drowned — that's fine. If you want to believe they escaped, went into the north to live a new life, that's your privilege too. The text doesn't resolve it as far as I'm concerned. It's left. You see, that's what I mean when I say I want the reader to be engaged with me. That's his fun and his responsibility. Those are interpretations, aren't they? Those are critical acts, if you will — and either — No, I'll shut up.

HANCOCK

Where do some of the other images come from? The Model-T on the flatboat, for example.

KROETSCH

In *Badlands* — Sinnott seems to arise out of the water. He seems to emerge; he's got feet that are sort of reptilian; his socks are full of sand and so on. I like the absurdity of that machine, that automobile out there. I hadn't thought of it that way, but your notion of moving through a landscape — which is going to haunt me for a while — there it is. An automobile going down the river.

HANCOCK

What is the basis for the great Canadian novel? Can there be such a thing? Is it burning with a hot light up ahead?

KROETSCH

Again — I'm fascinated by Lowry, trying to shape his ultimate book. Or Joyce, for that matter... The fiction about the world becomes the world. The story must be told again... The story must be told again.

CLARK BLAISE

This interview took place on a sunny June morning, Friday the thirteenth, 1980, at Clark Blaise's Toronto home. At first I thought it would not come off. Clark had a migraine headache so bad he could not see, but he said the interview would be a "distraction." He was in the process of moving from Toronto, where he was a visiting professor of creative writing at York University, to Saratoga Springs, New York, and the real-estate agent would interrupt with potential buyers later in the afternoon. To round things off, the batteries in my tape recorder burnt out in the last half hour of the interview, necessitating another visit. Yet Clark's life, like his fiction, seemed to thrive on chaos, disturbances, and the unlucky. He reminded me of the Al Capp character with the perpetual black cloud over his head.

In his fiction Clark deals with uprootedness and the search for identity in a North America that is always on the move. His prize-winning story collections *A North American Education* (1973), *Tribal Justice* (1974), and *Resident Alien* (1986) and novels *Lunar Attractions* (1979) and *Lusts* (1983) deal with displaced characters in strange environments that are in fact their homes. With his wife, novelist Bharati Mukherjee, he wrote *Days and Nights in Calcutta* (1977). This was not so much a collaboration as two separate books written without consultation apart from the simple agreement that Clark would "deal with external reality and she would talk about emotional and inner memory." Clark and Bharati's most recent book, *The Sorrow and the Terror* (1987), is a documentary account of the 1985 terrorist bombing of an Air India jet. As a visiting professor or writer-in-residence, Clark is always on the move. Currently he commutes between Concordia University in Montreal and Columbia University in New York.

HANCOCK

Clark, you're one of the most rootless writers I've ever met. You're always moving around.

BLAISE

Yes, a person gets a taste for movement and it's very hard to adjust to being rooted in one place. I'd like to be rooted, I think. I have a nostalgia for it, in a Norman Rockwell sort of way, but I don't think it's going to happen. That doesn't necessarily mean I'm rootless, though. Think of those banyan trees that drop roots down from their branches and just create roots out of thin air. I'll never have the long, long tap root (to exhaust the metaphor) that goes down in one place. I'm a kind of a tropical tree with an awful lot of shallow roots and I can easily be blown over. On the other hand, I can survive a lot of changes. I adapt very easily to just about anything around me.

HANCOCK

Are Canada and Florida somehow connected for you?

BLAISE

I haven't been back to Florida since I was nine or ten years old and I don't ever intend to see it again. Florida was not so much a landscape as the place of childhood, the place of opening-up, and if it had been passed somewhere else I would have had deep attachments to a different place. It turned out fortunately because Florida was physically, morally and historically an apt place for me: I exploited it ruthlessly and it exploited me in turn. It was a location (thinking back now to the still-rural, Deep South Florida of the mid- and late-'40s) that was made for the hounding out of some central worm-like creature in myself.

Florida was foreign to everything in my nature. It was a brutal confrontation, but it was physically so interesting and physically so unforgettable that it linked up forever a notion of nature, of water, of solitariness, and a kind of harshness that I lost myself in for hours every day.

It is just as harsh as the Canadian prairie, but solar in nature, not lunar. And in Florida you didn't have to worry about dressing for it, so that you literally passed through a wall at seven in the morning and came back at dusk and were out in it all day walking through jungle and water and you never felt as though you were in particular danger. Yet you were always seeing things that were dead or dying, or crawling up from the mud or down from the trees. You saw putrefaction, you saw the tropical world in which all the processes are speeded up and which the chain of exploitation is just so much more vivid than it is up here.

So I was the beneficiary of that and later on, much later on, I came to see the social and historical and economic analogues to that kind of nature. The myth was laid down for me pretty early, and it was a matter of feeding into the myth with plots and psychologies and characters.

HANCOCK

What do you see right now as the state of contemporary fiction both in Canada and the U.S.A.?

BLAISE

I think the state of the arts there, meaning the States, or here, is grossly inflated. Reputations are grossly inflated. I don't find very many authors around here or there that I can read with any degree of discovery or excitement or anything other than appreciation of competence.

I think we're in a bad period despite what everyone says about this being a glorious period. I'm fearful.

I've read a recent New York *Times* Book Review article, and a *TLS* article about "little magazines" which seem to glorify a truly disgusting, profit-and-sales-centered literary reaction. I was appalled at the number of so-called significant authors, and editors, and agents, and the number of publishers who agreed with the simple proposition there is too much writing, too many "first novels" being written, and that the great aching is to "communicate" (awful word), not to create; that art should be lucid (meaning straight and simple) and narratively strong (meaning, as they say in Hollywood, with a "good story-line") and that the rewards (of the six-and-seven-figure variety) will go to people who "perform." And there's going to be a real gloved fist for people who don't.

I see contempt growing for writing programs and for university courses in which young writers are encouraged to write the "art" novel. They are being sneered at for their pretensions, and professors who teach writing are being called failures because they obviously never made money. Fiction is being cut back; in magazines and in publishing houses. First novels are as despised as story collections. But it's even worse than that.

Worse than the first novelist (who can be excused, because of all the bad advice handed out by failed writers in universities) is the third or fourth novelist whose other books had gotten, oh, terrific critical reception but no real sales. *He*'s in big trouble. The books that are getting attention are, by and large, foolish books. The writers who are getting a lot of attention are, by and large, fulfilling a commercial expectation, confirming a kind of an expectancy.

The last book of any excitement that I read coming out of the States was Norman Mailer's *The Executioner's Song*. Sure, it was too much. I was disappointed in Richler's *Joshua*. Stick-figures, conforming to a mechanical vision. On top of that, it was messy, contrived in structure rather than organically complicated. I've liked Hodgins' stories, but his novels? As soon as someone started walking on water, I felt that South American literature ought to get its tubes tied and cut down on the number of illegitimate offspring we're taking in. I thought Atwood's *Life Before Man* was very well-written but "the world" of the book left me, well, cool, as did the characters. "Unengaged" is the word that comes to mind; the book aroused my expectations more than it satisfied them. (But that's the case with even very good books; there probably are not more than a dozen books in anyone's life that exceed your expectation and achieve their author's ambition.) Leaving aside the work of the older Titans (Joyce, Mann, Proust, James, Dickens, etc.) I'd say I derive satisfaction only from Mavis Gallant, among Canadians. Among Australians, from Kenealley and from Robert Drewe. In England, Paul Scott and occasionally Anthony Powell. Of Naipaul's work, *A House for Mister Biswas* is a masterpiece; his other works lag behind, whatever their merits. A writer who I feel, in the States, has been consistently underrecognized would be Thomas Berger. I think *Sneaky People* is one of the best books I've read in the last decade. Heller's *Something Happened* is a book of drab wonders, with real depth, scary psychologically and socially and stylistically. The *Collected Stories* of Hortense Calisher stand with Mann's novellas just over my writing desk. There are a few books around that I would like to see in fifteen years, after all the hoop-la gets shaken down, to see what really remains. I have found a lot of consistent interest in reading Ann Beattie's stories, but I don't know if it's not a fascination more with the times and places and encounters we've almost "shared." She too scares me the way Heller does, especially when I see her control of so much waste and aimlessness. She's like an illustration of what Pynchon was getting at in *Entropy* and *The Crying of Lot 49;* you can almost hear a scream in those quiet little stories. Just like you can feel the blood in some of Rothko's geometric canvases.

HANCOCK

The landscape that your characters move through is sometimes a grey world, though. It's the way we live now. They always move in an ominous landscape. It's mass-market culture, it's cheap hotels, transitional neighbourhoods. What does that say about the way we live now?

BLAISE

Well, if I use the market-world, I don't believe in it wholeheartedly. I've always tried to show that running behind a shopping centre is a creek or a stand of timber and if one simply steps outside the motels or walks behind the franchise-stand or simply looks long enough across the parking lot, he will find birds in the trees, fish in the stream and mud puppies in the swamps; in other words, eternal forces are still at work churning under the surface. You carry out the garbage from McDonald's but it's still the same flies that lay eggs in it. I simply mean that my eye is on dualities more than it's on satire or put-down. I've always tried to account for *why* a road dips suddenly or *why* a basement gets wet in the spring. I've tried to account for these things, to be alert to them because I was a geology major in college and I have a greater sense of subsoil and substructures and determinants from weather and from rainfall and from things like that, things I had to learn, than I do from purely literary sources.

I remember the drawing my younger son, Bernie, used to do before school tried to straighten him out. His stick-figure people would stand on very perilous ground in the middle of the paper, under the usual sun and tree, beside the usual house with the usual smoke in the chimney. But underfoot, he would lavish enormous, intricate attention. Those lines were "worm-roads" he said. His real attention was focused on the unseen, and he was flinging order on the wildest chaos.

I get impatient with satire and with pure realism, because I'm a moralist in my own way and I think I've always tried to mitigate the greyness of the landscape by saying that no matter how you transform it with bulldozers and concrete you are still having to deal with permanent forces that are unmoveable and that will come and get you. They're still there to change you, but you're never purely created by forces. We are formed by our

149

capacity to imagine, to make worm-roads under our feet as important as the clouds and airplanes overhead.

HANCOCK

To move right onto your stories, you always have an "I" narrator who is a very intense perceiving consciousness and the events are rendered exactly as the narrator perceives them or even misconceives them which sometimes makes them appear terrified because the focus is so tight. Is that a correct reading, that an emotional response always precedes that intellectual understanding?

BLAISE

I can't write anything until I feel I have come into contact with its depth. That sounds pretentious, but I hope all writers are like that. Unless I feel that I have seen behind the stage (so to speak) or grasped the texture of a given situation, I won't be content simply to say, here's a street, a house, a car, an attractive young couple. Which is to say unless I know far more than I can possibly use, I can't use a theory. I have to have some *other* sense about that street: what is the last thing I can say about this place? Until I've come to that point I'm not interested in rendering any of it. But once I have come into that awareness, then I can't stop from writing it. It simply grips me and that's it, I'm in its full power.

The first-person narrator is a way of controlling its power by limiting the world outside the self. I'm not using a first person right now in a novel I'm writing, or in my last three stories. First person at one time seemed a very rich, deep and natural thing as opposed to third person. Now I find first person rather tinny and I can't stand to write in it anymore. I want to link up an individual life with many things outside that life. Third person is a mode of community; first person, the voice of isolation.

HANCOCK

What kind of things do you want to connect with that you couldn't before?

BLAISE

I want to connect with randomness. I want to connect unpredictableness, shock, surprise, disorderliness, chaos. I want to connect those things, and happenstance, and the collisions of the most unlikely forces. I want *impact*. So I want to get an illusion of depth, and that sense of spaciousness in a work derives, I think, only from the demonstration of things failing to quite connect.

HANCOCK

Do you find you can also use humour and compassion and other subsequent insights with the third-person narration?

BLAISE

Yes. Third person opens up many, many aspects because the tone of voice can be varied. In first person the tone is so controlled you can't really exploit all the opportunities for humour. If you do then you end up with a funny story. Or an ironical comic monologue. Well and good, but if you're less than perfect with it, your comic scenes come off like gravedigger bits, transparent attempts at levity. I didn't want that, either. I wanted more *un*evenness of tone.

HANCOCK

Now could you tell me something about the victory of voice. That's what makes your work so compelling for me. There is a voice of an intelligent consciousness dealing with the tones, with the colours. I would also say that the mastery of voice is probably the most important thing a fiction writer can do.

BLAISE

Voice is finally *all* that he has because the other forms of writing have everything else under control. Obviously fact is more "important" (and often more *interesting*) than fiction. Most people would rather read factual, not fictional, accounts of most things, simply because facts work in more bizarre ways and they are more unpredictable and they're richer. The thing that makes fiction fiction is the kind of luminous, or at least *suggestive* space between quite ordinary facts. Other kinds of writing have to lay on facts densely, sentence by sentence and they have no trajectory, no sprung energy, nothing to sustain them when the informative level is lowered.

HANCOCK

Your stories are very visual. The surfaces were almost sculpted with the texture of words. Could you comment on this?

BLAISE

I try to see things in dimension and with texture. I don't feel as though I'm in possession of the detail until I can see the other side of it. "Sculpted" is a nice word, if it's meant to imply the use of space, the "other side" of the familiar surface, and if it also implies the hardness of the surface. Details are there because they have penetrated my own consciousness, and when a detail penetrates as it so frequently does, then I try to figure out *why* because my life is generally a fog.

When I'm going very well, a number of things stand out, and when I'm in possession of a story, everything stands out and I'm seeing linkages that almost make a story inevitable. Then I go back to my normal fog and to keeping these notebooks in which I copy down random bits that I see, read, imagine, or overhear. Well, trying to be responsible for those things that leap out at me, means that I have to write a story to it. I have to find the *why* behind each of them; I have to find a set of characters who can in some way provide a context for those details. It's often that way, finding characters who can justify the details rather than the other way around. I usually start with the light or the physical details that evoke a particular mood, and then the characters suggest themselves more slowly.

151

Is the image sometimes triggered off by an experience, an emotional ulcer?

Rarely, rarely. I get moved by a visual situation. Most of the deep emotional situations that hit me or that hit people I know are too hot for me to handle. I'm in possession of a great number of stories of vast interest. But they're thoroughly useless to me; I'd make pulp of them. If they'd give me a *detail* instead, then I could invent the situation. I think Joyce Carol Oates probably can turn such stories to fiction, at least I believe that she does that when she says, "someone told me the story and I wrote a five-hundred–page novel about it." I can't do that. I guess I'm in as much possession of emotional data about other lives as anyone is, and yet I don't really use them at all. It's one of those great wasteful areas in my life. I overwork a rather small area of my experience and I ignore vast areas of it that would probably be more interesting and more to the liking of the editors that we were talking about earlier. There's nothing I can do about that. That's how I work.

Yet even working within this small area are you conscious of style? Shall we invent a new term, Blaisian stylistics?

Oh, I'm always very much aware of style. The style is the situation. If I want to be true to how something strikes me, I have to be as stylish or as style-conscious as that very thing that I found so gripping. I'm talking about very small things: a hedgerow, say. To do real justice to a hedgerow would require the work of a great lyric poet or Monet or (in prose) Proust — the only author I know who gives every element of nature and of character its proper space. To do real justice to anything is a matter of generosity, and character and style and you can't use the language of the butcher shop or the language of the newspaper or the textbook to do that hedgerow justice. That's the great challenge: to find language that fits the things that do not yield to language. We have no agreed-upon formula for that. We do have visual formulas in the arts, in painting and film and in music but not in prose.

The moment we agree upon conventions they become clichés. As soon as we agree that "spun-gold" hair means something, it's become already part of the language of coquetry and of the marketplace, and thus off-limits for art, except for pop-art and parody. So the self-conscious (or simply respectable) writer is continually reinventing the world through language.

I might add as an aside here that most of what critics and editors call "new" or "exciting" concentrates on *formal* inventiveness, without realizing that one sentence of great writing (in a traditional formal shell) can be as "avant-garde" as the latest breakthrough in form. To put it another way, dazzling innovations in form are simple face-liftings if they do nothing fresh with language as well.

HANCOCK

Your opening lines nearly always suggest the opposite of what's going to happen in the story. So if it starts off with a sunny day, you just know that there's going to be stormy weather coming up. You suggested this in your essay, "To Begin, To Begin."

BLAISE

A writer is always trying to suggest the *other* side of things. He's trying to create a subject and an object, not only the centrepiece but the frame, and sometimes he feeds the frame first and withholds the picture. Other times he gives the picture and withholds the fact that he's going to hang it in the garage next to an old nudie calendar. Sometimes it may be a very beautiful thing to be deliberately destroyed. There has to be surprise, continually. You can't follow a single course. You can't shoot an arrow straight and expect to get anywhere in fiction. It's always a matter of working by indirection and by surprise and by suggestion, which means that everything you state directly has a shadow meaning, implied. There's an essay I wrote, called "The Cast and the Mold" (in Metcalf's *Stories Plus*), in which I tried to develop the notion at greater length: the story is a delicate, fluted, casting; what the writer is out to capture is the rough, shaggy and broken-open mold that surrounded it, at least in his imagination. This doesn't necessarily mean that you are committed to a path of irony at all times but it means that you are always trying to be aware of the sinister and of duplicities and of dualities.

HANCOCK

Does that mean then that the writing of the story is a line-by-line discovery?

BLAISE

Oh, it had better be! If the reading of a story is a line-by-line discovery, the writing of it has to be much more. It's not just line-by-line discovery, it's line-by-line creation and it's line-by-line re-presentation. It's not like choreography, with its illusion of spontaneity, and its hours of rehearsal. Line by line the writer is discovering the nature of his material and each line is like the finest nozzle point holding back a great force, and the best kind of writing (thinking of Gallant, or Calisher, or a few others) is that which comes out like a laser: very fine, very controlled, perfectly placed, able to do retinal surgery but behind it is the power to knock aircraft out of the skies. You are aware of the power and of the need to be very precise and very controlled.

HANCOCK

Because of the choices you have in creating each line do you do a lot of editing in your head or on the page?

BLAISE

I edit before, during and after. I am continually editing. I am continually writing and I am continually rewriting.

HANCOCK

I am making that distinction between rewriting and revising. Rebuilding the car as opposed to revising which is giving it a new paint job.

BLAISE

I tend to work from the small to the large. I can worry a long time over a word and then the sentence and then the paragraph but the real progress comes when I realize that all of that was useless. I didn't need the paragraph, I didn't even need the three or four paragraphs around it, and I can go from point A to point G in a single leap and a suture, but I don't see it quickly. I have to go from the very, very fine up, and that's how I work and I don't have the construction engineer's sense of "knock this out, knock that out" and it'll work. I'm a bricklayer in that sense, I have to go from brick to brick.

HANCOCK

As a result of that, your stories seem to point into their centre rather than follow that line towards a revelation, climax, or epiphany. Is that a strategy or is that just what happens?

BLAISE

Who knows? It's deeply related to one's own psychology obviously; introspective people write inward-turning stories. The stories, in my own mind, tend towards a kind of confirmation and towards the discovery of that which you wanted to keep hidden, and to a kind of confirmation of what you hoped was not true. If there is any kind of optimism it's in the fact that, well, "I've" weathered it and "I" can survive it and before the story, "I" would have thought I'd have died if this had happened. But it does happen and, look, you've survived it! That's to me the central message (if any) in most of the things I've written. Most of my own life experiences have been like that too. I don't think I'd have taken out an option on any year in the past five or six, if someone had shown me an outline of what the fates had in store. Well, I've survived, the family's survived fire and repeated uprooting, disease, disillusionment, all sorts of agony and we've swallowed it back and we're not destroyed. I'm older, that's all.

HANCOCK

Is that why your stories have a slice-of-life approach, in quotation marks?

BLAISE

Well, yes, only if slice means segment. I hope to imply that the world was not created when the story started and it does not end when the story's over, but rather there is a continuum and the story is a plucked thread, one of possible thousands, from a sweater that remains indifferent to the process. We tease the story into a very visible loop and we stare at this loop and it bothers us and it disrupts the harmony of the weave but it also goes back

154

into the weave and disappears. End of story. For a while, it snagged at our eye. We even felt sorry for the owner of the sweater. But we also noticed that snagged thread and all, it remains a handsome sweater. It doesn't destroy the sweater, it doesn't destroy the overall design, and there are millions more threads running in every which way which will eventually get snagged and which will become exposed and embarrassing. And that's my sense of the story. We are not talking about a whole sweater. We're talking about one out of several thousand intricately patterned, interwoven, anonymous threads and if we had the time and patience in our life we could look at every single strand, at every single moment of human life, and make of it a densely observed story. But no one has that. The sweater, however, is the shaggy old mold I was talking of earlier.

HANCOCK

So that means that rather than a bigger realization or a greater epiphany, again to use that well-worn term, you have little epiphanies, little realizations that light up each moment of a life, each part of a story.

BLAISE

I think it's what I'm trying to do. That's all I can do. I would like to make the big noise but it's just not in me to do it. I don't have that talent and I don't especially regret not having that talent but it's not of my background either. It's not of my personality; it's none of my concern.

HANCOCK

Is every story an allegory about reality, in quotes, or a metaphor for some aspect of reality?

BLAISE

It's not an allegory in the sense that, say, Hugh Hood's stories are. I don't have the moral patience or the scruples for allegory but I would imagine they are all metaphors. I think of a story as essentially a single metaphor and the exfoliation of a single metaphor through dense layers of submetaphors. My test, when I'm rewriting stories, is that every sentence in some way be a part of that metaphor. I try to understand what the largest metaphor that contains that story is, and that's my principle for cutting out things, that certain details may be well and good in themselves, and tangential to the story, but not really part of its central metaphor.

HANCOCK

Could you give me an example from one of your stories?

BLAISE

Well, say, "At the Lake," about the leeches. There it all is from the very first page, I say, "I was suckered into it." I use the name "Lac Sangsue" and I specifically say that the name of the lake does *not* refer to the bugs or the leeches, but rather to the shape of the lake. I specifically said of Lac Sangsue (meaning bloodsucker) that it's named for its leech-like shape, not its fauna. You see, the metaphor is of *naming* things, not *doing* things. My character places his faith, like many academics, in the names of things, in aesthetics. He wants to drain off the "health" of nature, he dreams of transforming himself simply by lying in the sun on his dock in "immemorial torpor." All of it is a denial of reality, all of it is a desire to place a faith in names rather than in reality, so that eventually reality comes, eventually what happens to him is that he is forced to pay the price for his preference to live in a world of aesthetics rather than realities so he ends up with bloodsuckers around his body. My feeling has always been that nature is ruthless and that nature is corrosive.

If I have any kind of "vision" it's a naturalistic vision. Everything shall be worn down; every life will be worn down, in 70 years, the way continents are reduced to bedrock. Everything that's been suppressed will eventually be exposed. Every doubt will be tested. Every weakness will eventually be exploited. A life consists of about two billion separate seconds; every second is like 6 months in the life of the planet but with the concentrated time-lapse of Creation to Apocalypse. Every second in a life relates to the beginning and to the end of that life; every sentence in a story relates even more intimately.

HANCOCK

Both of the story and of your larger world view.

BLAISE

Yes, yes, how each story is a metaphor. I can't say it's a metaphor with a paraphraseable meaning, but it's just a metaphor, an elaborate comparison, a way of suggesting something larger and more permanent. Then I have to create characters to satisfy the metaphor.

HANCOCK

Let's talk about some of those characters. A lot of your protagonists are watchers as much as they are participants and they're often detached observers. They're sort of artists if not real artists. They're interested in healthy mind-improving hobbies, astronomy and chess and all those things . . .

BLAISE

I don't think of those as mind-improving. I think of those as anxiety-ridden. Chess! I used to play competitive chess and I never knew a more ego-destructive and tossing-and-turning-all-night-long type occupation than chess-playing. You'd replay endlessly your mistakes. I think of chess as the epitome of sickly pursuits, something worthy of Thomas Mann or Nabokov — it's really out of that tradition. And astronomy too, is the most humbling of sciences. The concepts of astronomy are so humbling to human ambition and to the human frame, to the human context, that I look on it as an apprenticeship either to humility, or to cynicism. It's very hard to worry about your mortgage payments when you're also having to worry about calculations in space. So I would dispute the idea of either of those things being mind-improving or healthy. They're metaphors.

Your characters are in some way trying to triumph over the world's sordidness. What do your characters do to achieve that triumph? What's their strategy?

Cunning, exile, and silence. Their only triumph is that they have imagination and an ability to accept. A low-grade survival principle. They're not terribly ambitious for themselves in a physical sense, in a physical, sexual way. In very few of my stories, I think, the characters could actually think of themselves as competing in the normal world. They're on a continent of strangers. The young lover, Keeler, in Europe, wants to compete in all the classic ways, as artist, as lover, as man of the world and all the rest of it, but he was young, untested.

The other characters have more or less seen the eternal footman hold their coats and snicker, and the world has provided enough irony about their ambitions (or they have provided their own irony about their ambitions) and they realize the big gesture is not for them. So that their survival could be called a very Canadian thing, I suppose, in that the "lesson" of life seems to be don't try too hard, don't want too much, be satisfied with less and you'll get by, and too much ambition is a bad thing, and conspicuous success is inevitably going to bring the gods down on you.

I've never been comfortable with the kind of character who really is, let's say, Faustian. That's part of my essential psychological Canadianness, I think. I've always said I'm sociologically an American and psychologically a Canadian. I'll never possess the sociological information about Canada that I do of the States. I'm a trivia whiz if you put me in an American context. I was that moist-skinned, under-the-rock type child who simply knew everything, memorized everything and listened to everything and never fed it back, and I have all that and will always have that at my fingertips — but I think my use of it is decidedly Canadian. I read Alice Munro's childhood stories, or Margaret Laurence's, and that's me just as much as it is her. The *National Geographics*, the maps, the encyclopedias, the mother with genteel tastes, the father who's continually letting them down, the small towns, the hankering after a kind of respectability and gentility that is never really there, the sense that you are somehow superior to your surroundings.

But it's exactly the same world that Naipaul writes about in Trinidad. It's a Commonwealth experience. The very nature of the Commonwealth is, I think, precisely that; that you feel you were created for better things but somehow the centre has receded far from you and it's not there to certify you anymore so you're left with this vulnerability. And this arrogance. You've been exposed. You've come out of your shell expecting something and all you're getting is the boot.

How autobiographical is your work?

I feel quite often my life has been an imitation of my fiction as opposed to the other way around, that I have such an imagination for disaster I have merely accepted, until very recently, the shell of "my" life for my fiction: Canada, America, French, English, north, south, and a kind of reflective, observant, fat and phlegmatic child simply because I've always found it easy to feed the things I was more interested in, into those frames. The "stuffings," the plots have been totally invented.

If you have a basically passive and observant, fearful child, then you can create vivid, lurid nightmares for him to fall into. If you create the tension of a responsible and respectable mother and irresponsible, unrespectable father, you can create confrontations between them. That is again fruitful. If you're talking about such vast geographical compass points as Manitoba, Quebec and Florida, you can talk quite legitimately about North America. So I've been quite happy accepting the givens of my life autobiographically but I have not been dependent upon the contents of my own life. I'm a placid bourgeois. My ambitions are purely mundane. I don't lead an adventuresome life, and I don't hanker for it. Adventures have come — the India-aspect especially — and I exploit it for all it's worth. For someone my age (40), I am probably less rooted than most. That is, if someone would offer me a job tomorrow doing something else in a completely different place, I'd probably say yes. My house here is up for sale, I'm off on leave next year, without pay. The only adventurous part of my life is its restlessness and the fact that I'm likely to be just about anywhere, this time next month or next year. But if all the things that I've written about had actually happened to me, then I would obviously be a very different person than I am. They are merely all within me. I would say I'm beginning to be in touch with the possibilities that can derive from my life.

Another question springs off from this too, and it's a big one, the William Gass one: what is your concept of character?

The centre of my stories is not in my characters. The centre is elsewhere and so I do not set out to create character. I do not set out to write a psychological case study. I am really trying to talk about, as I understand it, the world, the nature of the world, the nature of event, happenstance, accident, beauty, permanence, change, violence. I'm trying to talk about things like that. You have to have in our humanist culture, in our humanist Western traditions, you have to have a human focus for those things or else you are writing allegory, or fable. And psychology has told us so much about probability that the character is bound to be fairly recognizable. I'm committed to representational fiction; otherwise you're doing stained-glass windows.

HANCOCK

Or sociology.

BLAISE

Yes, or sociology. So that the agreed-upon way of registering shock-waves is through a perceiving consciousness and so I do that. That's Jamesian, I guess; tinged with a bit of W.H. Gass. It feels natural but that's not to say that I see the character first and then devise a story for that character. Writing would be a lot easier if I did, but my own essential narcissism or egotism gets in the way. Things that really interest me are more aesthetic than psychological, so I'm willing to accept a fairly stable psychological receiver. I don't explore a great range of characterization, and I'm willing to accept that so long as I do have intensity and texture. To me that's where the interest lies, not in the characters. Or put it this way: my experiences have led me into interesting places, and my subconscious churns up confrontations that I find terrifying. So I follow those strengths into fiction. But what I can tell about character is probably deficient; I simply don't notice that much, and the thing that I do notice about disparate lives and about social patterns fail to move me. I'm very under-populated.

HANCOCK

So that leads to that gap between the author and the "I" narrators of your stories, characters like Dyer and Greenwood and Thibidault and that also explains the link between the three or the four, including yourself.

BLAISE

I've only written of three characters really and that's my mother, my father and myself. I am utterly dependent upon the family situation and the family conflicts as the source of my fiction. Now the "myself" character is sometimes female, sometimes male and the myself character is sometimes acutely analytical and cynically intelligent, and sometimes it's reflectively and passively intelligent, sometimes it's only cynical and worldly and abusive, but all those are within myself and I can as easily be one of them as another. The father character stands as all males, older, with authority, with physical power, with experience, with sexual charm, with confidence, with a fearlessness before the law, with a kind of lawlessness, people who *define*, or, who are continually pushing out against definitions. And my mother-figures are always the ones who are pulling in within definitions, anticipating, so acutely aware of restrictions and anticipating rebuffs, anticipating them so sensitively that you internalize them before you ever do anything. So that this is my landscape, my moral landscape and that's always been enough for me. Eventually it will not be enough for me either, and that's when you notice "crises," and "stages" in a writer's career.

159

Do you want to be a self-projecting or a self-effacing writer?

It doesn't bother me, self-effacing or self-projecting. It amounts to the same thing. That is, an artist might do two hundred self-portraits or he might do the Rouen Cathedral for twenty-four hours. Which one is more self-effacing? Is a self-portrait any more self-projecting than doing a landscape? I don't think so. The artist is as much present in his landscape as he is in a self-portrait. In fact he may even be curiously more self-effacing in his self-portraits because he may be seeing the parts of himself in a disembodied way.

Does that mean that the old notion of plot and character is worn out, that writers have to find a new way of dealing with a character?

For me and for me alone, plot is not planned but plot is the revelation of inevitability, the slow disclosure of something beautifully obvious, though hidden. That's plot and that's the kind of plot that I acknowledge. I feel sometimes that you hurtle through the vastness of time — those two billion seconds that we all have allotted to us — towards some point that was always there, something that you feared and hoped to avoid, but it was always there. And you embrace it finally and that's a plot, but until that moment, you've had (seemingly) an infinite number of choices, and ways to avoid it. With my strong sense of inevitability I obviously have a strong sense of plot, of a certain kind of plot.

Here's a bunch of easy questions. What are your writing habits? Do you have an average number of pages per day or a certain time of day? Do you set aside a certain place? You've mentioned you keep notebooks. Do you type or write in longhand?

Those questions are all too painful. I don't have a schedule simply because I don't have the time to write, so, given the ideal circumstance, I would be writing every day. I would begin writing as I do when I've had my month a year to write. I used to go to Yaddo, to the artists' colony in Saratoga Springs, and there I would finish breakfast at eight-thirty and I would write steadily till five. When I lived in India and we had servants looking after the house and the kids were in school I wrote steadily from eight-thirty to five and in each of those cases it was ideal. I wrote a lot, I wrote every day, never took a break. I would write about an hour and I would read about an hour and I'd play solitaire for about half an hour. That would be my way and I knew exactly where I wanted to get, not in terms of pages but in terms of scenes. I knew I wanted to move this far and if it took eight pages, it took eight pages, if it took two pages, it took two pages, but I wrote very carefully.

But I haven't written in the last year and a half more than three stories, three chapters, some reviews and some articles, because of my teaching job and responsibilities with the kids and the house. So I can't really speak with any legitimacy about work habits. I know that when I first was writing, I was an all-night writer and I loved to start around midnight and write till about five and then sleep till about ten and then get up and write some more; that's when I was in Iowa. Ideally I want a circumstance that allows me to write every day, read every day, write letters every day, walk every day, that's really all and if there is socializing to be done, fine. I like to see movies. I like to see my friends. I think I would like to be in a fairly confined setting, I mean in a fairly small town. I don't think I need the cities particularly but if I'm in a city and I like it I exploit the possibilities.

HANCOCK

Do you find the literature of India has an appeal for you?

BLAISE

I'm so restricted to reading what is written in English that I am really not able to say I know the literature of India.

But the *experience* of India is like that. It gives a new range of potential, a new range of possibility that to these tired eyes is very refreshing. You just can't match on the page the qualities and complications and dramatic pitch of daily life in India. You suddenly find your palette loaded down with new colours. The spectrum that you've conventionally been operating in has been widened, and you see what a tiny slice you've been in.

HANCOCK

How do you deal with that in your work?

BLAISE

I haven't written much fiction about India at all. I have a story, "Man and His World," and I have a book in germ with two or three beginnings about Africa and India and Canadian characters in those places. It's really a matter of feeling confident enough to control those settings and to allow for greater degrees of accident and collision than I'd ever done before. I would deal with it by plotting on a larger scale. Character remains character throughout the world. But it is a matter of plotting. Of feeling in command of so many points on the compass that you can navigate much farther out.

HANCOCK

Would you deal with the African or Indian experience in the same way as someone like Margaret Laurence, Audrey Thomas, Dave Godfrey, David Knight, even Hugh Hood?

BLAISE

I would choose to do it in Canadian terms rather than American because Americans simply by nature of their national and psychological involvement in other parts of the world have muddied the waters. It's largely impossible to be an American and still be a neutral creature in those places. The Canadian is a kind of clear veneer that you can put over the canvas. It allows the highlights. It's a good thing to be in those settings because it really doesn't interfere all that much with the native essence of the place. They can be more reacted upon than reacting.

I think of the Canadian as being your standard, decent, uptight soul who doesn't go with great ambition to transforming the landscape and saving these people for anything. He goes trying to be fairly open to experience and he goes a fairly vulnerable person. He can be destroyed more easily. He also has no historical linkage in a place, and to me, lacking a history in a place is almost a formula for vulnerability and destruction.

HANCOCK

Is that what you were doing in *Days and Nights in Calcutta* when you created the persona that wrote your half of the book?

BLAISE

Yes, very definitely. I exaggerated the qualities of lostness and wonder and ignorance on the part of the character who carried my name. All the things that I described are true, but I suppressed a lot of things too — things that I did know to create a character who was capable of wider degrees of wonder. It was necessary if I wanted to move him from a point of absolute ignorance to a point of some comfort and sensitivity. I had to create a character who was perhaps a little more naive than I was.

HANCOCK

To change directions here: do you think *Lunar Attractions* is an extension of your stories?

BLAISE

It's definitely that. I came to the end point of many of my stories in that novel. I can't see ever picking up on southern material again. I can't see picking up again on that particular quality of myself: the fearful, phlegmatic child, the spoiled, but neglected child. I'm writing a story in which the same American-Canadian-Montreal-French-English axis occurs, but here I found the mother character has all the affairs, is an extraordinarily attractive woman, with aggressive sexuality. The father is a poor shnook who's been on the lam for years and the son is not myself at all. At least not as I recognize myself. But it's a new variation on my side of reality.

HANCOCK

Does the novel have a form for you?

BLAISE

No, not at all. The form has to be like abstract expressionism in painting. Representations for the passions. Metaphoric equivalents. Dramatic equivalents for your deepest feelings. They just come, in the same way abstract expressionism came for painters. They may come in a rigorously controlled Rothko way, as two big squares, or they may come as they did for Jackson Pollock, but to impose an academic form on it — this is how it *must* be — violates the essential reason for the novel. The story is a formal piece. The novel is an experience the story couldn't contain.

HANCOCK

Do you feel part of Canadian literature?

BLAISE

Yes. Psychologically this is my home. Culturally I am a hybrid and maybe not bred true to either parent — Canadian or American. But if Canadian literature can't find a place for me, then Canadian literature is sadly self-restrictive.

LEON ROOKE

A prolific writer, Leon Rooke has published several story collections, including *Last One Home Sleeps in the Yellow Bed* (1968), *The Birth Control King of the Upper Volta* (1982), and *A Bolt of White Cloth* (1984), as well as the novels *Fat Woman* (1980), *The Magician in Love* (1981), and *Shakespeare's Dog* (1983), for which he won a Governor General's Award.

This interview was done on Leon's terrace in Victoria, B.C., in July 1980 and revised by mail throughout 1981. The view from the sundeck swept down through a ravine, past a heritage mansion, and up and across the tops of oak trees towards Oak Bay and the American San Juan Islands. An exhilarating — nearly distracting — place for an inverview. Sunny day, breezes, and a never-ending supply of Harvey Wallbangers made it, as Leon described his hilltop home, "someplace we'd all like to be."

Leon is a quiet man who rarely talks about his work or himself unless cornered by an interview such as this — his first. Still tanned from a few weeks in Barbados with his wife, Connie, and their son, Jonathan, he was relaxed and as generous with his time as with his hospitality. His North Carolina accent still retained its deep southern twang. He spoke slowly, carefully, looking across the treetops for answers.

By then I had known Leon for several years, and he has always moved at a comfortable pace — easy, not slow — whether making pancakes, raking leaves, or just going from one place to another. His real force and energy cut loose in his writing.

HANCOCK
Do you like to do interviews?

ROOKE
No. I can think of any number of things I'd rather be doing. Driving a gaggle of geese to market; walking the shore in Long Beach; sunning myself in Barbados. An interview is not at the forefront of my desires.

HANCOCK
Why not?

ROOKE
I'm not that much in love with the sound of my own voice. I don't like the idea that the voice we hear now will come back later to haunt me with its ignorance.

I sense some irony here. Some would say your own work is nothing but voice.

I've yet to decide whether that is an insult. In any case, the voices in my work are only infrequently my voice. My voice is somewhere underneath all those others that one hears. It is the one saying, Listen, this speaker is **human too. Hold your judgement until the voice falls silent. I take the old-fashioned notion that one of the writer's jobs is to project a multitude of** voices, of identities, and not simply to write of the self. To write of the self only is the power of a few, the disgrace of many, someone said. The voices in my fiction I regard as authentic; mine I see as a thing made up from day to day. Shapeless. Mass without form.

Now that you're co-editor of *Best Canadian Stories*, what do you see happening in contemporary short fiction, both in Canada and in the United States?

It's an exciting and fertile area. A lot of excellent work is being done. The **short-story form, over the past fifty years particularly, has been a vigorous** one. Despite everything editors could do to kill it — in the sixties, for instance, when so many magazines closed their pages to fiction, and while so many of society's overseers were saying that people no longer wanted fiction, they wanted fact — the short-story writer has persevered. There's **probably more activity in the form now than there ever has been. And it** keeps getting better. It is always getting better. It is always getting worse too, but one invariably goes with the other. It's a growing, living, vital form and one ever seeking new directions.

Compare any anthology of the forties with one published last week and you can see how the form has altered. Enough front-line established writers have remained faithful, not content to repeat the same victories; enough new writers keep coming along, firing away with a totally different arsenal. Change but no change: that describes pretty much the whole recent history of the short story in North America. It describes any art form where the evolution is constant. In Canada, the vitality is not always as evident. But our golden age is approaching.

Do you have a quick lesson to offer story writers in Canada who want to try new things?

Good things often happen when a writer paints himself into a corner. How do I get out of here? Houdini was ever concocting new schemes of entrapment. This time, chained and in a box underwater. Next time around, a stronger chain and the water is shark-infested. There is too much sameness in Canadian short fiction. Not enough risks taken. Too much timid breathing. Not enough channel swimmers. Too many readers — critics too, I guess — saying I don't want much, you have given me exactly what I wanted. Not enough love of the big surprise.

HANCOCK

Do you mean vitality in the form of structure, innovation, language, exploring extremes of character?

ROOKE

You bet.

HANCOCK

As a story writer you're precisely in the American tradition now, more so than in the Canadian, if we use, say, Alice Munro as a comparison.

ROOKE

I was astounded, a short time back, when I made my virgin's appearance on CBC radio and the host referred to me as a member of Canada's literary establishment. Me? Jesus Christ, if so, God help all others. I have somewhat the same reaction to your statement. The only tradition I dimly perceive is that one where we find the writer attempting to write well and knowing from the start the likelihood of failure. An international community of thieves raiding whatever landscape is before them.

I became acquainted with Alice Munro's work 10 or 12 years ago when I first came to Canada. I felt an immediate closeness to her work. The emotional bondage to time and place was familiar to me, and very southern, and I wasn't surprised to find, when I later met her, that we had read and liked the same people. We belonged, emotionally, to the same territory. And it is a territory without boundaries or borders, which is to say that it can be found anywhere. Writers do from time to time worry about another writer's work. About the work of friends. I feel good about Alice's. I think it would be a mistake to predict what she will do next year, or the next five years. I sense spectacular new horizons for rural Ontario.

HANCOCK

You've spoken several times of form. What do you have in mind with that word?

ROOKE

Form as a thing apart from structure. That includes not only the pattern with which lines are formed and which guides the eye along a page — how a work falls on the page — but also as the overall shape which holds the work. The mould. But a mould that isn't fixed, varying, as it does, with any given work. What it is that makes a good reader, finishing the story, catch his breath. Pure form is like a ship that has had good passage and has, out on the open sea, come to anchor for the night. You've got where you were going and everything is perfect. That's why many of the typically traditional stories being written today no longer satisfy. You know the route too well and you know before you get there that you've been there before. Such stories can have form, of course, but it's form manufactured by the thousands, and the magic is absent.

What constitutes innovation and change in the short story?

You're better equipped to answer this than I am. A reliance on newer techniques, of course. But the techniques — the innovations — that have the greatest interest for me are not the games that one can have with the typewriter or by folding pages over or by producing triangles of print or by asking the reader to read from right to left, or by introducing the page-phonic muse or by inserting mirrors or by listing 64 descriptions of one inch of the female thigh. So what is one left with if one discards these more obvious elements of gamesmanship? I'm not sure I know. I know you have to have a fresh approach to what story is, to what constitutes story, to what story can be. I know you say to yourself a story is anything I can make it be and get away with. I know you scrap the old advice about beginning, middle, and end, and instead see them as a stretch of shifting coordinates that relate in ways unpredictable.

And plot? Do you change the order of "and then, and then, and then"?

Plot, which was always the least important element for everything except Agatha Christie mysteries and Dime Westerns, takes an unlamented back seat. Language, which a lot of writers try to disguise as something else, tries not to be ashamed of itself. What beguiles me most is a liberated approach to point of view and delineation of character, and precious little is new about that. The point to be made about innovation is that it is re-sisted every step of the way by publishers and readers and yet it still makes inroads, makes them until it alters the mainstream literature, so that we find ourselves always arriving at a point where what we think of today as traditional is not what we meant by that word yesterday. Is a period piece a period piece because it's trapped by a curious pocket of time, or because it's trapped by the dictates of the traditional fiction of those times? I would venture a guess that several Morley Callaghan stories, several Hugh Garner stories, some lesser Hemingway stories, three-quarters of the 1,000 or so stories reprinted by Martha Foley, and probably a fair number of stories John Metcalf and I will select for *Best Canadian Stories,* suffer more from the latter than the former. I've never read a Camus story I could say that about.

Is that what you're trying to do with your fiction? Alter the mainstream? What makes your fiction innovative? Different from Alice Munro, let's say, who once lived down your street.

167

I would be happy to have it recognized that I, like many others, travel a legitimate diversion of the mainstream, and one no less important just because the flow is less thick. Am I more innovative than Alice? Perhaps it only seems so because she writes more out of the single unified voice while I shout the tidings of many. I'm in a peculiar position. I'm a traditional writer, but at times a more experimental one. Most writers are one or the other. My position isn't fixed, it isn't firm. It's always at the mercy of whatever material I'm dealing with. Some stories demand a traditional form. I don't think the traditional form is exhausted or ever can be. Because it always changes. Frequently, the two come together in an amalgamation that is both traditional and experimental.

My "Adolpho" story from the *Cry Evil* collection would be an example. The framework, the structure supporting the story, is utterly in the traditional. Some old men gathered around the club fireplace, one of them telling a story. The English, especially, have given us dozens of such stories, and this one is straight out of Conrad. So what's the difference? Interior narrative? Not much new there. The story progressing along two fronts, current action and old action, until the point of revelation, where both fuse? Nothing new here. An ending that makes a difficult reach: the narrator, already passing or passed over into death, recoiling from the illusion that has summoned him there. All right, a curious authorial attempt, but nothing revolutionary. Authors frequently strain the final page. So it's the unexpected content, what goes into Adolpho's peculiar vision, that brings us into the 20th century and gives us the sense of "something experimental" going on here.

And, deep-down, I don't even see that. If a work is successful then it is no longer "experimental." It is the state where narrative development, where craft, has naturally got itself. It is the New Traditional.

What is fiction? What is it supposed to do? Who is it for?

Fiction is real life coming at you from another angle. It's for all those people out there who want and need and often are enriched by that "other" angle.

How do you know, when you start a story, whether it will be traditional or experimental? Does the material dictate that? Are you a theorist? Or do you just write?

The material has to do it. One thing that keeps me in the traditional camp is that I am unwilling to relinquish character. It's important to me to see characters in fiction as living human beings. I extend this to include even the extremes. In my "Magi" story in this issue I've got several "spirit" people running around. I believe in them. Whether I believe in them outside the pages of the story is beside the point. I believe in them for the purposes of this fiction. In Derk Wynand's fine book *One Cook, Once Dreaming*, recently published, he's got this strange person, this cook, sprinkling flour over his wife. The cook takes out his roller and rolls her flat. She's then a wide sheet of dough and he takes out his tins and cuts the dough into crescent moons. I see the moons, see the dough; the book is beautifully written and Derk from the start makes me believe his cook exists. The poet is then free to do with language what the cook does with dough, but the book is stronger because the cook was there first.

HANCOCK

Does innovation occur just in form? Or do you expand it, as I gather you are saying Derk does, to include language? By language, I also include the voices that you use for your various characters. How do we open up the possibilities of short fiction? Or do we even want to in Canada? Or can we get *too* innovative? I'm thinking of Donald Barthelme's "one-shot" innovations. We don't want to see those tricks a second time. And *thin* innovation seems worse than none. Think of the two volumes of *Statements* (Fiction Collective).

ROOKE

The two Fiction Collective anthologies leave a lot to be desired. I suppose most Fiction Collective members would agree that the volumes issued to date contain much that is silly. But some strength is there, even if hidden. My guess is that we become too innovative when we have innovation merely for the sake of innovation. Innovation is meant to serve the demands of the thing that contains it, and to serve the larger purpose of maintaining a powerful, energetic fiction. What we call literature. Winter lettuce never made it to a lot of tables before the invention of ice. I'm straight-laced enough too to accept the cliché that you learn the rules before you break them. Or that you learn them *by* breaking them. But the one thing you don't do is say they are not to be broken. Thin imitation is as bad as thin innovation. Remember that the death bell tolls for fiction every month that *Chatelaine* makes an appearance. That stuff, their stuff, is not even fiction; they are little blurbs for the crematorium. The writer on automatic pilot. The prevalence of such material has to be fought. People see it called fiction, and they get confused, just as they do when Rod McKuen's work is called poetry.

Barthelme? I don't know. We don't have to worry about his "one-shot" so long as it's not another writer doing it. He walks a fairly large battlefield. There is a lot of distance between an early story like "Some of Us Had Been Threatening Our Friend Colby," and a 1980 story like "The Emerald." Both fascinating. Both absolutely different.

HANCOCK

Do your stories start from character? Or with situation? How do you arrange for that first sentence, that often oblique leap into a story?

ROOKE

They start from any number of things. Occasionally from character. Occasionally from "idea." What is a situation? I wrote a story a few months ago called "Standing In For Nita." I had overheard two people introducing themselves. One of them got the name of the other person wrong, and was not corrected. So this one person thought the other was in fact another person, the Nita that this person was standing in for. The mistake changed both of them. Because of this, both had an evening they would not otherwise have had. The story came out of that situation.

"Fromm Investigations" developed out of idea. I thought wouldn't it be interesting to consider what would happen if you had a guy who thought psychiatrists were lazy and no-account and criminal for not going out and investigating the various things their patients told them? Wouldn't it be interesting if this guy fancied himself as a kind of souped-up private eye? And wouldn't it be even more interesting if this guy was pretty much messed up himself? If he had some baggage in his own past that kept getting in the way of his investigations. That's "idea." I've also written ten or fifteen stories that came out of nowhere. I sat at the typewriter, typed out one sentence, and that sentence invited another sentence and that demanded a third. Several hours later I had the first draft — even sometimes the final draft — of a story. These stories happen very fast, and where they come from or where they're going I don't know until I get there. "Wintering in Victoria," published in your magazine, is one of these. "Deer Trails in Tzityonyana" is another.

HANCOCK

Do all your stories have that same line-by-line discovery? Or do you have some Holy Grail at the end that you're aiming for?

ROOKE

The Holy Grail usually appears about two-thirds of the way through. But of course, the Holy Grail has a nifty habit of disappearing too. Sometimes when you think you're two-thirds of the way through, you're actually at the first page, starting over. The more complex stories take the longer time, and often have to develop at their own pace. I have to work at it; the story won't do it by itself. There's no way of telling how long it will take. A handful I've done in a few hours. Others I've worked on for a couple of years. And I don't want to give the wrong impression; some are planned very thoroughly in advance.

HANCOCK

Are you a linear or a lateral thinker? You like fragments, bits, discontinuous narrative. Notes, even drawings.

ROOKE

Yes, but I like something beneath all that, to bind it. Tone, perhaps, if nothing else.

170

Is fiction an entertainment for you?

Art is entertainment, plus. Society's idea of what entertainment means is not necessarily my idea. Or yours. One of the functions of literature is to change society. To change the way people think. To redress grievances. To mould society, to pace out, confirm, and secure certain desired directions. I'm a stoop-shouldered moralist.

So literature reflects the world more than it is an addition to it.

It reflects, it adds to, and somehow it redeems. There is nothing so stunning as excellence. It absolutely rivets the backbone, it stirs about and resurrects the always-tired soul. One of my projects over recent months has been to put together *my* list of the Top Forty Modern Miracles, to itemize a few of those performances that have hit the charts. Karen Kain when she's out of her tutu and into her tights. Violinst David Oistrakh performing Shostakovich, Concerto No. 1. Paul Scott's novel *Staying On*. Mado Robin singing the "Bell Song" from *Lakme*. Sonny Terry and Brownie McGhee doing "De Waw Is Over But De Battle Go On." These things are all around us and would be recognized almost as commonplace, but for the fluff that is around us too. But they are stunning; they allow us to forgive or at least live with all the shoddy evils alive in the world.

Traditionally, the novel is more reflective than the short story because it deals with a community, deals with historical times; but the short story deals with characters who are somewhat apart from the times. They're lonely voices, as Frank O'Connor called them. Submerged populations, loners, outsiders, eccentrics, fringies. Can the short story be as powerful as a longer fiction?

I think it can. The perfectly-moulded short story is every bit as complete as a perfectly-wrought novel. Everything is in there that needs to be in there. Is a large painting more powerful than a small one? The sense of a person's life that one takes away from the reading of a short story is as satisfying as that one which is taken away from reading a 400-page novel. What more can a reader want out of the 75 pages of "The Death of Ivan Illych"? Or out of the 30 pages of a good Chekhov? Or out of Jack Hodgin's "Three Women of the Country" or Metcalf's "The Lady Who Sold Furniture" or Walter van Tilburg Clark's "Hook" or Alfred Chester's "Berceuse" or Allen Wheelis' "The Illusionless Man and the Visionary Maid." Or out of Flaubert's "The Legend of St. Julian the Hospitaller" or Flannery O'Connor's "Resurrection", Jane Bowles' "Camp Cataract" or Paul Bowles' "The Circular Valley" — or from Bill Kinsella's "First Names and

Empty Pockets" or Spencer's "Prelude to a Parking Lot" or, for that matter, Guy Vanderhaeghe's "The Watcher," in *CFM* #34/35. Such stories exist by the thousands and are every bit as powerful as the novel. But I recognize that's not a commonplace view. Too many readers of the short story would argue against that view, and certainly all novelists would.

HANCOCK

Do you sneak in myths and archetypes and patterns which might be evident from an overview of your complete works? Do you even want your work interpreted in these ways?

ROOKE

I'm aware of a number of recurring patterns. Mostly these are character patterns, people patterns. Gode, in my old short novel "Brush Fire" later stands in as the lover in the "Field Service" story; still later he's reborn as the film-maker Martin in "Biographical Notes," with time off to be Jake in "Wintering in Victoria," to be the frustrated husband Talbert in "Leave Running." The wife from "Leave Running" turns up as the fun-loving schizophrenic diarist in "The End of the Revolution," having taken time off, while healthy, to be the cautious laundromat woman in "The Love Parlour." A lot of story-hopping. Same character, but new relationships, new set of circumstances.

And other things too. The pattern in "Adolpho", for instance, where current action and pre-story action fuse and old Philby goes off to meet his illusion Orpha, duplicates the life and death swirl at work in "Broad Back of the Angel" when the paraplegic wins final release from his chair — which is itself predated in the skirmishings of "The Third Floor" and a number of other stories.

HANCOCK

What are your necessary disciplines when you work on a story?

ROOKE

I'm unable or unwilling, emotionally, to structure tomorrow. My wife Connie and I have had numerous discussions about that, because she takes considerable pleasure, actual joy, in planning what she will be doing and where she will be six months from now. But when things are more or less what one would call "normal" I like to mess about for a couple of hours in the morning, and sit down at the typewriter about 11:00, after the mail has arrived. Whenever I've moved, the first thing I've wanted to know is when the mail comes. Work until the middle afternoon, take a break, get back to it later that night. Or sometimes my work day is just made up out of 15 or 30 minute patches. I've always been a night worker. My best hours are usually between ten at night and two in the morning. But if I'm really going strong then I have an around the clock attitude towards it.

But there are days, weeks, from time to time months, when this is not true. I don't see the typewriter at all. Or if I do I curse it. Also, I get my best work done in the winter. The lure of the outside isn't as strong. When I'm really into a story, however, it's hard to leave it.

172

HANCOCK

Do you find it a schizoid existence? You're so into it that the story world overlaps the real one?

ROOKE

I don't. Perhaps those around me do. Do find me schizoid. And sometimes there is a monologue, or dialogue, or scenes going on endlessly in my head, connected with story, and this can cause some social ineptness on my part. But my social ineptness has other explanations, I fear. No. Often I'm working on three or four different things at a time. One thing one day, or something in the morning, something else in the afternoon, and something different the next day. Sometimes it's like that. I don't have much trouble; I'm like an actor in rehearsal for three plays. I can do it with some ease.

HANCOCK

Do certain situations, or certain characters, haunt you?

ROOKE

From time to time. Usually not. I've lived with this "Magician" character for years. Ella Mae, of *Fat Woman*, did so very early. The character that haunted me for a long time, when I was beginning, was the one who was outside of things, outside of life. The face at the window, looking at what was passing by. Cut off. Sometimes I was the one passing, and cut off. Sometimes I was the window face and cut off. But the effect was curious because it presented me with that awful sense of isolation and at the same time it told me that I was not alone. I still feel it. And much of the wonder of fiction, of course, is in making that cross. Crossing that boundary. You want patterns? That's one.

HANCOCK

That's why you have such characters as lifeguards, magicians, conmen?

ROOKE

You may have put your finger on something with that. In those early days too I was attracted to characters wounded somehow. Both in my actual day-to-day life, and in my day-to-day fiction. The "Wounded Creature" syndrome.

HANCOCK

Which brings us back to Frank O'Connor. Could you talk about why you like revising? Do you start to discover the possibilities that are hidden in a story? The artifice of the art?

ROOKE

Yes. Everytime now I sit down with a piece, I see stuff that I missed. Stuff that is just *wrong*. It seems like absolutely vital stuff, even if it's only a loose fingernail. In the old days I would rather have uprooted a tree than retype a page. I would have thought, "Nah, that's not very important." Not so any more.

HANCOCK

When you do a revision, is it just for details? Or is it the overall shape? Do you add characters? Take them out?

Sometimes one, sometimes the other. Often the entire form of the piece changes in its revision. When I first started writing, I believed in the authenticity of the original effort. It came down through my fingers and into the keys and onto the page. It firmed up like concrete. It felt so *good* doing it, and if it felt that *good,* it couldn't be wrong. Over the years I discovered that pieces are rarely set. You come back to the material a little later, and you see the gaps, see all the things that are missing. So now I take some pleasure in taking out what doesn't belong and putting in what does. Or in honing a sentence. Unless the piece is dead to begin with. Then it's no fun at all.

HANCOCK

How many times can you revise a piece? Rikki said the most marvelous thing to me yesterday. She said writing was like clay. You can only work clay so much. Then it starts to break apart.

ROOKE

Yes, I like that. I love that. I've worked with clay enough myself to know exactly what she means. Clay just goes limp and dead after awhile. But it can be revitalized by mixing it with unworked clay.

HANCOCK

Are you like Bill Valgardson? Do you do forty complete rewrites and only then are you satisfied? What do you think of the kind of story Valgardson writes?

ROOKE

I'd begin to get a little tired after the fifth or sixth rewrite. Let me look at the stories in my Mexican series for a minute. The first two came rather rapidly. The first overnight. A month after I wrote it it was in print. The second, "For Love of Eleanor," took three or four months. I kept getting trapped by the opening. I'd sit down, write what I thought was a terrific first page. Then four or five pages, ten pages, twenty, then I'd look back at the first page and say, "Well, I've started it at the wrong place." Then I'd write another terrific beginning. Eventually I had fifteen or twenty different beginnings and several reams of paper. All of them fine. I had been backing up on the material, starting each new beginning at an earlier point in time. By then all my beautiful beginnings were too close to me to be thrown away so they were incorporated and helped form the heart of the story. I think that's why the sky moves so slowly in that story.

No, Bill Valgardson's approach to fiction is very different from my own. It's been some time since I read your interview with him, but my impression from that and from the stories of his I've read is that he operates out of the textbook rules of long ago and far away. Fortunately, the writer is often better than his theory. I can often admire a Valgardson story. Just as often, though, my admiration is tempered. Take his story "Trees," for instance, or "Bloodflowers." Both excellent, I would be pleased to have written either. But why do I feel I've read them before? Would it be fair to say that "Bloodflowers" owes a little too much to Shirley Jackson's "The Lottery"?

HANCOCK

Could you tell me about growing up in the South, in North Carolina? Did that have a lot to do with your view of the world, with how you approached fiction?

ROOKE

That question has a lot of complex answers.

HANCOCK

There's a rich and complex literary tradition in the South.

ROOKE

Which I was opposed to. I felt myself apart from the Southern tradition.

HANCOCK

Meaning who?

ROOKE

Let's go back a bit first. I went to the University of North Carolina at Chapel Hill. I remember my first evening on campus, thick fog swirling around the old lampposts, thinking "God, this is a dream, something is going to happen to me here!" The great literary ghost at Chapel Hill was Thomas Wolfe, of *Look Homeward, Angel,* and *You Can't Go Home Again.* Not a bad ghost to have around. Read "Only the Dead Know Brooklyn" sometime, a knockout story. I read Wolfe as an undergraduate and loved him, as most undergraduates do. And there were Faulkner and Eudora Welty in Mississippi, Carson McCullers in Georgia, Peter Taylor in Greensboro, Tennessee Williams up to New York and early Truman Capote out of New Orleans, William Styron in Virginia. There were the newer and brand-new writers such as Shirley Ann Grau in Louisiana, Flannery O'Connor in Mississippi, and Elizabeth Spencer there too. There were actual writers in Chapel Hill with whom one could rub elbows: the Broadway playwright Paul Green, the excellent novelist John Ehle, the beloved novelist Betty Smith, and high-power story writers like Max Steele and Doris Betts, Doris only a year or two ahead of me. So, yes, there was a sense of stepping into a tradition. Then came the sixties. Martin Luther King singing "We Shall Overcome" and a strong sense of too many in the older order singing "You Shall Not." And that did something to my sense of loyalty to the region. It took away some of the ghost's power.

HANCOCK

Who did you learn from?

ROOKE

I learned a lot from Max Steele and John Ehle, just by having them as friends. I learned from Dylan Thomas that prose could sing in the same way poetry could. I learned from Tennessee Williams and some of the others mentioned, something about mood, about youth and innocence. Story, story-*telling*, was I think something that I had a fair start on, that came perhaps with the tradition. What I had to learn was language. And the dimensions of story. Of form. And what to do until I found my own natural material. You remember the old *New World Writing*, possibly the finest magazine ever published? It appeared twice a year for almost a decade, and was everything it said it was. *World* writing. I learned a lot from that. I recall I had just written a one-act play when I read in one of its early issues my first Ionesco. "Christ," I thought, "this guy has stolen my stuff. He's doing exactly what I'm doing." Naturally my play was rubbish, but learning that this guy on the other side of the world had something in common with me taught me a lot about writing. It made me look more closely at what was being written around me.

And from the start I was gravitating towards the strong stylists. Wright Morris, for instance. Stylists, I find, are rarely disappointing. If the style is strong then the content usually is as well.

HANCOCK

By style, you mean the surface of words? The music of the language, the pushing of language towards its razor's edge?

ROOKE

Yes. The unique imprint of the single writer. Style to me is like a woman walking in high heels. The way they know how. And one never exactly the same as another. The way the toes are pointed right, the way the legs shoot up straight, how the head is carried. That's style. Put the woman in high heels and give her a name and put her on the road: that's what the stylist does, putting words onto the page.

HANCOCK

Were you aware of this when you wrote your first collection, *Last One Home Sleeps in the Yellow Bed*? Tell me how it came about? All at once? In a year or two?

ROOKE

I had published maybe 25 stories by then. One was the lifeguard story, and Charles East, director of Louisiana State University Press, saw it and invited me to send a collection. I sent everything published, along with a list of those I thought were the best. His own list agreed with mine.

HANCOCK

Where did the stories come from? The lifeguard story, the army story, and so on.

ROOKE

Ah, the army story, "Brush Fire." I was living in New Orleans, after serving 18 months in the army, a line company in Alaska. Drafted, I was certainly not in the army by choice. So I had this little apartment in the French Quarter and I sat down one day and started this story. It had as its trigger an actual incident that had happened in my company. A Hungarian was locked up in the freezer unit by a cook who got angry at him. Both had been friends of mine. So I sat down and two weeks later — I've never again written so fast, some days I'd do forty pages — I had this short novel. Amazing. A new magazine had just been born, *The Noble Savage*. Edited by Saul Bellow. Jack Ludwig was, I think, the only Canadian associated with it. Eight or ten top-notch writers among its contributing editors, including Wright Morris. Max Steele, living around the corner at the time, liked my piece, suggested I send it to them. I did. And got this extraordinary letter of acceptance in return. This was actually before any of my stories had been published, although I had a bucketful.

My first book was, I suppose, more than a little late in coming. I'd been messing about with novels for a long time. Learning to write. The life-guard story in the LSU book is actually from one of those novels. As is the "Field Service" story.

HANCOCK

You call "Brush Fire" a short novel. It has a particular formal structure. You like that kind of story, I think. Stories that have structures. "Biographical Notes" comes to mind. Does a story have to have that structure?

ROOKE

I certainly prefer that a story have it. I like form. Shape.

HANCOCK

Where does that come from? Were you a mathematician at one time?

ROOKE

No. But I can count. I don't know where structure comes from. It's a lot of fun to sit at the typewriter and let words gush out. In an informal and uninstructed way. But I've never felt that was enough. Most things are seeking a form. Space wants to be filled, but it doesn't want to be filled by nonsense. It demands a form. A tree has a form. A seed of any kind thrown into the ground will grow up and have a form. Roots will go far, searching for moisture. I like things when they come out of the human consciousness to find whatever form is natural to them. It's often laziness not to seek that form. Of course, some things never find it. The pretty flower dies.

HANCOCK

So the form doesn't always find itself easily? Are you like Michelangelo, looking at the stone until you find the essential shape in it? Are titles important to you?

ROOKE

The stone, I suppose, would much prefer to remain a stone. Some stories resist their form-taking every inch of the way. "The Broad Back of the Angel" story, one of my favourites, was a painful one to write and partly because it kept wanting a form other than the one I wanted it to have. I wanted the man in the wheelchair to tell me what it was like being there, but stuff *outside* the chair kept insisting that *it* had validity too.

HANCOCK

You had to share his agony to understand it? Where did the story begin for you?

177

ROOKE

It came out of the year I was teaching in Minnesota. Southwest State is one of the few schools designed and developed for the handicapped, and up to one-third of the students is afflicted in some way. Wheelchairs scoot up and down the halls. One of my colleagues in my department was chair-bound; he had to brave *blizzards* in his chair. What might it do to you, I wondered, to be locked in those ugly machines? So the story came out of what was around me, although the character didn't.

HANCOCK

Do you keep notebooks?

ROOKE

I have many. Mostly empty. I scribble on the odd loose sheet.

HANCOCK

Do you do this to sort out technical problems that you're having? To authenticate details?

ROOKE

I guess so. These notes that I am speaking of have to do with the complexity of the material, lines that I will need ten pages down the road, exchanges of dialogue, assessment of characters, a phrase snippit. Often a note to myself to remind me of something I want later to work in, or an idea about how I might do what I want done when finally I get there. "Look back at page 25." "Remember Esther has red hair."

HANCOCK

Do you write poetry? Plays?

ROOKE

I have a little portfolio of the worst poetry imaginable. I haven't done any plays recently. I do have a full-length play called *Mary on Piano, Oscar On Horn* that I want soon to get at with a hacksaw. And a few uncompleted one-acts that I want to get back to.

HANCOCK

Some of your plays have been on the boards. In New York City.

ROOKE

I started out as a dramatist, in college. Then I went over to fiction and it was six or seven years before I got back to the play. Yes, the full-length *Sword/Play* was done Off-Off Broadway by The Cubiculo. Pretty good production. What I liked about it was that they brought their imagination to my imagination. Didn't change anything, I mean, just added to it. I like that. It's one of the few productions I've had where this has happened.

HANCOCK

That explains why dialogue is so important in your fiction. The rhythms, and the sense of character that comes through often simple phrases.

ROOKE

Print is expensive. One looks to be brief where one can.

178

HANCOCK

Do you find yourself constantly listening to people to get the sounds of their voices right? To capture that dialogue correctly? To use dialogue to reveal character?

ROOKE

This goes back to your first question: do you like being interviewed. I remain the watcher, not the participant, in most social situations. It's a nasty habit, hard to break. Dialogue does reveal character. It also reveals that your character has none, if that's what you want it to do. No, now I don't listen nearly as well as I once did. After a while the head gets filled up with all of the voices you've already heard.

HANCOCK

Do you get many rejections now?

ROOKE

A fair number. More than I would like.

HANCOCK

How do you deal with them?

ROOKE

Rejections have never bothered me. I don't dwell on them for more than a few seconds. They don't make me feel inferior, or that my work is inferior. I've always taken the idea that if one editor refuses it, another will take it eventually. If no one takes it, I'll look at it. Rework it. Dump it. Pull it out five years down the road and start again. In fact, many of my stories rejected five years before I've pulled out and had accepted immediately. Without making much of this, I prefer to think that *they* have caught up with *me*.

It bothers me a little when I *know* the piece I've submitted is good, and — funny thing — it is often the best work that's rejected. "For Love of Eleanor", not a bad story, was turned down by any number of minor magazines before it occurred to me to send it to *Southern Review*. "Wintering in Victoria," not a bad story, was rejected by *Prism*. Second time around, *CFM* took it. Did that tell me something about the relative merits of the two magazines?

HANCOCK

The literary magazines are very important to you.

ROOKE

I like literary magazines. I like the sense of vitality in literature that one gets from little magazines. That is precisely *where* one gets it. Corners. I like those funny little corners.

HANCOCK

But you don't send stories to *Esquire*, the *New Yorker*, *Saturday Night*.

ROOKE

Only if invited to do so. It doesn't matter to me a great deal where my manuscripts appear. I don't think I would feel very differently if a story appeared in the *New Yorker* (not that I've ever had one) or in some struggling little magazine with a circulation of 200. I like picking up a little magazine and finding really solid stuff in it, as is frequently the case. I've come to expect to find it there more often than it's found in *Saturday Night, The Atlantic,* etc.

HANCOCK

But they pay so well.

ROOKE

Yes, yes, yes. (*Laughter.*)

HANCOCK

What literary magazines do you admire in Canada and the USA? Of course, we'll include *CFM*. This is for the benefit of fiction writers out there who are looking for new markets to send the stories.

ROOKE

In Canada, I see most of the mainline literary reviews. *Descant* has made giant strides. It is now one of the best-edited journals in North America. *CFM* is a true rarity. Aside from *Fiction International, Fiction,* and maybe one other in the States, I don't know of another like it. That exists exclusively for fiction — fiction in the broader sense to include photographs and nonsense like this interview. But meant to serve the art. *Quarry* is slipping. Maybe I only mean that I wish they could return to their former format. *Fiddlehead* does a good job with the traditional story. Awfully uneven. *Exile* is beautiful, but why do I frequently get the sense of emptiness? The *Windsor Review* has never decided what it wants to be. Or even that it wants to be seen. *Wascana Review* is so bad that I'm actually fond of it. *Malahat Review* has wonderful resources: the world. And it is better with that world than many give it credit for. The fiction hand flutters too much. *Ontario Review* is dreadful, but for its poetry sometimes.

I've lost track of what's happening in the States; it's been a couple of years since I've sent anything in that direction. But . . . *Fiction, Fiction/International, Salamagundi, TriQuarterly, Ohio Review, Iowa Review, Southern Review, Partisan, Ploughshares, Sun and Moon, Antaeus, Crazy Horse, Massachusetts, Paris Review.*

Hell, we can applaud all of them. It's lonely, whether editor or writer. Maybe it's lonely for readers too.

HANCOCK

Do you concern yourself with a theme in your work? Obviously in *The Love Parlour* you have stories of love, the love that just eludes us. *Cry Evil* is about the evil within us and others. The Magician stories and the forthcoming novel that you are doing with Aya Press deal with magic. Do you always conceptualize a book that way?

ROOKE

No. In a collection, five or six stories are culled from, say, twenty that are maybe, just maybe, worth reprinting. Those that are worth it, we hope, have something to do with each other. And there are threads, motifs repeated. The "mole" for instance in *Cry Evil.* One wants a book to be read that carefully, but they rarely are, and the threads remain invisible. Short story collections shouldn't have to possess these patterns, but editors want it, reviewers want it. They want the pattern, want the overlapping, want the connections, and want the obvious ones.

HANCOCK

In other words, they want a novel . . .

ROOKE

Want anything but what I give them. What most writers give them. It's cruel, isn't it? (*Laughter*.)

HANCOCK

You have an extremely wide range of characters. Are readers disappointed because they can't follow that single voice? Do you like getting inside these characters? Do you add bits and pieces of real observed pieces to them?

ROOKE

My conception of what a fiction writer ought to be is one who can move into and occupy all sorts of human frames — and take on all sorts of vastly opposed human voices. I find it peculiar that many writers are only willing to write out of one voice. This may be because I don't have a single voice. The wider the possibilities, the wider the framework of achievement. And then there are writers like Mordecai Richler who have one voice but that single voice contains many. But he's a novelist, not a short-story writer, and so his "many" voices are more easily seen as a part of the one fabric.

HANCOCK

Are these characters outside yourself? Or are they extensions of yourself? What are the possibilities for characters in fiction?

ROOKE

When they are successfully created, I become them. When I leave the typewriter I'm not them anymore. But while I'm there, I feel they are a part of me. My other identities. But at the same time I have to judge how well it is all working, so from time to time I have to come outside.

Most people, I think, have personalities in excess of who they think they are. High one minute, low the next, feeling joy one minute, feeling sour the next — when nothing has happened to induce those changes. I think it's the other person trying to get in. One thing I like about my "End of the Revolution" story is that my schizophrenic diarist lives in a neighbourhood where *everyone* has these multiple identities. That's intriguing, I think, and it's not the madhouse you think it is. All the visors of the armour are raised. A healthy situation. But of course "Revolution" is idyllic; no one hurts anyone.

HANCOCK

Do you *ever* intrude as Capital A Author?

ROOKE

I can't say never. But rarely. Well, the spirit is there. But I don't do cameos. The rare Hitchcock. This is not one of the avenues I find promising in the New Fiction.

HANCOCK

You have an optimistic view of the world?

ROOKE

I'm always puzzled, baffled, confused, distressed by people who see my work as work of despair. By friends who won't read me because they don't want a writer in the family or because they have the notion that I'm gloomy. I don't know how the writer who feels only despair can continue to produce. What's the point? At the same time, one can't turn one's back on those occurrences in life that make one despair. Charlie Manson, Jamestown, poverty, the cruel way we often are with each other.

HANCOCK

Is humour one way of dealing with that despair? Or black humour? Or as a satirist? A parodist?

ROOKE

Life is often funny.

HANCOCK

Side-splitting, knee-slapping funny?

ROOKE

If we are lucky, we have known those times. But I'm not good at writing that. The best I can manage is the aggrieved chuckle. My strokes are too broad. Metcalf has a high-frequency range of side-splitters. In *General Ludd,* to mention his latest. And he combines this rich humour with deep, raw, driving emotional power. That's why the book has been so mangled by the critics. They want one or the other. It simply by-passes their understanding that a novel can combine both. So they either deny the slashing wit of the first part, or trample on the riveting intensity of the second part. Christ, we should get down on our knees for a book like that.

Stanley Elkin is another one who can plaster the face with sunshine. The rafters hum. Huckleberry Finn also still has a foot in the door. Evelyn Waugh. Joyce Cary.

HANCOCK

Many of your characters are quite obsessed. They are not passively sitting back there, or casually doing the shopping. Extraordinary things happen to them. Or they push themselves to make something happen.

Your main character in "Biographical Notes," for example. He is pressed with a morals charge. He wants to be the greatest pornographic film-maker ever because he thinks it's art. He's really plugged into what he's doing.

ROOKE

But the narrator of that story is doing what most of us want to do in our lives which is to validate ourselves. To justify ourselves. Note also that my character justifies pornographic films *only as he makes them.* He's a Freedom Fighter. He may be screwy, but his heart's on the right side.

HANCOCK

Who's your ideal reader?

182

Myself, I suppose. I write to please myself first. I have to be my ideal reader because I don't know that I have any readers.

I'm guessing, but I think you are more interested in your female characters than in your men.

It has seemed funny to me that I am interested more in my women characters than in my men. Most male writers are interested in writing about male characters. I may be wrong; I may have a total misreading of my own work, but I am also better at women characters. They simply interest me more. I don't really know why. I think I *understand* them better. I am attracted more to the female personality than I am to the male.

There's one simple explanation for this. I grew up without a father. I just know women better. Or think I do.

Do stories sometimes come to you out of dreams? Nightmares? Insomnia?

No. I make almost no use of dreams. As a rule, I'm usually not interested in people's dreams. I know I ought to be, and by themselves, dreams are fascinating. But I don't find a rich source of material there.

So you always use the real world, real happenstances?

I don't do that either. Rarely. I spoke earlier of the Mexican stories which was my response to the real world. My Mexico. Most of my stuff is invented. It may be of the real world, but it was not found by me in the real world. I have by writing it put it into the real world. Or tried to.

Is there anything you won't write about?

I think every subject is taboo until it is written about. That's more or less my approach. There is nothing that I will not write about. But there are some things I don't care to write about. We were talking a couple of days ago about Canadians and bears. I'm a little tired of graphic sex, simply because every writer has felt compelled to do it. As I was for awhile.

Could you please repeat what you said about Canadians and bears?

I made the observation that it would be invariably healthy for Canadian writers to assemble in a single room along with representatives from the animal world and for those writers to screw their favourite animals to get it out of their systems so they can then go onto something more rewarding. This was said in response to scenes in Susan Musgrave's *The Charcoal*

Burners, and Marian Engel's *Bear.*

Compare those with Stanley Elkin's scene with the bear in his story, "The Making of Ashenden." I measure all such scenes against the bear-loving scene in that story. All else pales. It's just so incredibly well done. All the juices run! They *pour* off the page onto the reader.

HANCOCK

Let's talk about the effect you were trying to achieve in your novel, *Fat Woman.*

ROOKE

Fat Woman was interesting to me because it was the first time I returned to material I grew up with. It's one of those rare times in twenty years that I've gone back to material familiar to me from my childhood. I loved doing the book simply because I found that the language I grew up with hadn't been lost. It all came back to me. Quite often when I was working I felt I was a simple vessel that the story was being transmitted through.

HANCOCK

Where did the story originate?

ROOKE

I started it in London, England, about two years ago. I had this simple idea of a man who locks his wife up in a room. I was working on the Adolpho story at the time. I put it aside one night to scribble out a little note to myself about this fat woman situation. Two or three hours later I was still working on the note to myself and had twenty or thirty pages. I put aside Adolpho and started working on the Fat Woman in earnest. I was fascinated by that woman and I saw that I couldn't handle it in a short story. I kept going on. The language came so easily. I remembered the voices so well. I could hear the single voice of the fat lady running through my head.

I suppose it was material that I had been sitting on for twenty years that through no wilful act of my own was suddenly there.

HANCOCK

Was part of that wilful act to include as many clichés as you could? The novel is an absolute thesaurus!

ROOKE

She lives in a region where clichés are an active part of the language. Where clichés are not dead. The cliché still has the sting of the whip to it. The cliché is a way of visualizing one's life. It is for her. Her life is composed of just these clichés.

HANCOCK

The novel follows a rhythm of optimism and pessimism.

ROOKE

That's life. But the critics are wrong about Ella Mae. She is not one of God's Ugly People. Her spirit is beautiful. Hope and love can not be stamped out.

You asked earlier about hope. I think Gomez is a good example of a character of whom we can say we know why he acts the way he does. Why he treats women the way he does. We can explain the evil surrounding him. I find something in his method that is actually ennobling about humanity. It isn't his evil. What he is doing is healthy for him, and in fact, healthy for the ladies who enter his environment. Madeleine, for instance, who winds up swimming in his mucky pool, finds the swim good for her. It's where she ought to be. She has dived into this pool with algae floating on the surface. That she has willed herself to do so is an act of hope. She's telling us that she recognizes her failures as a person. And I think, and Gomez thinks, that she will come out of it a better person. It's a *happy* ending, I'd argue.

HANCOCK
Marital strife seems to be one of the constant conflicts in your fiction.

ROOKE
A number of stories have gone in that direction, and I'm surprised myself by their frequency. But I ought not to be because it's a natural area in which to find conflict. Friends who know *my* marriage, who know Connie, are ever trying to read *us* onto those strained relationships. Ours is not exactly a *serene* marriage, but it *is* nine-tenths bliss. There is no tongue in my cheek here. We would both say that. I delight in her, to tell you the truth.

HANCOCK
You found the ending to *Fat Woman* difficult. You said you had *ten* endings.

ROOKE
Not difficult. There was something in all ten endings that I quite liked. They were not bad endings. It was finding the *right* ending that kept my head buzzing. My ideal ending would have been a blend of all those ten.

I should say something here about the pleasure of having a great editor working with you on a manuscript. Gordon Lish at Knopf is one of these. He *served* the novel. He kept saying, "I like it, I like it, but is it your best?" Nudges, the just right push that kept me digging away. The ending that finally came into being was written up in Knopf's office one beautiful day last summer. Traditions? It felt good to be hooking into a living rich past like that.

HANCOCK
What do all these endings say about your sense of resolution?

ROOKE
I had here a situation I really didn't want to resolve. I was tempted not to resolve it. I am often in that situation. I don't like resolving situations because most situations are not resolved. I like the open ending. I like the reader to say, "This is the ending," and the other reader to say, "No, this is the ending." I like to leave a situation poised like that. Readers, strange to me, want all ends tied.

ALICE MUNRO

In May 1987 Alice Munro received her third Governor General's Award, for her short-story collection *The Progress of Love*. Previous awards went to her collections *Dance of the Happy Shades* (1968) and *Who Do You Think You Are?* (1978). In addition, she has produced two other collections, *Something I've Been Meaning to Tell You* (1974) and *The Moons of Jupiter* (1982), and a novel, *Lives of Girls and Women* (1971). For many years her stories have appeared in *The New Yorker*.

CFM's long-awaited interview took place at my apartment in Toronto on September 15, 1982, on the eve of the publication of *The Moons of Jupiter*. The paperback rights had just been sold for $45,000 — a record for a Canadian fiction title and a triumph for the short story. Visiting Toronto from Clinton (about seventy-five miles to the west), Alice was staying in an apartment at Queen and Bathurst. From there it was an easy walk to my place. She brought a bottle of wine. The mood was casual, though she concentrated intently on each question as she prepared her answers. Afterwards, we reminisced about China, where we had recently travelled as part of Canada's first literary delegation to the People's Republic.

before she said she didn't think about writing

HANCOCK

Why don't you like to do interviews, Alice?

MUNRO

I don't like to do interviews because they seem, *to me*, a waste of my time, a waste of my energy when I'm trying to think about writing. This takes me away from the mental state I feel comfortable in, out of which writing comes. And, I suppose, I'm frightened of anything that cuts into that too much.

I do spend a lot of my time engaged at whatever this process is. If I'm called upon to back off and describe it, not only do I do it badly but it doesn't help the process at all.

This doesn't mean that I don't enjoy the sound of my voice after a while and a few glasses of wine, because I do; anybody does. But it still seems all a lot of flim flam.

HANCOCK

I see you as much a poet as a short-story writer.

MUNRO

I like you saying that but I've written very little poetry. I began to write poetry when I was about — oh — twelve, I guess, and I wrote it all through my teens. And then during my first pregnancy I wrote a lot of poems which

I sent off under an assumed name and they weren't very good. They were all sent back. That is the only time in my adult life that I've at all wanted to write poetry. What is the difference that makes you see me as a poet rather than a story writer?

HANCOCK

I see you as a lyricist, as a songwriter. You give voice to our secret selves.

MUNRO

That's absolutely what I think a short story can do.

HANCOCK

Do you see yourself as part of an ongoing literary tradition? Hugh Garner wrote the foreword to your first collection of stories.

MUNRO

I'm not interested in any literary tradition. I read things that I enjoy, that nourish me. But I never seem to put things together. I never see myself, even now, as having a steady career as a writer. Maybe it has something to do with being a short-story writer. I see everything separate. Right now, all that matters to me is making a new story. It's as if I had never made any in the past. When that story's finished, it's only the new one that will matter. That's why I can't talk about myself developing as a writer. I don't see a career. Because I look at things this way I also don't see a tradition. It's probably all there but I have to concentrate so hard just on this little bit that I've got hold of. I have to work very hard to be a writer. And it hasn't gotten any easier, at all. It's the one thing in which no facility has come to me with increased practice.

HANCOCK

So you don't see yourself related to people like John Metcalf or Clark Blaise, Leon Rooke, Mavis Gallant? What do you think of critics who make connections between you?

MUNRO

I see we are all writing at the same time. And that we may write stories where it seems the things we are trying to get at are similar. That's about all I can see. And I can never make much of critical attention so it doesn't matter to me except in a superficial vain sort of way, whether I get any or not.

HANCOCK

What are you trying to get at?

MUNRO

I never know. In each story it's different and I can't quite define it. But sometimes I can feel it in another person's story. And sometimes I can greatly admire it. I admire Mavis's stories tremendously without feeling that they're quite the kind of stories I could ever write myself. With Clark and John and Leon, I feel that sometimes we are working at the same kind of story. And I can feel greatly helped sometimes, overjoyed in a way, by a story or a book that isn't particularly successful but I like the spirit behind it; I like the direction it's going in. This is hard to describe. But it isn't always a writer's most successful stories that move me the most.

HANCOCK

In trying to reach that success, you seem to be your most severe critic.

MUNRO

No, I don't mean it that way. I hate talking like this because it sounds as if one is terribly modest and snivelling. And that's not what I mean. But I just mean that I have never written a story that got all the way.

HANCOCK

Is it for that reason that you are constantly rewriting? You seem to have a four-step pattern. You go from manuscript to magazine publication. Then there's usually a revision, before book publishing.

MUNRO

Sometimes. Sometimes I figure a story is just as good as I can make it. Other times, a story isn't anywhere near where it should be. The last story I published, "The Ferguson Girls Must Never Marry," in a small New York magazine, *Grand Street*, is a long story that's the kind of failure I can't leave alone. Even though it's been published, and I've spent the money I got for it, I keep trying to rewrite it and figure out where I should be going with this material. And I think I'll just have to drop it, leave it alone. I think there's a point beyond which you can't work the material any more. It's as if it dried out or something. And yet, it's extraordinarily hard to stop myself from trying to do this. The story has good things in it; these very, very nice chunks.

And this is what bothers me — I don't know why the whole thing isn't working. I have a suspicion it's because of an underlying ... mmmmmmm ... not a lack of interest in the main character but a lack of total honesty. I'm making an effect which I don't completely understand.

I'm doing something in this story which is sort of fictional and works on one level. But I don't truly believe in it. I think that's what's wrong but I'm not sure. I haven't perceived it well enough. I have thought I knew how to write it. I thought I knew what was going on and I haven't. It's almost a kind of humility, backing off and *waiting* to see what this story is really about instead of telling myself I know what it's really about.

HANCOCK

Is this constant revision somehow tied into your sense of a fictional aesthetic?

MUNRO

You know very well I haven't got such a thing. (*Laughter.*) I have an idea of a story. Stories I'm just never quite sure if I've got; when the final story is finished there always seems to be ... some diminishment between the idea and the story I've written. But with some stories much more than others.

Can a story be perfect? Have you written one?

Certainly I haven't written one. Maybe one can't. There are short stories of other writers that I've read that seem to me pretty well near perfect. Eudora Welty's "The Worn Path" is close to a perfect story. Some Chekhov stories are nearly perfect. There are lots and lots of good short stories I'm coming across all the time. I read an American writer called Elizabeth Cullinan. She writes very, very good short stories. All I am trying to say is a lot of people who aren't very well known are turning out excellent work.

Are you a compulsive story writer? You couldn't stop yourself.

I don't suppose so, no. For a long time I didn't want to go on writing stories. And even now, I've got a book of stories coming out this fall and I will have to go out and face all these people who say "Well, how come you're still writing stories and do you think your next book . . . ." Half the people who say "What about your next book?" say "Is it a novel?" and when I say no they say "Oh, well is it connected short stories?" and I say no. And then everything just falls away. "Well, I mean, she didn't even connect them?"

And yet, I think the most attractive kind of writing of all is just the single story. It satisfies me the way nothing else does. I will probably, from now on, just go on writing books of short stories which are not connected as long as my publisher will consent to publish them. Of course, you know you are not very popular with a publisher if you do this. For years and years I would convince myself that I really had a novel there and I would take these ideas I had and bloat them up and I would start writing them and they would go all — they would just fall. It was just a total waste of time. And I'd become very depressed. So it took me a long time to reconcile myself to being a short-story writer.

And yet, the interconnected story sequences you have written can't be seen as failed novels.

No, I don't think they are failed novels. They work okay. But I don't at all think that there's something more difficult or somehow a better achievement about writing those kind of stories than writing just the kind of stories that are complete in themselves.

Do you get a form of catharsis in the Aristotelian sense or do you think in those terms when you find a line or part of a story that connects with you?

Oh, sure. I get a big excitement when I think that I've done something right. I get the best feeling from having done something that I think is funny. That I think is *exactly right*. I like that. I get the big rush, the true feeling of tremendous excitement at the very beginning, before the story's begun to be written. When somebody says something. When I see something. When it hits me. Then I feel terribly happy and excited and grateful and glad to be alive and able to write this story or able to even think about writing it. I think that beginning perception, that first perception, is the total moment and from then on there's all this work. Then when it's finished there's a sort of workmanlike satisfaction rather than a tremendous exaltation about it. It's seeing the thing at first. A few weeks ago one of my neighbours began to tell me about her church group and how they were visiting the sick that day. I can't tell you more about this because I'm writing a story about it. But this was one of those perceptions. What a church woman told me about her group's visits to the sick. I was just flooded with excitement! There is no way I can't try to write that story! So things come on me like that and then I'm really very happy about the whole thing.

HANCOCK

So you write from the heart more than from the head.

MUNRO

It sounds like it, doesn't it? (*Laughter.*)

HANCOCK

In your books there seems to be a chronological connection between all the stories. That all the books seem to start in youth and move towards adolescence and then old age. Is that just my reading? Is that a deliberate strategy on your part?

MUNRO

No, it's not deliberate but it probably just reflects what I've been thinking about. When I started writing, I wrote stories about old people. When I was about eighteen, twenty, that's what I was writing. My first published story is about a couple in late middle age.

It was published in a magazine called *Mayfair* which you may not even know existed. It was published in 1953, the year my first child was born. It was one of those heavy stories where there's a whole lot of atmosphere. I think there was an overgrown garden and lots of ripe fruit and the wife's name was Goldora, and (*laughter*) it showed I was reading the southern writers and absorbing the wrong things. But I didn't dare write about young people or anyone at all close to myself for years. Not until I was in my late twenties. Then I probably did begin doing a fairly straightforward thing of writing from the place I was at in life, at that time.

I still do occasionally, a story that's about people quite different from myself. But I don't do those stories very often. Only when something overwhelms me and makes me do it.

191

Which southern writers were you reading at the time? Did anyone in particular help you begin to write? Will you tell me the story of the publication of *Dance of Happy Shades*?

My ex-husband, Jim Munro, helped me, just by believing I was a writer. Not that I would become one, that I was one. Bob Weaver just kept patiently prodding me. I'd sold my first story to him for broadcast when I was eighteen. Then Earle Topping at Ryerson Press invited me to get the stories together for a book and Audrey Coffin, an editor there, pushed me to write a couple of new stories. This was wonderful. I didn't have to peddle a manuscript myself. Ryerson did have a good idea about publishing new Canadian fiction. They just didn't have much of an idea about what to do with it once they got it published.

I was reading Katherine Anne Porter, Eudora Welty, Flannery O'Connor, Carson McCullers. Some Faulkner, but he wasn't very important. Later on I read Peter Taylor and I read Reynolds Price, who's a much younger southern writer. His first book is very, very good. And his second, which has a heroine named Rosacoke, *A Long and Happy Life*, is a lovely novel.

What did you learn from them? At that time, you wanted to write a story and you had some vague feeling that you knew how to do it? And from them, they gave you some kind of a sense of how you can move language, how you can use characters? How you can get a stage set?

No. It was nothing that definite. It was more like a way you could see ordinary life. A way of seeing perhaps grotesque things, comic things. It wasn't anything technical, though I imitate techniques without thinking about it. So, of course, that's what I was doing. This is because I have no academic background and no training. So, where someone else would say "Here I am doing this," I will just be doing it and not realize what I am doing. I probably waste a lot of time that way.

For you, then, the dramatic action — the meaning — of a story is more important than event.

What happens as event doesn't really much matter. When the event becomes the thing that matters, the story isn't working too well. There has to be a feeling in the story. I said I think "The Worn Path" is a perfect story. It's about an old woman going into town to get medicine for her grandchild. At each successive stage nothing much happens. She doesn't come back to find her child dead. She doesn't fail to get the medicine. Nothing happens. I don't feel it's important what happens in my stories.

Sometimes, when I have a story that doesn't work, I've made something happen. I've made too much happen.

HANCOCK

So you don't try to write a dramatic story. You don't look for drama in the sense of cause and effect and consequence.

MUNRO

Not particularly. I have written some stories recently in which there seem to be surprise endings and I didn't mean them to be that way. I think I was writing about kind of random connections of lives. I just wanted a feeling of this randomness. Well, in one of the stories in *The Moons of Jupiter*, "Hard-luck Stories," a woman meets a man she's had an affair with, an ongoing affair, a long time ago. It's over. She introduces him to her friend and they all get to know each other. She realizes some feelings she has for this man and then she discovers a few months later that the friend is having an affair with him. You see, that seems like a surprise ending but that isn't what matters to me about the story at all. . . . It's just a quality of these people's lives that matters to me. And, yet, I'm afraid that I have worked it in a way that was too easy. I think that's what I've done. So that someone might read it and think "Oh, my, what a neat twist." (*Laughter.*) And twists aren't what I have in mind at all.

HANCOCK

Did you write that story out of a scene? Did it begin as a scene for you? As a scene observed or a scene recreated?

MUNRO

I observed a figure of a woman. Yes, the woman who appears in the story and she's wearing a nice striped summer dress, the sort of dress a nice woman wears. A sort of self-effacing, good-taste kind of dress. I saw this woman wearing this, and a huge straw hat with fabric roses on it which was a southern belle's romantic notion of herself. The woman was middle-aged and tall and skinny and very happy. That's what started the story. I was thinking about what might have happened to her. Why she was dressed like that. If she was going to meet her lover. Then other things attached themselves to this story. Material comes from all over. Something someone tells me will attach itself. . . . The story "Wood" is a story which follows closely something that did happen. I don't usually do a story that way but that's what it is.

Other stories are just completely a feeling, as I've said. I want the characters and what happens subordinated to a climate.

HANCOCK

How do you create that climate?

MUNRO

That's what the whole story is trying to do. You don't do it by passages of descriptive writing or anything like that. It's the writer's angle of vision that will do it. In a story called "Bardon Bus" I want to have a kind of feeling of hysterical eroticism. Very edgy and sad. This came to me from the feelings I get sometimes in women's dress shops. It's a feeling about the masquerades and attempts to attract love. But the particular things that happen in the story aren't what I want people to remember. I would want them to have this feeling as strongly as I had down on Queen Street, in Toronto where I have an apartment. I would see the shops and the clothes and all sorts of ordinary women, like shop girls and typists dressing like prostitutes and making their faces up in brilliant and very artificial ways. Also, there are old women dressed the same way, made up the same way. From that I got the feeling that goes into this story.

HANCOCK

Do you see the story in its entirety or do you have to work at it scene by scene?

MUNRO

Oh, I have to work at it scene by scene. Oh, yes, yes. This business that I have been telling you about comes into the story as a very little fragment. Then other things came to me that seemed to fit into this climate. And I worked at them.

HANCOCK

How do you keep that mood growing in the story?

MUNRO

If I've got a good hold on the mood, I don't have any trouble keeping it growing. In me, it's there. Now, how to keep it growing in the story or how to sustain it or how to make the story work is what I never know from one story to the next. I just keep trying. I just keep trying! I write it! And then I see it's wrong and I write it again. But I'm not capable of making judgements, even simple judgements. I change things but I never can tell you why. You know, I might think something was too long-winded or too pointed. Things like that. But it's quite hard to see what was wrong. And I'm not sure about it's being wrong. But I would go at it and change it. Even when I look at my published stuff, it's torture to look at one of my books because I just want to pick up a pencil and change things. And take out things, usually. I feel awful because I can't do it. When I read aloud at readings I do. I change as I go along.

HANCOCK

So there's none of your work so far that you are completely happy with?

MUNRO

No. With some I am happier than others.

HANCOCK

Which are you happiest with?

MUNRO

Hmmmm. Let me see. There must be something in the new book that I like. I like "The Moons of Jupiter" okay.

194

HANCOCK

In that story you have the remarkable image of the Planetarium as a metaphor.

MUNRO

Yes. That's "Moons of Jupiter." I like that. Yes, I think that works all right. There's not much I'd want to change about that story. There's a story called "The Turkey Season" I think works pretty well. I think "Wood" works very well. I think it's a well-crafted story, but I don't think it's a very interesting story. I don't like it very much.

HANCOCK

What don't you like about it?

MUNRO

I don't know. Maybe that there is nothing in it that is sort of rough and unfinished.

HANCOCK

Rough-hewn wood?

MUNRO

I think it's a bit, just a bit too well made. It's a bit too easy to read and was a bit too easy to write. But, you know, I think sometimes you do a story like this. And fine, I expect I'll do more. But the real excitement I have is often about stories that haven't worked that well. In the new book, I like the story "Dulce." And I'm aware of some problems with that story. I like the first two stories, "Chaddleys and Flemings," which go together. I like "Bardon Bus." They are stories that I'm totally at sea about, you know. I really don't know if I've got anywhere near them. But still, they're the stories that I'm most excited about. I'm excited about having written them and I think that was worth doing. So it isn't always how they turned out. At all.

HANCOCK

Would you rewrite *Lives of Girls and Women* if you could?

MUNRO

I don't know. When you've written a book, you've exhausted something so much that you really can't say if you would rewrite it. That should be written the way it is. I might tone it down a little bit. I think it's over-written. But I may be mistaken. You see, I'm not very interested in that book any more. It's pretty hard for me to talk about. And that's just what happens as a book recedes from you. I'm still sort of interested in *Who Do You Think You Are?* but not all that much. It's receded quite a long way, too. There are things about it I think could be an awful lot better.

HANCOCK

What would you improve in that?

MUNRO

The section that I really like is the story "Mischief." But I don't think I've quite got it right. There again, I'm not sure why I'd like to work at that.

And, maybe a part called "Simon's Luck" I'd like to try again. But these are open-ended stories and it's because the vein I'm working is still there in me. It's still alive. And I'm still going back to whatever I'm finding there. I don't want to rewrite "Dulce" but I want to write another story from the same place. I'm not at all finished with that or convinced I have done the best I can with it. Whereas you read a story like "Wood" and it's finished. In a way, it's an anecdotal story. It's about something important, too, I think, but it just doesn't excite me as much.

HANCOCK

You like the story to have several layers of meaning and intent.

MUNRO

What I like is not to really know what the story is all about. And for me to keep trying to find out.

HANCOCK

What makes a story interesting for you?

MUNRO

The thing that I don't know and that I will discover as I go along.

HANCOCK

That's in the character, the meaning, the language?

MUNRO

I'll discover things about the characters that I didn't know when I started out. Or just ambiguities in the situation.

I will be interested because of the picture, the image and then I will just keep finding out more and more about it. But not about the craft, that's the one area where I just never seem to find out anything at all.

HANCOCK

Is that one of the reasons you write about writers? It's a curious question because writers are the questers, the seekers. They have the craft.

MUNRO

I try not to write about writers because for one thing, everyone thinks its autobiography.

HANCOCK

"Moons of Jupiter" has poets and painters.

MUNRO

Is there a painter? You read it in *The New Yorker*.

HANCOCK

Yes.

MUNRO

Well, you read it in the book. It's a writer. *The New Yorker* made me change it. They said, "No more stories about writers!" They have this editor at *The New Yorker* called Mr. Shawn. And Mr. Shawn never communicates with you directly. He sits upstairs somewhere so you get letters from your editor that say, "Well, it's nothing to do with me. And I like this fine. But Mr. Shawn says . . . ." And one of the things he said was no more writers. And so I said okay, I'll make her an artist. But I don't think I know very much about painters and so I changed her back.

I've heard it said "drop the last paragraph and you'll have a typical *New Yorker* ending." Is there such a thing?

No, of course not. What's more, I think they can smell "a typical *New Yorker* story" and turn it down.

What's your definition of a good editor?

Somebody who has some idea of what you're trying to do and can spot where you're getting vague or precious or windy or stiff or soggy.

In some ways, painters and writers are trying to make a better world. And they are creating, aren't they? Don't artists unify the creative impulses of humanity to make this world a better place?

No. As far as I am a normal political person, the kind of person who contributes money and gets involved in causes and thinks about things, I would say I was trying to make a better world. But as a writer, I don't think that way at all. I just get excited by looking at bits of the world here and there and trying to pull a story out of them. Take the story that begins *Who Do You Think You Are?* "Royal Beatings" contains, among many other things, a child being beaten by her father. There is *no* way I started out to write a story to alleviate the lot of children who are beaten by fathers. As a person this is a cause that would concern me very much. As a writer I just want to look at the situation to see what's going on. I just want to see what's there. I just want to write about it. Then, when I transform back into my ordinary liberal, maternal self, I would immediately want such things stopped. So, do you see what I mean?

Now, it's very hard to say in that sense I want to make a better world. I just have no time for thinking about anything like that because the writing is so hard. I think that's why I don't have answers to a lot of questions. Many writers know exactly what they're doing and have thought things out. Whereas I go into this peculiar limbo and this kind of shady area to look for the story and this takes up a lot of my time and I don't think very clearly about it. And I always think, when I finish this story, I'm going to take — What do I mean? — take a rest where I use my mind. Because I feel I never have. And there'll be time for it someday. Sometimes I will try to put everything aside, try to put this whole queer occupation aside and become a thinking person. And I've never done that. I've never been able to do it.

Do you find success as a pressure? Or do you see yourself as successful?

197

No. I don't find sucess a pressure. Because I'm usually unaware of it. I don't like being well known. I know that it has to happen if I'm going to be able to make my living as a writer. But when I find that I've become a public person, that I'm said to have said this or that, and people talk about even the way I looked or anything, then I'm horrified to discover that I have this separate existence. So that part of it is something I'm kind of afraid of. But I just don't think about it very much. As for success, I don't feel that. I was very surprised to hear someone telling a Chinese writer, when we were in China, that in Canada we have serious writers and popular writers. Alice is a popular writer, he said. I was upset because I think I am a serious writer. But I was also surprised to think that I was thought of as a popular writer. Because I think of someone who sells millions of books, like Harold Robbins, as a popular writer. Then I thought about it and decided that anyone who makes a living in Canada is probably a popular writer. And therefore you must accept that you cater to the popular taste in some way unbeknownst to yourself.

If you weren't either a popular or a serious writer and you went and started to become, as you said, a thinking person, what would you think about? Mathematics?

No. No. I'd try and find out about writing. And what people are talking about and understand how it was done. Because I realize that most writers don't grope around. They know what they're doing. Some grope around a bit. I don't think I would write any better by doing this, or any worse. But I would sort of like to know more about it. Well, I'm not really in a total fog. I'm just always on a search that is touch and go.

What don't you think you know about writing?

Well, you asked me about craft. I really do not know any of those things. I don't know why one uses the words. I don't know about using language. I think that's it. And I don't know about traditions of fictions. I've read quite a bit at random but I don't know about the things that people are doing purposely.

So, it's strictly intuition.

Well, I read a bit in your interview with John (Metcalf). He knew why he was using words. He did. I was terribly impressed. That's like knowing carpentry or something. And I am really impressed by skills. Yes. And I thought, if I had written that, I wouldn't be able to explain why I used any of those words. I would have laboured over them. It wouldn't have come out in any divine flood of inspiration.

HANCOCK

Are there stories you don't finish?

MUNRO

Lots of them. Probably more than I do finish. Well, that's not true any more. At first, I was writing a lot of stories that I didn't finish, of course, because I was learning to write. Most of them were exercises. Now there are stories, yes, over the last three or four years — big stories — that I have worked at off and on. Worked at off and on and haven't finished. And I don't know if I ever will. I read somewhere that Ann Beattie, an American short-story writer, says that if a story doesn't work in about four days, she knows that she should give it up and, I thought, my, now, that's very drastic. But it's probably very good. I would tend to keep on at that story for several years to see if maybe I couldn't get it to work. And keep going back to it.

HANCOCK

In the original draft of *Who Do You Think You Are?*, Janet of part two was, in fact, the author of part one. It sounds like one of the ultimate books. The portrait of the artist *and* the artist's work. Why didn't that version work?

MUNRO

That was just too fancy. I liked the idea. But it was one of my ideas from the top down and I eventually rejected it. Because ... it just didn't feel right, somehow.

HANCOCK

So it wasn't pressure from the publisher?

MUNRO

Oh no. No.

HANCOCK

It was just a pressure from yourself?

MUNRO

It was a pressure from myself. That's always the pressure.

HANCOCK

When you say too fancy, shall we put that in italics?

MUNRO

Yes, yes. I don't know what I mean by that. It was a little bit pretentious or precious, or something. It's like you think of something, you know, oh, I'll do this, wouldn't that be clever. You really mustn't do those things.

HANCOCK

After five books now, do you feel any kind of a theory on short fiction is emerging? A poetic?

MUNRO

You know, by this time, that I'm just lucky if the short fiction emerges, let alone the theory. (*Laughter.*)

HANCOCK

Is there something underlying them? That fits them all together?

199

No. I don't see this at all. That's why I like doing books of stories that are unconnected. Because then I feel I can just do any story by itself alone without having to worry.

HANCOCK

There's also a global vision that's starting to creep into your stories. You've moved away from Ontario. You're writing about other continents. Australia, in "Bardon Bus."

MUNRO

Yes, I have a bit but, to me, that kind of geography is very unimportant. I don't think that a story in which the characters go through their actions in, say Tokyo, is somehow a deeper story with a kind of meaning in it you can't have if the characters do those things in Moose Jaw. I don't think the setting matters at all. A lot of people think I'm a regional writer. And I use the region where I grew up a lot. But I don't have any idea of writing to show the kind of things that happen in a certain place. These things happen and the place is part of it. But in a way, it's incidental.

HANCOCK

One of the things that I have noticed in your work, which, I think for me, underlines a lot of it, is the way time passes. There's a very strong sense that your stories are about how time is remembered. There are gaps. It's not just chronological time. It's "felt time." The story isn't realistic in its time. But it's realistic in the way time is felt to be real. And often, you use time as a catalyst.

You like to open up a character's old life. A beginning might be "Many years later, as Rose sat in a cafeteria, she remembered . . . ."

MUNRO

That sounds pretty heavy-handed, doesn't it? Well, I like doing that a lot. I like looking at people's lives over a number of years, without continuity. Like catching them in snapshots. And I like the way people relate, or don't relate, to the people they were earlier. This is the sense of life that interests me a lot.

HANCOCK

Do you like the feeling that something happens in the gaps between the scenes?

MUNRO

Yes. Something happens that you can't know about. And that the person themself doesn't know about. I think this is why I'm not drawn to writing novels. Because I don't see that people develop and arrive somewhere. I just see people living in flashes. From time to time. And this is something you do become aware of as you go into middle age. Before that, you really haven't got enough time experience. But you meet people who were a certain kind of character ten years ago and they're someone completely different today. They may tell you a story of what their life was

200

like ten years ago that is different again from what you saw at the time. None of these stories will seem to connect. There are all these realities. The reality a person presents in the narrative we all tell about our own lives. And there's the reality that you observe in the person as a character in your life. And then there's God knows what else.

HANCOCK

In your stories, you look back to that moment, that turning moment in a character's emotional centre. When something does change. When characters don't become the persons they thought they would be? That the past shapes the present, that time tramples childhood dreams.

MUNRO

Maybe. Yes, in some stories, I may look at a choice. In a story like "The Beggar Maid," I'm looking at a choice someone made. The interest in the story isn't particularly what happened after the choice. Because everything can be foreseen. It's like a picture, the whole inevitability, inescapableness of the wrong choice. . . . I don't think I have a sense of time as brutally diminishing or hurting people. My feeling is probably too random for that. That we are liable to get hurt at any time and that things can get better at any time too.

Mostly in my stories I like to look at what people don't understand. What we don't understand. What we think is happening and what we understand later on, and so on.

HANCOCK

When you write a story do you create a challenging situation for the character? Not in the Jack London sense of a challenging situation. But at that moment when either an accident or an indecision is the ignition that starts the fictional motor running?

MUNRO

No. No. It's nothing at all that definite. In a story like "Wood" something like that happens. There's a moment. The transfer. The man's accident when he's alone in the woods brings him out of that ordinary world of control and inquisitiveness and into a completely different world.

HANCOCK

That story was based on a misunderstanding, too. In which he thought he would lose his business because of something which he had overheard that didn't even refer to him.

MUNRO

Yes. But what's important to me in the story is what his experience is like when he is crawling back trying to get to the truck. So that is one of the pivotal moments but I don't always write stories like that. It's hard to generalize at all because I think that each story is quite different. That they are quite different in whatever it is I am trying to get in them.

HANCOCK

Should each story have a pivotal moment for the character?

201

No. That's one of the few stories that does. "The Turkey Season" is one of those looking-back stories. Just trying to discover or describe what a certain feeling is like. It's an adolescent girl's strange feeling about a probably homosexual man.

That's partly what it is about, but it is also about the whole scene where these people are working. And what everybody is like just in this period in their lives.

HANCOCK

Can there be wisdom in looking back?

MUNRO

No. I don't know if there could ever be wisdom, Geoff. I was going to say "Well, I would hope so" but I don't know if that is true. I don't know if I do. If, by wisdom, you mean looking at something and thinking you see more about it now that you did then, sure. You usually see more about things. But you might not be right.

HANCOCK

Are titles important to you?

MUNRO

Oh, yes.

HANCOCK

What's a title supposed to do? And why do you have such long titles?

MUNRO

I don't know. I'm so sick of those long titles. Like "The Ferguson Girls Must Never Marry," I mean that was really going a bit far. Well, I like the titles.

HANCOCK

Take *Something I've Been Meaning to Tell You* and *Who Do You Think You Are?*. There's a very big vision implied behind those titles. Even *The Moons of Jupiter,* there is almost a cosmology implied in that title. About satellites. Characters as satellites.

MUNRO

I know. But I didn't really think of that. I just called it that because that's what we saw at the Planetarium. (*Laughter.*) I hate the way I'm coming across. I sound like a *medium.* But I think a title should be hinged onto the story in some way that is just right. And, of course, I like titles that are funny, too. I think (Metcalf's) *Private Parts* is a nice title. But there is almost, now, a terrific fashion for titles, you know, commonplace words that have an extra depth in meaning. Like *Who Do You Think You Are?* has that kind of double meaning. I'm not sure I like titles to be that fashionable.

HANCOCK

Well, the American publishers didn't want it to be that fashionable.

MUNRO

No. They said to me nobody in America ever said to anybody, "Who do

you think you are?" Because Americans were too self-assured. (*Laughter.*)
Just people in rural Ontario went around saying things like that. I think
probably it is an expression that's not familiar to New Yorkers or to the
people who were editing the book but I would imagine it is familiar to
people in rural Wisconsin or anyplace. But I thought it was a much better
title than *The Beggar Maid. Beggar Maid* is a very *still* title. It isn't bad but
it doesn't do anything either. It has all kinds of dreadfully unfortunate
connotations. People think it's an historical novel, which badly affected its
sales.

HANCOCK

Or a fairy tale.

MUNRO

I never thought of that. The title in Norwegian is *Tiger Pikken*. And if it
is pronounced just a little bit off — Piggen — it's obscene. And so I was
pronouncing it this way and talking about it loudly in the cafeteria in
Norway and wondered why all the men were sort of looking at our table,
until the girl who was interviewing me — an embarrassed young journalist
— told me not to say that any more.

HANCOCK

Who do you learn from? If not form and style, then vision.

MUNRO

I don't mean that I don't learn form and style. I just don't know how to
talk about it. I probably absorb it. I learn all the time from just about
everybody I choose to read now. Because a lot of things I don't read any
more. You know, I used to read everything I thought I was supposed to
read. I think a writer is probably learning from everything they read from
the age of fifteen on.

HANCOCK

I think you are a shrewd reader, too, and you read very widely. I
remember talking about Exley's *A Fan's Notes* and other books which are
obscure. Jean Rhys said, "Books are the only reason for carrying on." Do
you agree?

MUNRO

Oh, yes. What I have been reading in the past year? Well, I read Elizabeth
Spencer's stories all over again. And I read John Cheever's all over again.
And Singer's. But they are writers I have been reading for years. I have been
reading Kundera, the Czechoslovakian writer. And Woiwode, an
American. I've been reading him actually for five or six years — and I read
Wright Morris' *Plains-Song* and Katinka Loesser's stories. And Peter
Handke.

I like to bring to attention short-story writers that are really good and
who most people don't read. Because, mostly when I'm asked to name, I do
have a list ready. If I'm doing this to a college audience, they won't have
heard of anybody. You know, most people haven't even heard of Peter

Taylor. Or Cheever, until very recently. I do read Ann Beattie. I don't like everything she does but some things I like very, very much. I have a feeling of absorbing something from her. Because, in a way she's a very different writer. She's cool. I read Anne Tyler. I like her a lot. And David Plante. William Trevor.

HANCOCK

And the Canadian writers?

MUNRO

Well, I read nearly all of them, I think. But writers who write short stories are probably closest to me. I like Clark Blaise and John Metcalf's stuff very much. And Leon's, and Jack Hodgins' stories and Guy Vanderhaeghe. And Audrey Thomas. I like the collage thing Audrey does. I would like to work with it. But anything I do has to come out just because it evolves that way. I can't say, I will try this new form and we'll see what happens. Any writer who's been writing for a while can do quite passable imitations of any style going. Of any form going. Dead imitations. And sometimes I think people mistake the imitations. When I was starting I wrote, as I told you, imitation Flannery O'Connor stories. But I wasn't writing them consciously.

HANCOCK

I was going to ask about Flannery O'Connor. And ask if Southern Ontario was Canada's deep south. Some of your stories seem to have that Calvinistic sense of sin, the biblical images, the sense of family, that sense of gothic and the grotesque.

MUNRO

The racial thing is a big thing that isn't there. You know, the black-white thing. A hatred of French Canadians would be the closest to it. A hatred of Catholics.

HANCOCK

More in Peterborough, though.

MUNRO

No, it's the same in Western Ontario. Very much the same. Eastern Ontario's the same. Rural Ontario's the same. But I suspect rural Michigan is the same, too. It's a rural culture with a strong Scots-Irish background. Possibly, a culture that has become fairly stagnant. With a big sense of righteousness. But with big bustings-out and grotesque crime. And ferocious sexual humour and the habit of getting drunk and killing each other off on the roads. There's always this sort of boiling life going on. I'm always surprised when people say your stories are about such — ohhhh —well they don't say *dull*. That wouldn't be polite, but *restricted* lives and people. I always think the country I was born and brought up in is full of event and emotions and amazing things going on all the time.

HANCOCK

Your characters, in fact, just surge with that event and emotion. In fact, there's an extraordinary gallery of grotesque characters in your fiction. I'm thinking of the Honey Man in "Privilege". The old man and his house in "Wild Swans." Flo as she becomes senile. I mean, it's extraordinary. You have bizarre stuff.

MUNRO

Yes, yes. It is bizarre stuff. And there's lots of it there. The school in the second part of *Who Do You Think You Are?* is the school I went to. It's the most autobiographical thing in the book. One of the more autobiographical things I have written. But that's exactly how it was.

HANCOCK

And for anyone who thinks Alice Munro writes a bourgeois middle-class story, there's excrement frozen in the snow and outhouses knocked over. There's incest in that story.

MUNRO

Yes. That is the life I was observing when I was seven years old. And, of course, this is also the sort of thing that has made me terribly unpopular in my native place. I get threatening letters, really bad letters because of this kind of thing.

HANCOCK

Because they have a different view of themselves.

MUNRO

Yes. The view of people who were in this life and to the people who live there now, things were never like this. And if they were, why talk about it? It's very understandable, really. Because this is the way most people view their lives. You edit your life as you go along. That's one of the things I was talking about. The different editions people make of their lives. So people who could remember these things are editing them out.

HANCOCK

So what holds you to the region? Or are you moving about?

MUNRO

Oh, I move about quite a bit. Just practical reasons. Most people think writers have infinite choices. But when my husband and I moved to this region, it was to look after our parents who were not able to look after themselves any more. My husband's mother really wasn't able to look after herself. And my father and step-mother were getting old. So that was the reason for our choice. It wasn't any great desire to live in Huron County again. Then when we settled there, there are lots of practical reasons. It's cheap. I like the country. And there are the good things everybody knows about living in a small town.

HANCOCK

And yet, do your stories contain a veiled social commentary? As I read some of them, there seems to be a kind of class system in your work. We go down the social ladder in Hanratty to the other side of the tracks. The really poor have their own kinds of social ambitions. I'm thinking of a story like

"Half a Grapefruit" which has various ideas as to what passes for sophistication.

MUNRO

When I came back to live in Huron County, I thought I had written it out. I didn't intend to write any more about it. Because I had written *Lives*. When I came back, one of the things I noticed immediately was the class system. As it operates now and as it operated then which is very different. I immediately became awfully interested in it and realized this was something I hadn't really touched in the other book and I wanted to do it. Oh, and another thing that made me do it was a friend of mine was teaching a class on *Lives of Girls and Women* and one of the women in her class actually came from where I grew up. This woman put up her hand and said, "I think the class should know that Alice Munro came from the wrong side of the tracks." So to her my vision is suspect. I thought, yes, I did, and I never realized how much this influenced me and how much it is still in this reader's mind. So, therefore, it must be an important reality in our lives. It made me want to really look into that.

And of course, not only do we have this social system but we tend to make great leaps here and there or across it. There are all sorts of in-between classes that think they are classless. I think I am classless. Which of course, isn't true. In that book I was doing some exploration of that. I've done it a bit in *The Moons of Jupiter*, too. About how you feel, and this is personal, if you come from a fairly low, a fairly underprivileged class of very limited expectations and then make a big leap into another class. I think there's some guilt involved in this.

HANCOCK

Does the writer have a social function?

MUNRO

A person who has a social function does what? Gives people some guidelines? No. No. Then a writer doesn't have a social function. At all. But of course, good writing, honest writing is a necessity for some people, so a writer is providing a necessity. But I think the writer should be unaware of this function. I am saying that the art which doesn't set out primarily to rouse any sort of social attitude or action probably succeeds more than that which does. Though I know propagandistic art succeeds often very, very well. *Uncle Tom's Cabin* is an enormous example of what propagandistic art can do. So it is quite wrong to say that it doesn't work. It does work, as propaganda.

HANCOCK

You're certainly not going to say that poverty is ennobling.

MUNRO

No.

HANCOCK

That there is a right and a wrong side of the tracks.

But I just say that it's interesting. I feel, myself, that I have this enormously good background for a writer. Part of that was not being a member of the middle class. And not living in a neighbourhood where people were more or less the same. And, perhaps not having to carry the burden of expectation that's put on the middle-class child. You make a living and your parents aren't going to be embarrassed if you make that living as a waitress. So you're free.

And that's one of the reasons you would write about, as with your characters Rosemary and Patrick, the effects of owning property and the effects of climbing up the social ladder. And one sees that the ambition that one aspired to wasn't always to be preferred to the alternative.

Yes. And the betrayal that's involved. But, of course, there's a betrayal involved in leaving home anyway. If you are lower-class. For instance, you begin to talk differently. And I feel very guilty about that. And did for a long time.

I know I haven't lost my Huron County accent entirely, but believe me, I have lost a great deal of it. I tried to lose it. To me, this seemed a cowardly thing to do. To change oneself. To become more acceptable in this way. We always spoke grammatically at home because my father and mother knew how to. But we knew we should speak ungrammatically outside so that people wouldn't be offended, or make fun of us.

So you had no problem capturing the texture of the place when you started to write.

I have trouble with everything, getting it right.

So you didn't need notebooks and journals of how-was-it-then in Hanratty.

Oh no. No. I remember everything. I'm oppressed by it. A huge baggage of memories. I remember all this stuff about West Vancouver, where I lived when my children were growing up, that I haven't used. Sometimes I get a housewifely sense of needing to use all those scraps that are in the attic. When I feel this so vividly and can see it, can see the whole texture of that life. I haven't done much with it.

I will never, never run out of things to write about. And I never have to search for a visual detail or for the way people talk or look or anything like that. I have to search for the words, though, and I'm not very smart at noticing how things are done. You know that stuff in "Wood" about how a tree is cut down? Well, that all came from my husband and he had to write down notes. I had to learn it just the way you do in school. And I wrote a story about my father, recently, which is called "Working for a Living." It's in *Grand Street*, in the New York magazine. I wanted to talk about working in the foundry. He worked at the stove foundry in Wingham. So I went to the foundry and had them explain. They explained all their present processes, which are marvellous. But it wasn't what I wanted. They also had to explain to me how they did things in 1945. Things like that are not easy for me. I have to go and learn about them. But I love it. I love doing things right. All that accuracy. I did this in the "Turkey Season." I learned about gutting turkeys. I can't tell you the satisfaction it gave me. Why does it give me this satisfaction? To describe the process and get the steps right.

A writer I like to read is John McPhee, who is a non-fiction writer. I like that in him. He'll make the limits. And then he will tell you exactly. I love those things he does. He can do it about oranges, or canoes, or atom bombs, or anything at all. And sometimes I just think I would love to write non-fiction of that sort, of that kind of marvellous investigation of things as they really are.

HANCOCK

The opposite of texture is space. It's the kind of floating quality in a story that gives it drama. It's something that just makes a story hang there as if it's in perfect control. Do you know what I mean?

MUNRO

Yes. Yes.

HANCOCK

You have got that extraordinary balance between texture and space.

MUNRO

If that works, it's the writer's confidence. The writer's belief in the story.

HANCOCK

The tone is governed by the attitude that you bring towards the story that you are writing?

MUNRO

Yes. It's governed by the writer's total faith in the story. And the writer's abdication of . . . well . . . you abdicate from being the writer writing this story so that there is just the story. I think that's important. Even though you may make what looks like a very personal beginning and it may be a very personal story. There's still got to be some, some terribly basic respect of the writer for the material. And then, I think that's what will give the story that quality.

HANCOCK

Why choose the short story? Why not write a novel? Why use the interlocking story sequence? At one time it was suggested that it was a publisher's ploy for books like *A Bird in the House* and *The Road Past Altamount* and so on.

They were published because people were really wanting novels. They didn't really want that self-contained experience which is the short fiction.

That's true. It's certainly what readers did want ten years ago when I was a bookseller in Victoria. I don't know if it is so true now. I suspect it isn't nearly so true now because so many books of short stories have been published in Canada. I think they sell reasonably well. Mavis Gallant does and Clark and the new book by Guy Vanderhaeghe. Guy Vanderhaeghe's book is published as if it's a major event. They don't say apologetically that this is only a book of short stories. They say this is a book of good writing. And the same with Jack Hodgins' books. I could point out that most of these books are published by my publisher, Macmillan. So they are more tolerant perhaps than some other Canadian publishers about short stories. And I think they've begun to prove that people will read them. I think there is something occasionally very attractive about these linked stories. I will just find that I am writing stories all about the same character. Or I might find I was writing a bunch of stories all about the same situation. I'm toying now with a bunch of stories about marriages. But I don't want to do anything that will box me in.

I wouldn't like to start out saying I am going to write a book about inter-locking stories and I will write this one and so on and so on.

And when I write ten and eleven stories, I'll have it all finished. Instead you might start writing stories and find that this is what you are writing. That they belong together. And the same with a book that had a theme. If I find I'm doing short stories all about marriage, which is a kind of a gloomy thought, really, then that's what the theme of the book will be. But I don't start out to do it that way. Since writing's the thing I do, presumably for my greatest pleasure and satisfaction in life, it's pretty stupid not to do what I want to do. I like to feel free. I like to write any story that comes along. And not feel that it has to fit into any sort of pattern at all. There's an exhilarating feeling about responding to the demands of just this material. And never mind if it links up with any other story you have written in your life. And then, of course, you publish it in a book of stories and the critics say, "Well, this is kind of a hodge-podge and these things don't seem to belong together." Or they say, "Well, you can see these stories are skillfully related, one to the other and this is why she has put them in this order." I don't see why you can't be allowed to publish a collection. Just like a tray with a lot of different sandwiches on it. And what on earth is this feeling that somehow things have to connect or they have to be part of a larger whole?

When you write a story, do you block out its structure? Do you use outlines or do you just follow the story with its intuition? You talked about travelling around the world and picking up bits here and bits there. And after you've ransacked the world and you've got all this stuff what do you do?

MUNRO

Let me think. I start writing at some point in the story and I just write and I write a scene. That I think is the first scene. I think that I am writing a story in a very simple, orderly fashion. I know what's going to happen. I start at the beginning and I start to write it.

HANCOCK

You visualize the characters moving about.

MUNRO

Yes. Yes. They are there. It is hardly me visualizing them. They just are there. And then quite often what happens is all this peters out. It just totters to ruin. After eight pages it isn't going anywhere. And then I start again. I just keep starting over and over again. Some stories I've rewritten first scenes maybe thirty times and they haven't taken off yet. I don't know why. Sometimes I'll see where to start a story right away. But not often.

HANCOCK

When you try a story opening as many as two or three dozen times, do you get a sense that that is either the wrong starting point or perhaps the story is not meant to be?

MUNRO

I know one story I've been doing for fifteen years. Because I can tell by the age of my youngest child. So it may be you can't write that story and you don't know why. Or I can't write it *yet*.

HANCOCK

It's an accumulation of life experience and literary experience that finally gels and you know now is the time.

MUNRO

Yes. But you can also get beyond a story. One of these stories I've been working to death is the kind of story I would have written when I was thirty. . . . I can see it as a nice artifact but I don't really want to write it any more. That's a problem you have sometimes. There's just that imperceptible drawing away of your interest — that you won't even admit is happening. And you can't write the story.

HANCOCK

Do you think consciously of things such as symbols or metaphors?

MUNRO

No. I don't think consciously of those things.

HANCOCK

Because houses appear as theatres for various acts of the characters' lives which can be like a poetic technique. And houses are quite interesting because they get run down by time.

For example you've got the house as a symbol of solitude in a story like "Time of Death." It can be a symbol of ambiguous desire like in "The Executioner." It can suggest a failure as in "Lines." It can hint at history or the contradictions of history, or the family, or religion in "Heirs of the

Living Body." There are many ways that houses appear in your stories.
MUNRO

Well, houses have a great interest for me. When I look at a house, it's like looking at a person. So obviously they are important but I never think of them being symbolic of anything but themselves. There's a story with a house in the ground. You missed that one.

HANCOCK

Which one is that?

MUNRO

In the first book, "Images." There's this burned-out cellar, the cellar of a house that burned down. Then people have roofed it over and are living in it. Somebody writing about me made this into a symbol of something. But I just thought I was using it because I do remember when people did live in houses like that. They couldn't afford to rebuild.

HANCOCK

In "Thanks for the Ride" and "Trip to the Coast," there are also houses there.

MUNRO

In "Thanks for the Ride" and maybe in "Who Do You Think You Are?" the houses are about what we were talking about earlier about social class. The way people live. The way houses are furnished and all the objects in them. I am crazy about doing this. I have to stop myself. I just love doing everything in the room and everything in the cupboard. You know those things Salinger used to do where he told you everything in the bathroom cabinet. Updike does that a lot, too.

HANCOCK

It's like Balzac. That's how he created theatre. You know the characters before they walk in the room.

MUNRO

That's right. I love that kind of thing. I like people's clothes, too. I like doing that. I do a lot on surface things. Then I read with great admiration the stories where nothing is described. And I think how wonderful. To go straight to the heart of the matter like that and not bother about what they were wearing! Or what the lampshade was like or anything. I think that's great but I don't do it.

HANCOCK

Somewhere else, too, you suggest that objects contain a kind of treachery. It's a way of suggesting that there is something beneath the surface. That what you see is not always what's there. That there is a pretense, a mystery that plays on the surfaces of your stories.

MUNRO

When I was a kid, like all kids, I felt that about objects and their becoming animated by sort of hostile or benevolent spirits according to what is happening in one's life. Of course, I didn't know it was because of

211

what was happening in my life. I just felt the whole world was seething around me. And everything was to be noted. An object was to be just as important as an animal.

I remember in one of the stories I used a roll of linoleum that was in the attic.

HANCOCK

Someone said that that was actually a key word in your work.

MUNRO

What? Linoleum? Well, yes. That's part of being poor, you see. We didn't have any rugs. We had linoleum on the floor. It's as simple as that.

HANCOCK

What colour was it?

MUNRO

In my bedroom it was green and red and sort of beige. And then downstairs my mother used to paint the linoleum to make it look more like a rug. I remember it was all painted black. It had a red and white border. Then she got carried away and she did the red and white V-for-victory sign in the middle because it was during the war.

HANCOCK

Are all your stories linked by the same metaphors or the same objects?

MUNRO

Well, I don't intend them to be. When I find myself using the same kind of thing, I try to stop it. That's pretty boring.

HANCOCK

The grandmother in "Marrakesh" says there is in everything something to be discovered.

MUNRO

Oh, yes. Everything. Even totally commonplace things like a shopping centre and a supermarket and things like that are just sort of endlessly interesting in their physical reality. I find them that way. That they seem to mean something way beyond themselves. But I can't explain it much more than that. But I know I can get very excited by ordinary things — things like a bus or something and I won't really know why. And sometimes this leaves me. Everything, all the physical objects in the world begin to look as if they are just constructed out of material. They don't mean anything but what they seem to mean. You know, a bus is then just a conveyance for getting people around. Then I'm greatly depressed. With me this is a sign of depression. When I can't see things with this kind of rim around them.

But usually I do. And it has nothing to do with judgements about things being beautiful or ugly. Which is why, in a way, I don't get as upset as I might about ugly things. There again, there's a difference between the person and the writer. The person that I am, living in a house across from a beautiful wood, would get upset when the bulldozers came in and knocked all the trees down and put up a Texaco station. The person would hate to see that such things were happening in the world. But the writer wouldn't mind at all. The writer would start watching what went on at the Texaco station. It's going back to what I said about how, in the story about the child being beaten, I didn't make any judgements about whether beating children was a horrifying thing.

I just wanted to look at it and think about it and it was a drama in my mind. And I feel the same way about ugly things. Rows of town houses and things like that.

HANCOCK

Are names a clue to your characters?

MUNRO

Well, they might be but I don't choose them that way. I usually choose names that sound right. But with difficulty. I change names a lot. And then part way into a story I realize that the name I've been calling the character isn't his or her name. I know what the name is. Did you know, by the way, that Tess of the D'Urbervilles was not called Tess until the story of the book was almost written? I think she was called something like Rosemary. And Tess is so perfect.

HANCOCK

So it has to tie in with the story. One thinks of Del Jordan as the automatic association.

MUNRO

She was called Lonnie for a long time.

HANCOCK

One thinks of the Jordan river, a crossing has to be made.

MUNRO

I never think of things like that. But then I have no idea why I called her Jordan. I like J sounds, I think. I called the town Jubilee. I wasn't sure why, either. But I like naming the people and I like naming the towns and I like naming the rivers and the counties and all that. I like that nice sense of the imaginary country or the fictional country. That I'm in control of. I like the sound of Wawanash, which is actually the name of two townships in Huron County. I just love the sound of it.

HANCOCK

Would it be fair to say that your characters move towards discoveries? And throughout are seeking for self knowledge and sometimes the discoveries they find are not desirable ones?

MUNRO

Well, they move towards discoveries. Because everybody does, I think. But some people don't admit their discoveries and turn aside from them. Or maybe just don't even see them. They come up against discoveries but don't discover them. That's what the characters do sometimes. The discoveries may not be pleasant.

People sometimes criticize my characters. They will say that my characters don't find proper fulfillment, or don't find much of anything. I think critics expect, perhaps, something different from a female writer's characters, or maybe, female characters. The questing male is familiar but the female is not. There's still some expectation that the woman will find a solution to her life. The solution used to be marriage. Then in recent years, it's been walking out on your husband. You know, living on your own; finding yourself. I don't have these resolutions because they seem quite ridiculous to me. What I have is people going on. Just as if every day had its own pitfalls and discoveries and it doesn't make much difference whether the heroine ends up married or living in a room by herself. Or how she ends up at all. Because we finally end up dead.

There are just flashes of things we know and find out. I don't see life very much in terms of progress. I don't feel at all pessimistic. I rather like the idea that we go on and we don't know what's happening and we don't know what we'll find. We think we've got things figured out and then they turn around on us. No state of mind is permanent. It just all has to be there.

HANCOCK

It's like Nabokov said, "Our life is really just a brief crack of lightning between two extremes of darkness. And that's all there is to say about it. We're born, we live and we die. But it's the details that make it interesting."

MUNRO

Yes. They do. They do. They do. Yes, it's the details, it's not one situation, particularly.

HANCOCK

Are your characters religious? I was thinking of Addie who sees Christianity as a big American hoax.

MUNRO

Yes. The character of Addie has a lot of qualities of what I would like to call, without condescension, an old-fashioned feminist. She also has the ideas of people early in the twentieth century who thought the enemy was organized religion.

You just got rid of these things. Everybody got simple and rational. That was the solution. You know that line, "There's a change coming in the lives of girls and women." I meant that to be ironic because the changes I think Addie sees as possible and the whole situation as she sees it is touchingly oversimplified. I feel very affectionate towards her and there is something very, very touching to me and endearing in the way she sees life as a simple matter. For instance, she totally disregards sexual passion. It's just something you forget about and it will go away. And she disregards the impulses that make us religious. She thinks the whole dark side of nature can be easily dealt with. I meant that language that people have taken so seriously to be sort of sad and funny.

214

I didn't mean to make fun of her. But I meant her vision to be quite inadequate.

Are my characters religious? I don't think religion is a big preoccupation of theirs, at all. There's that big section in *Lives*. But that's there because every child, maybe it doesn't happen any more, but children in my generation went through some kind of religious crisis.

HANCOCK

You like to work with pairs of characters. There are sisters and aunts in the older stories. Mothers and daughters, older women and younger women, strengths and weaknesses. You like that balance, and that harmony.

MUNRO

Yes. I've noticed. It did certainly occur to me that I was doing this. I never chose to do it. But I've done it over and over again. I don't know why though. I really don't know why. But it's with female characters. I'm always doing this. Sisters, I really like to do it. I feel that I am two rather different people, two very different women and so, perhaps, that's where I'm working from. That I would like to get them separate. And the whole mother-daughter relationship interests me a great deal. It probably obsesses me. The way fathers obsess some male writers.

HANCOCK

Why?

MUNRO

Probably because I had a very intense relationship with my own mother. She became ill when I was quite young. The incurable illness of a parent makes a relationship — its stresses become more evident that way. And so her illness and death and the whole tension between us — she had Parkinson's disease — was very important. The first real story I ever wrote was about her. The first story I think of as a real story was "Peace of Utrecht." It's about the death of a mother.

And the "Ottawa Valley" which I like a lot is about her. It's one story which is autobiographical. Most of my stories aren't nearly as much as people think. But that one is. This is something I just keep going back to over and over again. I don't know what it is. Some writers are just always busy with this parent-child thing. According to how deep it went with them, I suppose.

HANCOCK

And the parent they were closest to.

MUNRO

But I've written quite a few father stories too. So, it's just something I've had a bit of an obsession with. I don't think I'll write any more. But that's always a bad prediction to make — I won't write any more of those kinds of stories. I was going to say, I think I am through with my childhood. But one is never sure.

Of course, that's the great blood mystery of women, isn't it? It's that bonding between mother and daughter. Between mother and child. Menstrual blood; the bleeding that bleeds but doesn't cause death. And blood to milk. Blood to child. These are the three big transformations of blood in women.

MUNRO

I've never written much about childbirth or any of that. I don't know why. It's interesting to me. It's one of those great dramas. You usually write about all the dramas. I've skipped something in the kind of personal material I use. I used all that child/adolescent stuff and then I skipped to being a middle-aged woman. I've never dealt with the in-between material. Maybe because so many people seem to be dealing with it in ways that I didn't much like. But that can't really be why. Maybe some day I'll find I have to do a story about something like that.

HANCOCK

When you write down an image, does that generate a series of other images?

MUNRO

Yes. That's what I started to tell you about how I wrote stories. I have this picture. It generates some other images and attracts them like a magnet. Things stick to it. Anecdotes and details.

I just feel that so much of it is dark. The structure of the story is building up, and you don't see the final shape at all.

HANCOCK

And yet you know it's there and you are moving towards it. That image that is there somewhere.

MUNRO

Audrey said a nice thing to me once in a letter. She was writing a novel and it was like a jig-saw puzzle but she didn't even have all the pieces yet. Or she didn't have the outside pieces. And you certainly didn't have the picture. And that is exactly what it's like. You just take the pieces and put them here and there.

HANCOCK

Do Audrey Thomas and yourself, as close friends, give each other advice?

MUNRO

No, not about writing.

HANCOCK

Your stories always move outward towards that final picture.

MUNRO

But the point is not all stories are the same. A story will start like this and another story will start rather straightforwardly. And will present itself all at once. Fairly clearly. And probably a story like that will come more directly. From life. "Dance of the Happy Shades" is a story that comes from a complete anecdote that I heard. From there I just had to flesh out the anecdote.

It was about this old music teacher giving embarrassing recitals that everybody had to go to. The whole story was right there. It was there in the attitude of the people telling the anecdote. The only episode not in the anecdote was the idiot girl playing the music. But the idiots were in the anecdote. That's one of the words one doesn't use any more. The retarded children were in the anecdote.

HANCOCK

On those rare occasions when you do become writer-in-residence and talk to fledgling writers, what do you tell them about dialogue, the opening lines of stories, resolutions?

MUNRO

I'm not good at discussing theories. What I am good at is working with an individual's work, even if it's the kind of writing I don't do. I'd make a good editor. I can pick up the story and I can see what it lacks and why it's not working. Or at least I can have a pretty good idea. And then I think I'm fairly good at directing a person's attention towards this. I never say this is what's wrong with your story. Because it has to be discovery. So we talk about the story and I ask questions about what the story is doing. Why the person is writing this story. What interests them about the story. I love this. I love doing it. It's quite exciting work.

HANCOCK

Do you ask those questions of yourself?

MUNRO

I don't back off enough. I just keep worrying the thing. When I'm talking to you, I might ask them. But, I like doing this work with the students. I'm not at all good in classroom work because I don't, I can't talk generally and I can't talk to the group. And I don't like doing anybody's story when there are other people around. I don't like the workshop situation. I like the one-to-one situation.

HANCOCK

In John Reeves' portrait of you, a Diane Arbus book appears on the bookshelf. Are photographs important to you?

MUNRO

Yes, very important. I just love looking at them. John Metcalf hates that book. He thinks she's a phony. But I like it.

HANCOCK

You don't think she's phony?

MUNRO

No. No. I don't think it's fashionable use of the grotesque. I think it's responsible.

HANCOCK

I was going to say that controlled mixture of light. The attitude a

217

photographer brings towards the subject. The formal technical process of using a camera is remarkably similar to the way you use your prose.

MUNRO

What I want to get changes with different stories. It's got to be dictated by the material itself. And sometimes I want to get something that is very grainy and I don't want any artifice at all. I don't want the choice of words to seem anywhere elegant. I want awkwardness. I want to get a kind of plainness. And then I would be doing another story with different material and I want it to be, I feel that it should be, well, lush isn't the word I mean. But there should be a kind of luxuriance. The feeling of the story should be of lots and lots of words and resonance. Things level upon level. And this means the writing has to change completely.

I don't do this consciously. I'm talking about it now and I know it's what I do. But I don't say I'm going to write a very sort of deadpan (deadpan's the wrong word) dogged kind of prose. Or I'm going to write a fancier prose here. I don't say that but it's what I do. It's not that I want a different effect. The story is different and has to be told a different way. And then, also, you look at something a year later and it's not the way you want it to read at all.

HANCOCK

Do you try to render a scene like a photographer might?

MUNRO

Well, I see the scene. I see it awfully clearly. And I want the reader to see it the way I see it.

There's a story in the new book called "Visitors" where there's an important scene for me. It's at the beginning of the story. It's where two women are sitting out in the shade of a driveway on little camp chairs, crocheting tablecoths on a hot summer afternoon. The story is around that scene and I want that scene there so strongly. But I don't do much with it. I just say that they were sitting out crocheting tablecoths. That's all. So, I don't know how a reader's going to see that. Maybe I've buried it.

I would feel it was wrong for that story to tell any more detail about that scene. It's got to be just like that.

HANCOCK

So when you do something such as suspending the narrative flow for description which happens in "Wood," that's something that feels right.

MUNRO

That's self-indulgence. I love that. I love those trees. I just had to put them all in. No. To be serious, I felt to be right the story needed them. That they were part of the story. But I didn't exactly know why. I did wonder if I was going on a bit much. But I just wanted to do that. It was more important. It was terribly important to that story to list those trees. But I have no idea why.

HANCOCK

So, you don't feel completely secure in your style. You are still working towards that.

218

No. That's not it. I don't want to work towards a style. I want to go with the story the way it has to be. I do feel a kind of inner bell that rings when something is okay. I'm never sure it's as it should be but I have a certain amount of confidence. It has never occurred to me to work towards a style. I don't think I have a style. I don't recognize a style. I would probably call it something else. I would call it a way of telling a story. Or something like that. There I like to be fairly flexible.

HANCOCK

The story "Dulce" seemed to be a new way of telling a story for you.

MUNRO

That's one of the stories that interests me a lot and I'm not sure, yet, that I got it right. I should ask myself those questions that I ask students. What is this story about? It's just about the ways people discover for getting through life. Which is what every story is about.

HANCOCK

Is that one of the changes that has in fact arrived in the *Lives of Girls and Women*? The discovery of how to get through life rather than raging against it? They simply accommodate their lives within its limitations.

MUNRO

It isn't just women who do this, of course. It's everybody. I'm not sure. That sounds a little bit more defeated than I feel. Let's say there are problems people come up against of loneliness and pain and that is maybe what that story is about. Because the two characters that are important to me in it are the old man who's getting through his life by worshipping someone. And the woman who has been getting through her life by being in love, and who is now drifting beyond that a bit. She looks at the other men as possible lovers, but there's a sense of speculation that you know she would rather speculate than act.

HANCOCK

And characters can also find relief in their daydreams.

MUNRO

Sometimes people talk about my work as really depressing. I don't find any of this. The fact that we may live in daydreams or that we suffer. Somehow I don't find it depressing. I think if you find life really depressing, then you don't write about it at all.

HANCOCK

In fact, I can remember when I first heard you read. It was at Simon Fraser University. I was quite moved by how funny some of the stories actually were.

MUNRO

Well, I hope so.

HANCOCK

Not just ironic. Not just satirical. But actually funny. I thought there is a tremendous optimism here.

MUNRO

I like to think so. Sometimes it fails me. Sometimes I write a story that has a bad, bleating tone. But usually I can do some funny stuff. Because I think, you know, stories about really tragic things should have, are bound to have funny parts or to be funny as well as tragic. The whole thing is to be funny as well as tragic. I feel when I can see things that way, I'm on top as a writer. Sometimes I'm not and I see things one way or the other. Sometimes I write a funny story that I think is funny but it doesn't work terribly well because I haven't really cared enough to give it depth.

HANCOCK

I'm always interested in process. Do you keep notebooks and journals?

MUNRO

No. No. I don't do any of that. Because I spend all my time writing. Or writing these interminable first drafts. I suppose I don't need notes because things stay in my head pretty well. I'm always attracted by the idea of writing a journal. But I'm too self-conscious when I start to do it. I don't think it's natural for me to write a journal. And I wonder if this has something to do with being a Canadian and coming from such a totally unliterary environment.

I have several times written a bit of a journal and I find myself doing very good descriptions of things. And then I think what nonsense. That's when I become self-conscious. It seems I have to be writing fiction in order to let myself write. I write very, very ordinary letters too. Very, sort of rambling, pedestrian, not good letters. And there's something of the same feeling there. To write a more careful letter would be insincere.

HANCOCK

Do you write on the typewriter?

MUNRO

Yes. Yes. Except if I am first-drafting and travelling around a lot. Then I take a notebook with me and try to write in that.

HANCOCK

Do you like to sit in front of a window or a wall?

MUNRO

A wall. No windows for me.

HANCOCK

Calendars on the wall?

MUNRO

Nope. Nothing. Boards. It's a varnished wall. Upstairs in our house sloping down in front of me. You see, it's very closed in. Very tight. I like it that way.

HANCOCK

Do you have a regular routine and quota?

MUNRO

Yes. But I often don't keep to it. When I set out to write something like

220

Lives, and I got the shape of it, sort of, in my head, I then had a very definite quota. Well, I knew where I had to get to every month. So much a month.

I would take a month to write the first draft of a section. And then I would take a month to rewrite it. And that wouldn't be the second draft, it would be second, third and fourth. And so on. And so I had the whole book to that point at the end of a year. And then I rewrote the whole thing. But I think I had to do that because I had a very heavy domestic workload and I was working in my husband's bookstore. And I had to chain myself, in order to get it finished, to this kind of routine. I've never done anything else quite like that.

HANCOCK

Do you have a different routine now? Five pages a day?

MUNRO

When I get going on a story, I'll do two or three pages a day when I'm doing the first draft. Then I do a lot more after that. When I'm doing the final re-write I'll work all day.

HANCOCK

Are you a tense writer or relaxed?

MUNRO

Are there any relaxed writers? (*Laughter.*)

HANCOCK

I think so. Don't some relax when they are writing? The tension comes in getting it down. And once you make the step to the page, relaxation sometimes takes over.

MUNRO

Well, yes. I'm probably more relaxed when I'm doing later drafts. That's true. But then there's all that typing and I hurry to get finished. I'm always aware of the other things I should be doing. I never can shut them out. So I think I am fairly tense. On the other hand, I kind of enjoy doing final drafts. I'm so relieved to have the thing done. I sometimes even take a glass of wine and sip at it to celebrate as I'm writing.

HANCOCK

What do minor characters contribute to a story?

MUNRO

I don't know. They have to be there. It's just the same thing as I have to put all the furniture in and that sort of thing. I don't do people in any kind of a vacuum or a spare setting. I want a lot of different people in their lives.

Also I think it's probably because I grew up in a community which was just loaded with people you couldn't help but notice. Because they were pretty bizarre. So I always had the sensation of a crowded canvas when I looked out. I've worked with that. But I don't know why they are there. If I thought about it, they probably are necessary.

HANCOCK

I thought in some other way, too, they might add up to a life pattern. For exactly the reasons you just said.

221

You mean they are part of the whole scene people are living in. Yes. Yes. But sometimes a minor character is important. There's a story called "Images." The child's mother is bed-ridden because she is expecting a baby. Nothing very awful is in the story but the child keeps feeling a threat and a horror because her grandfather has died. There's something about the mother's being bed-ridden and the mother's pregnancy and everything that's just frightening. There's a nurse in that story. A relative who's come to look after the mother. And she, to me, is the embodiment, though she's loud and jolly, of terror, to the child.

So there's a minor character who serves a purpose. But I just thought that up right now. I didn't think it up before. Sometimes I have to think of very quick explanations.

HANCOCK

Like Trudeau who'd shrug and say . . .

MUNRO

"You figure it out." Someone asked me, at the last reading I did, "Why did you write that story?" So I thought up an explanation that sounded good, like a defense. It wasn't exactly a lie but it wasn't true either. The *only* answer to that question is "Because I wanted to."

HANCOCK

With your major characters, is it important to explain their motivations? Whether or not your characters care or don't care about each other?

MUNRO

I don't think about explaining anything. I just get the characters together and let them carry on. It's a little hard to decide what people's motives are. I want to know the protagonist well enough that I don't have to question whatever she would do.

Some of the other characters I will know only through the eyes of the main character. So as long as I know how she would see them, then that's all I need to know. As long as I'm sure of that.

HANCOCK

You are very concerned about how men and women characters draw out certain aspects of each other and how men and women find happiness, freedom, love.

MUNRO

Well, that's the main thing isn't it? This is endlessly interesting and you keep discovering more things about it as a person and as a writer. The whole subject of what men and women want of each other. The big drama of life as I see it right now.

HANCOCK

The feminine side of myself reacts very strongly to certain aspects of your work. Especially how women survive in a patriarchal society. Am I projecting? Is that a message coming across? Do you embed lessons in the stories?

Ahhhh! No lessons. No lessons *ever*. I didn't even think, when I began writing, that I was writing about women, at all. I just wrote these stories. When I wrote *Lives of Girls and Women*, it didn't cross my mind that I was writing a feminist book. Because I didn't know what I was doing. It just occurred to me once that I wanted to write the kind of thing about a young girl's sexual experience that had often been written about boys'. I was doing it when I thought of this. I thought, I'm glad this is what I am doing. But I didn't think, then, that I was writing about women and their ways of survival.

I just wrote it because I know a great deal about that. In that same society there are men surviving. But I haven't written about that, yet. I don't know as much about it. But in *that* society of the fairly poor people, I don't think of it exactly as a patriarchal society. I think of our society as a whole that way. But on those lower levels, often, women have a considerable degree of power. That's something I'm very interested in. In the way women, for instance who are waitresses, or who have jobs like that, often feel quite strong though they will have very conventional opinions. They will probably believe there are all sorts of things women shouldn't do but in their actual behavior with men, they can often be pretty tough characters. And in a way I grew up with women who were like that. There was no sense in that community of the women being victims of society or the men. Now, I am consciously interested in the way women live. The way things are different for men and women at middle age, and so on. The particular conflicts between men and women seem to me to be so much more articulate at a middle-class, educated level. I see them now in a way that I never saw them when I was growing up. You know, in *Lives,* the grandmother and aunts have very definite views about the role of women and the things women shouldn't do. But the thing is, those people have very definite views about *everybody*. Everybody is in this structured society. In the actual society I grew up in, if anyone had asked me "Would you rather be a boy or girl?", I would have opted to be a girl. And for the very reason of more freedom.

I felt that it was easier for me to do what I wanted because I was a girl, and it didn't matter so much about girls.

HANCOCK

And, also, Addie talks about the Goddesses of the past. I've been reading a lot about the great Goddesses — female intuition, rebirth ceremonies, the role of the circle as the great central fact. Are there on-going mythic undertones in any of your stories?

MUNRO

Not that I am aware of. No. It is what I keep returning to. That I don't get time to think about these things because I am always involved in this immediate task. It is almost as if I always write from that small place out. I never write from an idea, a myth or a pattern. Or any of the big perceptions.

Now, I told you that sometimes an incident or something somebody's telling, or the sight of the two women crocheting tablecloths can get me all excited — as if it is tied into something far bigger than itself. But that is as far as my thinking ever goes. Then I just think how to make a story about this. Or I start writing the story and I don't know what it is about in those other terms.

HANCOCK

Could you talk a bit about your sense of resolution? When does a story end?

MUNRO

I know the ending when I start a story. But that sometimes changes as I go through it. I don't have any worry, ever, about the end. It may change a bit or something may be substituted but the ending is one of the things that is there very early. Almost as early as that kernel I was talking to you about, in the centre of the story. It's just a lot of stuff in between I don't know. I don't know how we get there.

HANCOCK

One last question. Where do you go next?

MUNRO

I just never know that at all. I have stories I've got in my head. So presumably, I'll go on to write them. Often I have a yearning and a great hope of writing something completely different. I would like to do a good non-fiction book. I'd like to do a kind of fiction book that is different than anything I have done. I can feel in my head what this book would be like but I haven't got a way of describing it properly.

HANCOCK

Like Audrey Thomas' *Blown Figures* with comic strips and street signs?

MUNRO

Yes. I really like that. And I like books like Elizabeth Hardwick's *Sleepless Nights*. It has some chapters that are self-contained short stories. Others that are fairly undisguised autobiography. Others that jump all over the place. The book goes together, but it doesn't seem to be in any premeditated way. I would like to be able to do that. But all the plans I make for big books tend to fall through.

I'm amazed when people say, "Well, are you going to try something different? Are you going to try something bigger?" I realize that's the way careers go. Yet, when I get hold of a story, every time, that is enough for whatever satisfaction I am getting.

JOSEF SKVORECKY

Josef Skvorecky lives in a white house in a row of houses on a quiet street in Toronto's Cabbagetown. The interview took place in his bookish living room on a chilly February day in 1983, with jazz records from the forties playing softly in the background. He pulled on the Cuban cigars I brought as a small gift, but claimed they were stronger than the brand he normally smoked. An old cat sprawled on the sofa, and Josef sat comfortably in his writing chair beneath a painting of himself as a jazz musician. The painting is also reproduced on the cover of *The Swell Season* (1982), his poignant recollection of a jazz- and girl-obsessed teenager in Nazi-occupied Czechoslovakia. A natural story-teller, by inclination he is given to long digressions on a wide range of topics, on some of which he maintains an encyclopedic knowledge. Jazz, Dvorak, Nazi cinema, detective novels, the Soviet threat, fellow writers in Czechoslovakia, and New Wave Czech film were just a few of the subjects that would set him assuredly off on lengthy tangents.

Josef's own career is unique by any standard. One of Europe's leading writers in the 1950s, he grew up in Nazi- and Soviet-occupied Czechoslovakia. His work had a profound influence on the New Wave Czech film. When the Soviet Union invaded Czechoslovakia, he came to Canada in 1969. With his wife, Zdena Salivarova-Skvorecky, he established the Czech-language publishing firm Sixty-Eight in Toronto, which is now the most important Czechoslovak publishing house anywhere, including Czechoslovakia. In the past decade they have published over one hundred books by leading Czech poets, playwrights, and novelists. Josef has been called "one of the major literary figures of our time." His works have been translated into fifteen languages. In 1980 he won the $10,000 Neustadt International Prize administered by the University of Oklahoma (previous winners included Giuseppe Ungaretti, Francis Ponge, Elizabeth Bishop, and Nobel Prize winners Czeslaw Milosz and Gabriel Garcia Marquez). In 1982 he was nominated for the Nobel Prize for Literature.

Although he has been writing for over forty years, many of his twenty-five books have yet to be translated into English. Among the titles now available are *The Cowards* (1970), *The Mournful Demeanour of Lieutenant Boruvka* (1974), *Miss Silver's Past* (1975), *The Bass Saxophone* (1977), *The Engineer of Human Souls* (1986), for which he won a Governor General's Award, and the non-fiction *All the Bright Young Men and Women* (1975), a history of the Czech cinema in the 1960s. His most recent work is *Dvorak in Love* (1986), a fictional biography of the composer.

Josef is professor of English at the University of Toronto. Several essays on his fiction were published in the Autumn 1980 issue of *World Literature Today*. But in spite of world-wide acclaim, this was the first major interview with Josef on his work.

HANCOCK

Josef, do you like to do interviews?

SKVORECKY

I have mixed feelings. On the one hand, it certainly gives me a chance to speak my mind. But on the other hand, because I am limited in time and space, I tend to present to the interviewer conclusions based on lifetime experience, or that come out of a long process. But I cannot simply talk about the whole process, about how I arrived at those conclusions. People read it or hear it and label me immediately. For instance if I say that I'm an anti-Communist, that throws a very bad light on me, because anti-Communism is a bad label. At least people think it's a bad label, and I'm rejected right out of hand. But I was not born anti-Communist. I arrived at that position as a result of many experiences.

It's sometimes quite discouraging. I wrote an article for a Czech magazine published in Canada called *Za'pad*. My article was a comparison of Communist and Nazi propaganda songs, based on well-documented facts. The point was to show that all these ideologies come up with the same propaganda songs. The songs used general words like "fight" and "struggle" and "flag" and "courage." One of my friends gave the magazine to her doctor who is an American. He saw it and said, "Oh, he is a fascist, I won't read it."

So that sometimes happens with people who read interviews. You say something provocative, and they just stop reading it. They put a label on you and you are finished.

HANCOCK

What is literature to you? What is a writer supposed to do?

SKVORECKY

Literature is simply my fate or my obsession. I came to literature in the classical way. When I was a boy I was very extroverted. I played soccer, skied, skated and so on. Then at the age of eight or nine I got pneumonia. In those days there were no antibiotics, no penicillin. Pneumonia was a serious illness and I almost died. I didn't attend school for a year and I became so well protected by my mother, that from an extrovert I changed into an introvert. My mother was afraid that I would start playing sports again and become sick, so I was isolated from the children's community and I started daydreaming. That's usually the way to become a writer. You just daydream and one day you start writing those daydreams on paper, and develop into a writer.

226

But the interesting thing perhaps for the Canadian readers is that my first finished novel (which was only eighteen pages long, typed) was the third part of a trilogy, the first parts of which were written by a Canadian writer, James Oliver Curwood, whose name few Canadians know. He's practically forgotten. But he was very popular in the late twenties and early thirties in Czechoslovakia in translations. He started a trilogy. But he died after the second part, so I finished it for him. It was a typical romantic novel about Mounties and the beautiful — I think Indian — girls with whom they always fell in love.

HANCOCK

Hemingway said, and you've quoted this often, that the job of the writer is to tell the truth. You've written novels, short stories, film scripts. You're an essayist, a broadcaster, a professor of American literature. Is part of this job of telling the truth to tell it in as many ways as possible?

SKVORECKY

Yes, but truth may be very complex — truth about what? Hemingway said that the writer must tell the truth about his own feelings at the moment they exist, which can be translated, simply, into sincerity. The writer must be sincere about how he feels, and that is his truth.

That was the stumbling block of my first published novel, *The Cowards*. I simply tried to be absolutely honest about my feelings during the events of May 1945, the end of the war, which in Czechoslovakia was called a revolution. I don't know why they called it a revolution; it was simply the end of the war, an uprising against the Nazis. This period in recent Czech history was the subject of many stories and novels. But all of them, before my novel, were written from the point of view of "socialist realism." The writer did not really present the events as they happened, as he saw them, but tried, I suppose, to colour them by using certain ideological concepts and putting them on reality. For instance, in a classic entitled *A Silent Barricade*, about the uprising in Prague, most of the heroes are workers and the traitors are invariably bourgeois. That is an ideological concept because there were as many bourgeois among the rebels as workers. The soldiers of the Red Army in those proper novels were always immaculate, chaste heroes who played accordion and sang songs. They wouldn't touch a girl and that is simply not true. The Red Army soldiers were like any other soldiers, and they had just survived a very deadly war, so they did touch girls because in a war you don't know if you will be living the next day. You don't have so much respect for proper behaviour, and they were dirty because they had just been through battle.

So my first quarrel with the establishment in Czechoslovakia was an artistic one. I tried to be true to my artistic convictions. They criticized me from the government point of view, they wanted writers to be hack writers, fulfilling their orders and describing reality as the government saw it. When *The Cowards* was banned, I received hundreds of letters from people all over Czechoslovakia who testified that they had been through the same thing, that it was exactly like what I said in the novel. So I had obviously struck a chord.

Is that why now you've continued to write your version of the truth in as many ways as possible?

SKVORECKY

I always tried to adhere to my feelings. I never strove for any great variety. I just belong to those writers who base their writings on personal experience. I had never any trouble finding my subject matter. I just described episodes of my life. That goes for what I may call my serious fiction. I also wrote detective stories and obviously I've never been a detective, so that's imagination. But in my serious fiction, I never looked for subject matter. That's probably due to life in Czechoslovakia where everybody went through so many different experiences within a lifetime that it's not hard to find something to write about.

I still remember the Great Depression. The Nazis came when I was fourteen, and they stayed for six years. I was twenty when they left, and that was a very dramatic time. My father was arrested by the Nazis. After the war the tensions in Central Europe were very high. Many people sensed or knew or suspected that we had just got rid of one troublemaker and we were headed for trouble of a very similar kind: a totalitarian dictatorship. So there are the three years between '45 and '48, the year of the Communist takeover. That was a dramatic time of political fighting, even attempts at killing Ministers. Then came the Communist takeover and the Stalinist years and the mass arrests and executions and the class discrimination.

Later I was drafted into the army which is an experience anywhere, but especially in those years. A Russian military system was imposed on the Czech army, which was absurd because the Russian military system was based on an entirely different tradition. It was designed for units that serve for two years somewhere in Siberia where there are no towns. Though the camp I was in was only about twenty miles from Prague, we were not permitted to leave it for one year. We just boiled in that little camp, bored to death.

Before my military service, I taught school. They sent me to the border regions, to a town called Braunau. This town was in ruins because the German population had been shipped out. It used to be a town of fifteen thousand, but when I came, only about a thousand people were living there. There was nowhere to live. So I got accommodation in the local cloister. I spent half a year in one of those monk's cells without heating in winter. There were so many strange and funny events.

After my military service, I got a job in Prague in a publishing house, in the Anglo-American Department which involved me in all kinds of interesting squabbles with censorship. I published my first novel which caused a big scandal. So my life was full of things that in Central Europe are quite ordinary, but in fact are quite adventurous if you think about it. Then I went into exile.

Was your father a cinema operator?

He was a bank clerk by profession, but he also managed one of the two local cinemas. That was voluntary work. He was an operator, a projectionist, and he also sold tickets and ordered films. I helped him in the projection booth. I became a film addict. For five or six years, I literally saw a film every day, and on Sunday, two. The other cinema, our competition, also gave us free tickets. They changed programmes three times a week in both cinemas, so that made six films a week, plus two on matinees on Sunday. So I saw everything. I probably am the greatest expert on Nazi cinema because this was during the war and most of the films were German or Czech or Swedish. I became a film buff of the first magnitude.

Not much is known about the films of the Third Reich.

No, very little is known about them. In the post-war frenzy in which I unfortunately took part, I burnt all the Nazi novels I had to buy as a student. I went to a high school during the war and had to study new German literature so we had to buy German books. So I'm probably the only person in Canada who read *Schlageter* which was *the* Nazi drama about a guerilla fighter in occupied Ruhrgebiet who is sentenced to death by the French and executed. That was a real historical person. That's for instance the play where you find that famous sentence "Wenn ich das Wort 'Kultur' höre, da greiff ich nach meinem Revolver" ("When I hear the world 'culture,' I grab my gun.") And this sentence is sometimes ascribed to Goebbels or Goering, and that's not true: it's in this play. And I read a novel called *SA baut eine Strasse (Build a Road)* which read like any socialist realism. It was about the building of the Autobahn, the first highway in Europe. It was built by Hitler. In the frenzy of the post-war elation, I destroyed them all, and now I am sorry because they can't be replaced. There are no new editions, and they are valuable documents.

I'm afraid the same thing happened to many of the films. I don't think they were destroyed, but they were shelved. The only film that is always being shown is *Triumf des Willens (Triumph of the Will)*, because it has become a classic. But Nazi films were not very political. They started making political movies before the war and at the beginning of the war. I remember the first war film was called *Stukas*, about dive bombers and their bombardment of Warsaw, but these films were not successful. Nobody during the war wanted to see films about war. The Nazis soon sensed that, so they started turning out musical comedies, and entertaining

229

films, but very few political films, just because they were interested in getting some escapist stuff to the people who were terribly tired by the war, especially when the raids came. Some of these so-called Nazi films were really very good. I remember one which was called *Friedemann Bach*, a film about one of the sons of Johann Sebastian Bach. Maybe my memory makes it even more beautiful than it actually was, but I don't think I've seen a better musical film since.

HANCOCK

From being a film buff, you became an actor in films; you were involved with the Czech New Wave during the 1960s.

SKVORECKY

I never was a professional actor. I appeared in a few Czech movies, but as a token appearance. All these young Czech moviemakers of the early sixties were graduates of the Film Academy, and they were among the few people who had a chance to see classical Western films. They picked up Alfred Hitchcock's signature idea and put me in films based on my stories. I never really acted. I just spoke a few lines.

But I was involved with the New Wave as a novelist. It all started with Milos Forman, whom I had known since the war. His uncle was a very good friend of mine; we used to climb rocks together. Milos, because his parents were arrested by the Nazis and sent to the camps where they died, was taken into the family of his uncle and he grew up in my native town. He was much younger. I just knew that this was the boy whose parents were in the camp. Otherwise I didn't even speak to him because he was a boy and I was eighteen or nineteen. After my novel was banned, Milos came to my apartment and said that he would like to make a movie based on another story of mine called "Eine kleine Jazzmusik." We wrote a script (the story is in my book *All The Bright Young Men and Women*) and eventually the film was banned by the President himself. The banning of my novel made me very popular; that's the best publicity you can get. I was then approached by almost everyone in the film industry to give them something to film. Eventually I had five feature films based on my books. I saw and knew personally all those famous directors like Forman and **Menzel, Chytilova, Nemec, etc. Czechoslovakia is a small country and the film industry is concentrated in Prague. Once you start working in the** studios, you meet everyone. In 1968 Forman and I wrote a script based on *The Cowards*. The film was to be shot in the summer of 1969. In the meantime, he was to make his first American movie and then return and shoot this movie. It never came to be because the Russians invaded and it was then impossible.

The Czech New Wave is much better known than modern Czech literature, although this movement of sincerity, of real realism, not socialist realism, started in literature with my *Cowards*. But books have to be translated, and that means additional expense for the publisher. Film is much more suitable for world distribution. All you need is a few subtitles. So these films became so much better known than the novels. The impression was created that the film people were the avant garde, but that's not true. The avant garde were the writers. But they were not known. *The Cowards* was not published in America until 1970, although it was originally published in 1958. Whereas films were shown a year after they had been made, at film festivals in the sixties, and they became known immediately. But if you remember Czech films made by Forman, such as *Peter and Paula* and *Fireman's Ball* and *Loves of a Blonde*, and Menzel's *Closely Watched Trains* and compare them to *The Cowards*, you will see that it's the same anti-ideological approach, showing people as they appeared to the filmmaker. The script of *Peter and Paula*, which is the first film by Forman (and was released here as *Black Peter*), had an epigraph, a motto, taken from *The Cowards*. Forman was quite open about one of the sources of inspiration. I worked with him for quite a long time on that script that we wrote together. Unfortunately the film was never made.

HANCOCK

What made *The Cowards* different? Was it the new style of writing? The little guy who became the main character?

SKVORECKY

In the first place what made it different was the vision. I simply described the events as they appeared to me, and as they appeared to most people. Secondly the style. I used slang in dialogue. Slang was taboo in the 1950s because Stalin wrote a piece in which he said that slang was an invention of the bourgeoisie. In the translation of *The Pickwick Club*, the censors corrected Sam Weller and made him speak as an educated man because for them "Cockney" was non-existent.

Czech literature has a great lyrical tradition. Lyrical poetry achieved a very high level in the nineteenth century. But Czech fiction lagged behind: that's what happened in all world literatures. Every literature starts with great poetry and fiction comes later. Between World War I and World War II, there were probably only two or three really excellent fiction writers. One was Hasek, the author of *The Good Soldier Svejk*. His excellence is of a special sort. He was simply a natural born genius who didn't care about how he wrote. He just put it on paper. The second was Karel Capek who is for some reason known here mainly as a playwright. He was a lousy playwright, but he was an excellent short-story writer. Some of the stories were translated years ago, but he's unknown. The third one was Karel Polacek, who has never been translated. He was a great Jewish writer who died in the camps. But I don't think he'll ever be translated because his Czech vernacular is difficult to translate. Czech fiction reached the standards that could be labelled as international only in the sixties, beginning with *The Cowards*.

HANCOCK
Do you feel at home in Canada? Or do you still feel in exile?
SKVORECKY
I feel very much at home in Canada. I don't even like to travel to Europe
as Canadians do, because I have become so attached to this country, to the
atmosphere it has. Because — this is probably hard to explain — but in my
life, since I was fourteen, I have never experienced this atmosphere of
liberal freedom. I have always lived under some kind of dictatorship where
you had to turn around if you had to say something aloud. If you wrote
anything, you had to think twice before you formulated a sentence, because
you knew this would be tough for the censors. The secret police were
always after you, and you were taken in for interrogation because of some
stupid thing. So it's the atmosphere of liberal freedoms that most people
here don't realize that they have, because it's like the air. To me, this was
such a great thing when I came.

I remember our first night in Canada. We came here direct from Prague,
after the funeral of Jan Palach. That was the boy who immolated himself,
and that was a time of great tensions and people were expecting horrible
things to happen because the Soviet General Gretchko was threatening
that if Dubcek was unable to put things in order, he would move his tanks
to Prague. It was a dreadful time. There were rumours about secret police
preparing lists of people to be arrested. So then we came to Canada, and we
spent the first night in the house of Professor Gleb Zekulin from the
University of Toronto. That was probably the best night in my life because
I felt that I had nothing to be worried about, that I could just fall asleep and
wake up in the morning and the worst thing that could happen to me
would be that some kind of natural catastrophe could befall Toronto, but
nothing else.

So we feel very much at home and also we both found interesting work
which gives us fulfillment. We have made friends here, both Canadians
and Czechs, and some old friends from Prague are here. The Czech
community in Toronto is quite lively. The Prague that I knew and the
Prague that I liked does not exist anymore. It's a different city, different
people. Most of my friends are either in the underground or in exile or in
jail. It's not the same city I left.

HANCOCK
Do you feel an empathy for the internal exiles — those writers in
Czechoslovakia who must smuggle their works out? Who risk harassment
by the police simply for writing?
SKVORECKY
We publish their works, and I have a great respect for them. Most of them
are my personal friends, so I feel strongly about them. I will do whatever is
humanly possible to help them. Just try to image that these people have
been living for fourteen years now in a sort of semi-legal existence. They

are interrogated literally every week. What possible questions can be put to them week after week? For fourteen years? That is beyond me. The questions make no sense. It's simply that the secret policemen have to do some work. So they just molest them. But it's not as innocent as that. Sometimes they are arrested for a few days, released, and so on. But it's a miserable existence. They have no jobs because they simply won't get any jobs, so those of them who have wives who work are supported by them. People send them money anonymously. It's quite encouraging because most of the people of course adapted to the new situation. That doesn't mean that they love the government, but they have families and they have jobs, and they don't want to lose them. Few people are made of heroic stuff. So they just adapt. They say the proper things at the proper places, but of course they don't change internally. But the writers can publish in the West.

For reasons that are very hard to understand — there are many interpretations — so far the government has molested them, interrogated them, but they have not jailed anybody for publishing in the West. They tried to send Jiri Grusa to jail. He's a Czech writer who published a novel **with Sixty-Eight Publishers, called *The Questionnaire*. The novel is now in English, and it was published by Farrar, Straus and Giroux in New York.** They arrested him, and said he would be charged with writing an anti-government novel. They even had readers' reports. I read them, they were incredibly funny. There were protests in the West. Writers in England and France signed petitions, so they just quietly released him. But they have interrogated all the dissident writers and warned all of them: if they continue publishing in the West, they will all be charged with publishing anti-state, anti-socialist propaganda. But I think they are bluffing, because it would be very unpopular to put dozens of people into jail because they write. But who knows, they are capable of doing it.

They are now expelling dissidents. They came to the conclusion, because they unfortunately can learn, that if you sentence a writer to jail, it is counter-productive, because of Amnesty International, and writers' organizations. They raise hell, and they sign petitions and protests. It's bad publicity for Communism. But it's much better to expel, to just send them out. So the writer makes a few statements and then he disappears. Because there are so many in the West nobody is interested. A voice is really silenced by the lack of interest. But if the same man is in jail! Havel is in jail, the playwright, and from time to time you still can read a little article about him. But he was not arrested officially for what he had written. Of course the real reason was his writing, but he was arrested officially for slandering the government, some trumped-up reason. I feel very strongly about my friends there, because they are our real heroes. It's not an easy life.

HANCOCK

How do you experience Canada? Do your students help?

I feel at home. The Canadian students are both a source of inspiration and also a source of information because of their terrible political naivety, at least some of them. But on the other hand, they are unspoiled young people and it's always nice to be able to be in touch with these youngsters who still are idealists, who still think life is good.

Do you see dangers in nationalism? Canadian or otherwise?

Nationalism, as everything in the world, can be dangerous or useful. That depends on who, and under what circumstances, is a nationalist. The worst is big-power nationalism. If a strong, numerically big nation like the Russians, or perhaps the Americans, gets nationalistic, that's a tragedy, because it very soon changes into chauvinism. They may not use that slogan "My country — right or wrong," but that's what the Russians are doing. So if such a nation that has a huge army at its disposal and that can really threaten the world becomes nationalistic, that's a real tragedy. That's what happened under Hitler. The Nazis were simply chauvinists. But if an oppressed nation becomes nationalistic, that's a way to survive. If a small nation which lives under foreign oppression becomes indifferent to its nationality, then that nation is lost. So it depends on the situation.

Nationalism is okay, but if you are not in the situation of a small oppressed nation, it should be pro-something, not anti-something. Here in Canada some people are anti-American. I'm not saying everybody has to love America; there are reasons you can criticize the States, and good reasons. But in the mind of a nationalist, it becomes generalized. "Anything the Americans do must be wrong, because they did us some wrong." That's where the trouble starts. Then you become anti-American and just reject everything, including democracy, because it came from the States. I had a discussion with a student about it just this week, and it's dangerous. In Canadian literature, it's true that undue preference is given to American books, because they are published by wealthy publishers and they are much better promoted, and not necessarily better than books written by Canadians. So certainly Canadian books, Canadian fiction, should be given every help. But what should be stressed is more the quality than the fact this has been written by a Canadian. That leads to a literature where every third-rate writer becomes an important writer simply because he is of a certain nationality. Then somehow the really good ones do not differ very much, in the mind of the reading public, from the bad ones. They are all Canadians. So there is another danger. That is a thing that happened in the States at the beginning of the last century. There was also this tendency, "Let's support the American writers, don't let us read the British, we have our own literature, we must read the American writers." As far as I know, one of the few great American writers who criticized this attitude was Poe, who said "Yes, I am also for American writers, but first they must achieve the same level of quality as a Charles Dickens, and then I will prefer them to Dickens. But you can't ask me to prefer some third-rater to Dickens just because he's American." It's an intricate question, and certainly I'm not speaking about support for Canadian literature, because I profit from it myself. But I simply want to point out this danger, that sometimes people become so nationalistic that they would reject a Faulkner because he was American. Although he spent part of his life in Canada and created the myth of his participation in World War I when he never went to war. There are some dangers in almost any situation.

HANCOCK

With that in mind, what can Canadians learn from your work?

SKVORECKY

I don't know, let them find for themselves. I don't like to evaluate myself. All I can say is I always try to do my best. Whether it's good enough or not, that's for others to judge. What they can learn from my work is — if it ever gets translated, not in its entirety, but at least the main novels that I wrote — about life in Czechoslovakia under the dictatorships. It's a source of information in a hopefully entertaining form, not as a scholarly work that nobody reads.

My ambition, really, is to be an entertainer. I never thought of myself as an artist, and I never strove to become a respected artist. I sincerely wanted to be an entertainer. Entertainment can be on pretty high levels. Charlie Chaplin certainly was an entertainer in the first place, and he was not a negligible artist. I'm not saying I just want to be a clown who does a few cheap tricks in the hope people laugh. But I want to appeal to a great variety of people. I don't want to appeal just to intellectuals or just to the so-called masses. I'd like to flatter myself that my books would appeal to every intelligent reader, not necessarily an intellectual, and not necessarily a boor.

HANCOCK

So you don't see yourself as a human-rights activist or a fighter?

SKVORECKY

To me the word "activist" associates someone who attends meetings and speaks at public gatherings. I always add my signature to protests and, if I have to, I go to meetings and give speeches. But I do other things which help the same cause. I can probably help the cause much better if I write novels than if I attended and spoke at hundreds of meetings. Other people can do this much better.

HANCOCK

Can literature combat a dictatorship, compared to non-literary writing?

SKVORECKY

I'm sure that good fiction is dangerous for a dictatorship. Otherwise, they wouldn't be so much against it.

What is the threat in fiction?
The threat to totalitarian regimes is that good fiction simply tells the truth, without ideological spectacles. Every totalitarian regime wants to turn writers into hack writers, into people who carry out an assignment according to the rules laid for them by the men who pay for it, the government. So that's their idea of a writer. Most writers who are honoured by totalitarian regimes are hack writers. You can compare them to people who write Harlequin romances. If you want to write a Harlequin romance, you write by a set of rules. The heroine must be between 24 and 27, and she must be either a secretary or a nurse, and the hero must be between 30 and 35, preferably an artist, or maybe this and that, and they must meet and split twice. This is hack writing. It may be done very well, but it doesn't tell you much about life.

Graham Greene once said that the totalitarians give the writer everything — no Western society can give him as much — in exchange for him ceasing to be a writer, stopping to be a writer. That's very true. So the danger is that a writer who is not willing to accept such an assignment simply presents reality as they don't want to have it presented. Truth about reality is always dangerous to any totalitarian ideology, because every ideology is false consciousness as Engels knew. It is a consciousness that is false because it believes that its biased *conception* of reality *is* reality. Some people who have this ideologic bent of mind start believing this is the reality. This is something that a good writer cannot do, and that is why they are so much against writers. The interesting thing is that in every totalitarian regime, the first victims are always writers.

You like your work to operate on two levels: the story that you tell and the message that you convey. The occupation, whether it's Nazi Germany or Soviet Russia, is always in the background. Is that a deliberate strategy? That's much different from how Solzhenitsyn would write. That's much different from the parables of the Polish writers.
I don't think it's a deliberate strategy. If I should characterize myself, I am a simple realist. I try to capture my life experiences, and it so happened I lived under dictatorships, so they are always in the background. That's one difference between a liberal democracy and totalitarian state. Here you can spend your life without realizing that there is something like politics. What is presented as politics here is simply local politics. There is no ideology in Canada. None of the leading parties are ideological parties. They represent certain views, interests, and so on, but none of them has a strict, well-defined and compulsory ideology. Whereas the totalitarian states are based on clearly defined, very oppressive ideologies. They poison

the entire life by the presence of aggressive politics. So if you lived in Nazi Germany you couldn't escape politics. It's simply interweaved in your life all the time. The same is true about the Communist state. So if you write a realistic novel about Czechoslovakia, you cannot omit political pressures. You cannot ignore the existence of the Communist Party. But you can write an absolutely honest and truthful novel about life in Toronto and not mention the Progressive Conservatives or the Liberals or the NDP because they don't oppress you. If you are interested, you can become a member, but if you are not, you can just forget about it. But in a totalitarian state, you cannot forget about it, because it reminds you of its existence all the time: censorship, compulsory meetings, screenings, questionnaires, and direct intervention by the police. So if you write realistically about life, you simply cannot omit it.

HANCOCK

Why didn't the literature in Czechoslovakia take the allegorical or the parable route such as Franz Kafka, who was one of your countrymen? Or the kind of indirection that the newspaper writers would sometimes take? For instance, the weather report might read: "A black cloud is moving across the land."

SKVORECKY

There are such novels too, but they have not been translated. There are novels set in ancient Rome which obviously were about Czechoslovakia. I myself don't like this sort of thing very much. I can't tell you how many were written. I could tell you some names, but they would make no sense.

We published a novel called *Maso* by Martin Harnicek, which means "meat," but in Czech, meat and flesh are homonymous, just one word. This is a typically Kafkaesque novel. It's about a society where ecology was so destroyed that people can only eat meat. There are no vegetables. In the first half of the novel, you simply think that cows and cattle survived, but then you find out that people eat flesh. They kill people who are deemed unnecessary for society, or criminals. It's a cannibalistic society. That's an allegorical novel, a powerful short novel. I have been trying to sell it to some American publishers with no success because Harnicek is an unknown writer.

There is also a glimpse of Kafka in the latest novel by Milan Kundera, *The Book of Laughter and Forgetting*.

HANCOCK

Do you see history as something that trespasses on the lives of your characters? Especially in Czechoslovakia, a nation at the crossroads of European history?

SKVORECKY

Yes, very much so. All my "major" novels, if I may use the word, are based on important historical events, or set at a time when something

237

historically important happens. *The Cowards* is at the end of the war, which meant a complete change of the political system. *The Miracle in Bohemia* is set in 1968, when Dubcek tried to reform Communism and of course met with disaster. And *The Engineer of Human Souls* is a re-examination of the past thirty years in the life of Czechoslovakia, which is framed by the Nazi occupation and the year 1968. These historical, crucial moments had a deep impact on society, much more so than in the West. In the West, World War II certainly meant some changes, but basically the system remained unchanged. Every system develops, of course, but there was no radical change. Whereas in Czechoslovakia, the transition between the first republic which was a liberal democracy like Canada, into Nazism, was nightmarish. We fell from a liberal democratic regime into the cruellest dictatorship possible. So such a change, which came literally overnight, must have an impact on everybody, both mentally and in the literal meaning of the word. People got arrested, Jews were sent to the gas chambers: that's an impact of history.

Then in 1948, there was a change from a democratic socialist system into a Stalinist tyranny, which again meant concentration camps and so-called "class approach." This class approach is a very dubious thing because theoretically it should mean that the workers are preferred, and the non-workers are simply oppressed or tolerated, depending on their behaviour. But in actual fact, if you joined the Communist Party, you were safe. So the class approach is a strange thing. You can easily avoid it by joining the Party. You don't even have to join the Party if you are active and a sort of fellow traveller.

It's difficult with Communism. Nothing can be taken for granted. It is unpredictable. Then the question is, what happens to the children of suppressed bourgeoisie whose fathers are sent to factories and made into workers? Their children in the questionnaire state their origin as "working class." And that's the truth. But now they've introduced a new category in Prague. Class origin now has three categories: worker, non-worker, and a person in a worker's job. A "person in a worker's job" means that originally you were a shopkeeper or something and sent to a factory. You are not a real worker.

HANCOCK

Is writing easy for you?

SKVORECKY

It depends very much on what I am writing and what mood I am in. I usually write the first draft very quickly. But then I work on it for several years, so I always do three, four, five drafts. I always write in longhand. Then I type it up. Then again I correct it in longhand and change it and cut and add then I retype it. This I repeat sometimes two, three times.

Occasionally — two or three times only — I wrote a novella which I did not have to rewrite at all. I wrote *The Bass Saxophone* in three days. I was at

238

home with the flu and I wrote it in a fit of inspiration. I had the idea for it for many years, and I somehow felt that someday I'm going to write it. Then I sat down and wrote it in three days. I don't think I changed anything in retyping it. But it was exceptional. That occurs in literature from time to time. Stevenson wrote *Doctor Jekyll and Mr. Hyde* in three days. There is so much that is mysterious about the creative process.

HANCOCK

Do you do a certain number of pages a day?

SKVORECKY

I put in a certain number of hours per day. When I was younger I used to write at night, because I had a job. I would come home at six and eat a dinner and then sit down at seven and write until midnight. I can't do that any more because I am too tired evenings, so I write during the summer months when I don't teach. I start usually at nine in the morning and keep writing until four, four-thirty. On the average I do the same number of pages. When I retype it, it amounts to about twenty double-spaced pages per day. But that's the first draft, so let's say I spend seven hours a day and I produced twenty pages, then I spend another twenty hours on every page. It's hard to tell.

HANCOCK

Do you like being by a window?

SKVORECKY

I write in this chair. I sit here and write. It's by the window.

HANCOCK

On this coffee table?

SKVORECKY

No, I have it on my lap. I write on my lap with my feet on the table. I write in little scribbles, so it's almost unreadable, illegible. I think I can decipher it, but most people can't. Because as you write for so many years, you develop a sort of script that is almost like shorthand. I suppose a researcher could learn to read it, but it's not easy.

HANCOCK

You're writing a more complex book now, with flashbacks and parallel time lines, such as in *The Engineer of Human Souls* and *Miracle in Bohemia*. That's a departure from the novella and the chronological story that you've been writing in the past. It's also a departure from the interlocked story sequence in *The Swell Season*.

SKVORECKY

This particular technique of using the flashbacks and so on has an interesting origin. When I started writing *Miracle in Bohemia*, it was just the first of two novels that employed this technique. I had so many stories in my mind, I had trouble organizing them. At first I thought I would just write it in the usual chronological manner, but then I realized it was impossible aesthetically because it would just be a string of episodes. The idea struck me we are living in a chaotic world, bombarded by impressions and events and ideas. So I got the idea that this chaotic accumulation of things should somehow be reflected in the structure of the novel. I wrote the episodes I had in mind on little pieces of paper, or even just the titles or certain characteristics. Then I sat on the floor and I shifted these papers until they appeared to me as order in that disorder. Then I wrote it on a piece of paper and started writing. In the process of writing, new episodes emerged and I thought of new ideas.

HANCOCK

Is structure affected by the time span of the novel?

SKVORECKY

The Bass Saxophone or *The Legend of Emoke* or even *The Swell Season* cover a brief span of time. *The Bass Saxophone* is one evening, *Swell Season* is one year, and *The Cowards* is one week, so there is no need for an innovative structure. Remember *The Bass Saxophone* is also very diverse, digressive, because the associations just branch off. But *Miracle in Bohemia* covers many years, and *The Engineer of Human Souls* covers about thirty years. So how to put that in chronological order? And it's interconnected. In *The Engineer,* the central story is set in Canada in the seventies and one of the things that happened is that Danny is teaching young Canadians, including young Canadian girls, and suddenly he realizes young people are not very different in different countries; that they are in fact similar. They go through the same emotional upheavals and they even act in similar ways. So that reminds him of his own young years, when he was young and the girls who are now fifty were eighteen. So the putting together of episodes which in actual life were divided by thirty years has a logic. It forces the reader subconsciously to compare. The main reason for that multi-level structure is simply that the novels cover so much time: thirty years.

HANCOCK

Is *The Swell Season* an important book for you?

SKVORECKY

For me it is a very important book. It is what books should be written about, the really important thing in life: human emotional relationships. The political and historic things unfortunately are a necessity that we cannot avoid. I wish we could avoid it, but we cannot. So to me, *The Swell Season* is the book of all my books which is probably the closest to my heart, because in a way it is pure. This is about a young boy who is after the girls. He cannot get any, but he never gives up, and he's happy and unhappy. And from time to time from the background comes this danger because I couldn't ignore it: the war. But this is how we lived. This is what made some reviewers question the authenticity of the thing. I read in some reviews that it appears that life under the Nazis was really not so bad. Well, that ignores two things. First, the Western image of what life was like

240

under the Nazis derives mostly from war novels. Most of the war novels are based on some very dramatic events. Few are about ordinary, everyday life. Consequently, life in these novels appears as one continuous adventure, full of cruelty and danger. The second thing ignored is that this is a novel about young people. And teenagers can live quite happily under almost any circumstances, unless the circumstances are really so oppressive that you cannot ignore them.

Also this opinion ignores the difference in the quality of life in different occupied countries. Here in the West, people often think of occupied Europe as one entity. The Nazis were the cruel rulers, so life was the same everywhere. That's not true. Bohemia is a heavily industrialized country. It's probably more industrialized than Canada. And at the same time, it's a very small country, smaller than Ontario. So most of the towns are industrial, and the Germans needed the industries desperately because Czechoslovakia produced some of their best guns, for instance the famous Skoda gun that could be used with equal effectiveness against tanks and aircraft, much of their tanks and light weapons. They needed the country. The terror in Bohemia was not indiscriminate. Poland was not so industrial. It was an agricultural country, and so in Poland the situation was much worse. The Nazis closed down all their schools, except for very basic schools. In Bohemia they only closed the universities, and otherwise the gymnasiums, the high schools were functioning normally. The Czech working class was really bribed because they needed them to work, and they did work diligently. They got special rates for alcohol and so on. The Nazis were not stupid. They were clever organizers and manipulators. So life in a small Bohemian town appeared more or less normal, as far as life can be normal in a war. There was the presence of the Nazis all the time. There were arrests, but they were not mass arrests. They'd pick up someone who they learned was involved in some sort of anti-Nazi activities—mostly intellectuals. Whereas in Poland, they just rounded up a city, or part of a city, and arrested everyone who happened to be in the streets and sent them to the camps without even interrogating them. That's a very big difference. Except of course for that period after the assassination of Reinhard Heydrich who was the Nazi boss in Bohemia. He was an important Nazi: third or fourth in importance. He was assassinated by Czech and Slovak parachutists sent from England. After the assassination, they resorted to mass terror, and five thousand people were executed in a month. And Lidice was completely eradicated. All men older than fifteen were shot, all women were taken to concentration camps, and all small children were kidnapped into Germany and adopted by German families. Many of them never returned because their whereabouts were unknown. That was only a brief period; it lasted maybe a month or six weeks. After that, it returned to normal.

But if you are seventeen, eighteen, you just live, and you are interested in girls and you are happy because of the girls, which doesn't mean that you like the Nazis or that you would not yearn for another sort of life. But this is how it was. Since Western information comes at best from novels like *Sophie's Choice* — which is derivative anyway because Styron is an American writer who just made research — at worst from sensationalist novels about the Holocaust (of course the situation of the Jews was entirely different — that's another chapter), or about heroic partisans, or guerillas, — here Evelyn Waugh is an honourable exception — then the impression created is that life under the Nazis was continuous hell and everybody was either collaborating or fighting them. That simply was not true. One of the functions of literature is to tell the truth. I probably would be better off critically if I could describe these youngsters as thinking only about anti-Nazi struggle, but that simply was not the case.

HANCOCK

Could you tell me about your interest in jazz, the Swing Era, Ella Fitzgerald, orchestras, obscure musical instruments? That all happened at the same time.

SKVORECKY

Well, that was a coincidence. I was fourteen when the Nazis came, and the swing craze came to Czechoslovakia about a year before that. I became, like most people of any young generation, an enthusiast, because I liked the music. I remember how I became an addict. I just bought a record in a local shop which was a Chick Webb song, "I've Got A Guy" sung by Ella Fitzgerald. I brought it home and put it on my record player which was not an electric one, just crank, and when I heard the saxophones I felt like I was having a mystical revelation. I never heard a sound as beautiful as that before. I had a sudden conversion. I became a jazz addict because of the sound of the saxophones, which was an absolutely new sound. Of course, like the rock craze, students would start little bands, and there was a jazz band, or a swing band, in every town. People played it; young people played it. Then came the Nazis and they were against jazz music, because it was American — black, lower race — and there were many Jewish swing men in America, such as Benny Goodman. So it had these three things: American, Negro, Jewish. They tried to suppress it but they were too clever to work very hard at this solution, so they tried to channel it into safe waters. They banned American compositions, but that could be easily solved by creating this mythological Mr. Patocka who wrote everything. The Nazis could be fooled easily. But since they were so much against it, that was one additional reason for us to play it. But in the first place, we simply loved it, as the youngsters now love hard acid rock or whatever. Music has also some political connotations. They love it because it speaks for them. Young people are very emotional. They need music that expresses their emotions, their mental states, their feelings, and every generation finds such music. So when my father was young, they had brass

242

bands, this march music, and in the old times it was folklore, all these dulcimer bands and violin bands and bagpipes. So every generation has it. That's why they love it. If it happens that music, that generational expression, is being suppressed by the authorities, they love it even more, because every youngster is in revolt.

You were in a band. Is that how you discovered an interest in more obscure instruments like flexatones?

That's part of the love affair, because you seem to love anything that has a connection with the object of your love. It's a sort of fetishism. If you love a girl and she forgets her gloves — she puts them on your night table and leaves them there — then it's simply part of her. When I became an aficionado, I searched for books about jazz. At that time there was only one book in Czech about jazz by E. F. Burian, written in 1932 and full of mistakes. In the twenties, in the early Chicago days — Paul Whiteman and all that — they used very strange instruments which later disappeared, like the flexatone and something called the sarrusophone. They even had something called the kastophone, which was a set of drums, tuned drums, like timpani, but it was really like a xylophone or a vibraphone but made of drums. They had Hawaiian flutes and cowbells and all kinds of things. I became fascinated by it because it was part of that beloved music. I bought a flexatone but it's very difficult to play. I don't think you could really play "Sweet Georgia Brown" on it. You can play a simple, slow melody. You have to press your thumb on it and shake it at the same time, so you can imagine that to play "Sweet Georgia Brown" which is fast, full of syncopation, while shaking your hands and pressing your fingers, is very difficult. You can play a slow melody like *Deep Purple* (*sings*, "When the deep purple falls . . .") maybe. So that's part of my image of this strange, beautiful music. I became quite an expert on musical instruments. I developed an interest in them, even in classical music.

When I started learning to play the saxophone. I had a textbook which listed all the saxophones that exist, all the tunings. So I learned that there was a sopranino and a soprano; that's quite common, but sopranino is very rare. I saw it for the first time in Italy in a military band. It's very short and it's very high. Paul Brodie is a marvellous sax player and he plays classical music in Toronto. I have a recording where he uses a sopranino. There was something called a C melody which was between alto and tenor. It was used in the thirties and it has a beautiful tone. I don't know why they abandoned it. Baritone was available in Czechoslovakia. There was a bass; I'd never seen it at that time. There was a contrabass and a sub-contrabass. To me it was so exciting to imagine what a sub-contrabass saxophone must look like. I only saw one in a museum, and it's just huge. It's like a kettle. I don't think it's even manageable. I read that Wagner in one of his operas asked a tuba player to hold a note over eight or ten or twelve bars which is physically impossible. In a slow tempo, you cannot simply blow one tone on a tuba for ten or twelve slow bars. You've got to have additional lungs. So I read they constructed a special device, a sort of foot pedal which pumped air into the corners of the mouth of the tuba player so that he could stay playing the note. I don't know if it's true. It would be very difficult to manage. I became a specialist in musical instruments because they fascinate me. I always correct everyone who says that the famous *largo* in Dvorak is a solo for oboe, because it's for the English horn. Not many people know that. Well, it's part of my love for music.

HANCOCK

How does music, especially jazz, operate symbolically in your work? Is it because it requires improvisation which runs contrary to the rigid rules of an ideology?

SKVORECKY

That's really for you to say, because I have never been able to start thinking about symbols when I write something. I'm not a symbolist. My mentor was Hemingway and he said that if something is written well, then it may have several meanings, and that is something I subscribe to. Obviously *The Bass Saxophone* can be interpreted in a symbolic way. The struggle with the bass saxophone is really a struggle for expression that every artist has to undergo. It can lead to frustration. So the huge saxophone player at the end of the novella takes the instrument from Danny and starts blowing it. I think he symbolizes the efforts of any honest artist who tries to express what he feels about life and himself and so on. To that extent I would be prepared to accept a symbolic meaning.

The entire novella was written at a critical time in my life. *The Cowards* was the beginning of the end of socialist realism. That really ended the era of socialist realism in Czechoslovakia. After that, nobody would dare to write novels in the way that had been written before. In a way it opened the way to the acceptance of modern literature. It would not have been accepted if only *The Cowards* was there, but also there was in-fighting in the Party and the more liberal faction prevailed. They rehabilitated *The Cowards*. Then came the Kafka conference and suddenly almost anything was permitted. So many of the same critics who prior to that were arch-Stalinists and demanded socialist realism suddenly became Kafkaesque and demanded Kafka and Beckett and Ionesco and Michel Butor and all these ultra modern writers. Because some critics have the tendency to become very snobbish, there came a time in Prague in the mid sixties when unless you wrote like Kafka or Beckett, you were thought of as old-fashioned, outmoded, outdated. People were still interested in realism, but the critics were not. So there are critical articles about me in which these people said, "Well, he's historically very important because his novel

244

broke away from socialist realism. He paved the way, but in fact he's just a traditional story-teller." So I became a living classic who was already outdated because I never wrote like Kafka or anybody else.

So I try to ignore the critics as every writer should, but it's impossible. In the end you do care what they write about you. Of course it's more important to have readers, but if the critics are against you, it's not pleasant. So I was in a crisis, because I could have easily produced *something that would sound* like Kafka. I am very versatile. I could certainly have written a novel like Robbe-Grillet, a kind of *roman nouveau*. That would not be such a great problem, but this is simply not my way or my style. That is probably why in that fit of inspiration suddenly I wrote *The Bass Saxophone* without really knowing the meaning of it. But then, I saw that it was my answer to that crisis. That's simply staying faithful to your way of doing things. I am this type of writer, a realist, a story-teller. If I should violate myself, I would lose usefulness and credibility and I would lose sense.

At that time, a very good friend of mine was doing a desk-drawer translation of Ezra Pound. Pound was naturally very difficult to push through censorship, although the things he wrote were really more critical about America, about capitalism, than most socialist realists. He was a racist, there's no question about it, an anti-Semite, a real fascist. And fascism was very different from Nazism. Some of the real fascists were, in a way, idealists. The Italian fascists were not racists. But Ezra Pound was. So he was very difficult to present to a publisher, so my friend was just working on a translation of the *Cantos*. In one of the cantos, there is a beautiful line "What thou lovest well remains, the rest is dross. What thou lovest well shall not be reft from thee. What thou lov'st well is thy true heritage." I suddenly realized that this is the basic truth about art. Unless you love the thing that you do and the way you do it, then it doesn't make any sense.

HANCOCK

So art is wider than music. As music operates in your work as alienation, it's the inspiration, it's a lifestyle, it's a metaphor, it's a social ritual, it's a catharsis too at times, it's vital to being alive. And then there is what you called the "hidden music," made by the players who played "Kansas City Riffs" in Buchenwald.

SKVORECKY

I always wanted to become a jazz musician. That was my sincerest wish when I was young, but I simply didn't have the talent to become a professional musician. Fortunately I realized that in time. I also had problems with breathing because of that early pneumonia, so I really couldn't play the saxophone. I started writing about it, but the love remained. Subconsciously in some of my books, I try to somehow express musical feelings in words. That was not very conscious. It was more like

245

subconscious. But whenever I come across a passage about music, it's always what I enjoy most in my writings. I think it shows.

There is a literary analysis of *The Cowards* which appeared in the *Canadian Slavonic Papers,* where the author maintains that the structure of the blues affected the style. It's quite interesting. You know the classical blues where you have one line, then it is repeated with minor variations, and then you add the third line which is different from the first two. He quotes examples from *The Cowards* which seem to be quite convincing. There can be something to it.

HANCOCK

What makes Danny and his friends cowards?

SKVORECKY

To be quite honest, I don't know why I called that novel *The Cowards.* I think I subconsciously wanted to make fun of the concept of the hero, because in those days you had to have a hero. In the literary criticism of the Stalinist years, you never used such terms as the "central character." Every book had to have a hero. The hero, usually, was really heroic. So there was an inflation of heroes. Especially in the novels about war, you had to have heroes. But I presented these absolutely normal youths and I called them cowards. (*Laughs.*) So that is probably why I called the novel *The Cowards,* because they are not particularly heroic, and they are not particularly cowardly. They just are caught in that situation and somehow get out of it.

HANCOCK

Were you reading Hemingway at that time?

SKVORECKY

I first read Hemingway during the war in a very bad translation, because I couldn't get hold of the English original. I read *A Farewell to Arms* which had been translated shortly before the war by a man whose name was Emanuel Vajtauer. In the war, he became one of the most obnoxious quislings. And he disappeared. Nobody knows what happened to him. He probably escaped and assumed another identity. Maybe he's still alive in Germany. The translation was horrible. I remember how puzzled I was by a remark that the hero makes after they cross the Lago Maggiore in that rowboat. He rows throughout the night, and when they arrive in Switzerland, he says "I am drunk with that grog." There is no grog in the boat. (*Laughs.*) Grog has to be prepared; it's hot. The book never mentions that they had any alcohol in that boat. So I was puzzled. Where is that grog from? After the war when I read the original, I found he says "I feel groggy."

As a young aspiring writer, as most such youngsters, I was quite good at describing nature and the atmosphere and mood and the rain, that is, at description. But I couldn't write dialogue. All my dialogues sounded like explanations, or information. The characters informed each other about things. I felt that this was wrong because it was not the way people spoke.

246

But I didn't know what to do with it. After the war in '45, I got hold of a Swedish edition of *A Farewell to Arms* (an English language edition). I read it, and it was like a revelation. I suddenly realized that you could write dialogue which doesn't really mean anything literally. It simply gives you the feeling of the characters and reveals the beauty of their talking about nothing. That was my inspiration, which I derived from Hemingway.

Also, of course, he was probably the most influential American writer, that is, influential in every literature. Even Russian. He demonstrated that you could use simple syntax effectively. It's not necessary to have flowery vocabulary in order to achieve great effects. So he certainly influenced me very much in that novel. But I flatter myself that I did not imitate him. I simply learned certain technical devices from him, but I used them with my material which is simply mine. It is not Hemingway's.

HANCOCK

So your books say something about our existence in the contemporary world. That makes your work so universally appealing in the dozen or so languages it's been translated into.

SKVORECKY

If that is true, that would mean my books are not so bad, if they have universal appeal. That every honest piece of fiction in a certain sense is universal, because the basic human situations and feelings are no different from two thousand years ago, and no different from America to South Korea. People are people. They are simply a species: the same, identical. So the basic emotions are the same. If you capture the specific variation of that human situation in a specific setting, it can be understood. It can be valid and paradigmatic.

I read a book about the tomb of *Tutankhamen,* the Egyptian Pharaoh. They opened the gold coffin and there was a silver one. Then four or five coffins, and everything was laid with gold and emeralds — very rich, Pharaonic luxury until you get to the mummy. On the breast of the mummy was a bunch of field flowers, very simple ordinary field flowers, which were obviously placed there by his young wife. Now this is a gesture which is timeless. Modern girls will give you a bunch of field flowers. So that convinces me the relationship between these two people, the Pharaoh and his wife, although they were demi-gods, was very normal, was really the same. He probably courted her and told her sweet stupid silly things, as any ordinary boy and any ordinary girl in any time. Good literature that captures this essence is universally understandable and speaks to people.

HANCOCK

Do you concern yourself then with the formal structure of a book, with the shape of a book?

SKVORECKY

That depends. *The Bass Saxophone* was written in a fit of inspiration. I wasn't concerned about the form at all. It somehow happened. But in *The*

Engineer certainly I gave some thought to the structure. My latest novel about Antonin Dvorak was a challenge because I had never written an historical novel or a biographical novel. I had to think about how to handle it. Again, to write a chronological story would be possible, but somehow it didn't challenge me. So I decided to write it in a fragmentary way, by presenting Dvorak, the hero of it, through the eyes of the different people who knew him, some of them Americans, some of them Czechs, and to use with almost every narrator an entirely different style and approach.

HANCOCK

Could we talk about Danny as a character? Over the years, his persona has changed from observer to participant. His reactions to Czech history in all his books is almost a counter-cultural guide to history. And Danny's version of post-war history is presented to history's subjects, that is, the readers of his stories. Is that something that links your books, all the Danny books? Who is Danny? Is he an alter ego, a persona, a symbol of the new man, a self-conscious character?

SKVORECKY

Obviously, he is a semi-autobiographical character: a sort of alter ego. The first book I wrote about him is *The Cowards*. When I was about to write this book, I read something about a literary trend called "magic realism." That was only a label, but the expression appealed to me. So I wanted to capture a week in May 1945, so that it would be in a way magic, that I could relive it again.

HANCOCK

You read it in relation to Latin American writing?

SKVORECKY

No, no. That was in a Czech essay by a Czech poet, a pre-war poet who said the best realism is magic realism. He didn't define it, but it just appealed to me, this magic reality, because I'm a realist. To me, magic is not connected with sorcery or fantasy, but with reality. So, when I started writing the book, intuitively I just created this "I," this Danny, who is certainly myself, but of course like every literary character, he is a composite. "Composite architecture" I believe Mark Twain called it. So there is part of myself, part of idealization, part of imagination. But in the context of Czech literature, Danny used to be compared to, let's say Svejk, who was also a counter-culture figure. He simply is a non-ideological man. He never subscribes to any official ideology. He goes after his things, which is what most people do. That's probably why he was so well received by the readers, not by the government critics.

I was always so irritated by this talk about Danny's cynicism. To me, cynicism is in the acts, not in the words, the attitudes that one expresses. The so-called cynicism in Danny and similar people is a self-protective pose, because if you live in dreadful times, you develop this seemingly cynical attitude towards murder, but you yourself would never murder

248

anyone. The guy who murders talks about lyrical and very noble ideals, and then he goes and kills somebody. So who is a cynic? The man who talks about nobility and beautiful ideals, or the man who, because he has to face the results of these idealists' deeds, develops a sort of cynical, a thick hide. So that's the cynicism of Danny. It's simply a protective mask. He doesn't want to get sentimental about things, and he doesn't want to express any noble ideas, because he resents the results of such things. Danny never has done anything bad, really. Well, maybe he harmed some girl, although the girls harm him much more. He develops because he grows older, but I think the basic attitude remains. He's an intellectual and he very often associates with non-intellectuals. In *The Tank Corps*, which has never been translated into English unfortunately, he is in the army and is surrounded by non-intellectuals, soldiers. So again, he observes their behaviour and has some cynical comments. But obviously he speaks out of the hearts of many readers. In Czechoslovakia there are even women who baptized their children Danny, because of that character.

HANCOCK

Is part of telling the truth the use of comedy within the context of a police state?

SKVORECKY

This tragicomic mode comes naturally to every writer who writes about dictatorships, because every dictatorship is pompous. And every pomposity is comical. Every dictatorship has its cruel and tragic aspect, but also its comical aspect. I remember when the Germans first came to Prague and they had their first military parade which was filmed and shown in cinemas. When the SS started the goosestep, it looked comical, because men are transformed into funny dolls, so people started laughing. It is a comical step, performed by very cruel killers.

Then there is "gallows humour." Again, humour in a sad situation is protecting yourself against simply going insane or succumbing. I had a friend whose name was J.R. Pick. He was a survivor of Auschwitz who wrote a humorous novel about a concentration camp, because he was irritated by all these novels about concentration camps that were pure tragedy. He said, "My God, it was so much fun there." It was gallows humour, but then it had this aspect, so he wrote a novel called *Society for the Protection of Animals*. That's about a group of Jewish boys and girls in Theresienstadt who steal pet animals from the guards, and eat them because they are hungry. But he develops an argument they are really protecting these animals against contact with these horrible assassins. In a way, it is a humorous novel. Of course, it has strong overtones of deep tragedy, gallows humour, but reality is simply a mixture of fun and tragedy, and especially in dictatorships. One of the responses to it is making fun of it. That's why they have so many political jokes, because that's a way of defending yourself against the basic danger and tragedy of such a life. That's not something that I would put in with an intention to make my books more interesting. It simply is part of the response. You make fun of it. It's like in the blues. "When you see me smiling/I'm smiling to keep from crying." That's not something specific to Czech literature.

I'd like to talk about your detective stories. You've done some very unusual things with detective stories. You translated Chandler and Hammett. You've written essays on detective stories, and you also made various alterations to the form: for example, the murder occurs at the end. In *The Sins of Father Knox*, you tried to violate the ten rules of Father Knox. You have a lady cabaret singer who's a detective. You have a society where the police are the criminals. You have moral detectives, who have to find a compromise with themselves when the criminals cannot be identified, perhaps because of political connections and so on.

SKVORECKY

My interest in detective stories started when I was seriously ill. I had hepatitis. I was infected during an operation, and that's a dangerous type of hepatitis. So I almost died. I spent four months in an infectious ward where books were allowed to be sent, but you couldn't send them out. They had to remain there, because they were afraid that they would spread infection. So my friends sent me detective novels, because they could part with them, not serious stuff. Anyway if you are seriously ill, you don't read Dostoyevsky; it's not the kind of literature you can appreciate if you are in hospital. There were no TVs, no radios. The hospital library only had socialist realism and Marx and Engels. So during the four months I must have read one hundred and fifty detective novels.

I discovered that this debased genre may be very useful in such situations, and they can be well written. I realized I could tell quite serious things through the genre. The name of my detective is Josef Boruvka. The first book about Boruvka was published in English in England: that's *The Mournful Demeanour of Lieutenant Boruvka*. At first he's just a regular grey detective who's sad because he is a humanist. He's sorry for the killers because they are so bad. Not that they are locked up, but that they are so bad. Then I started playing with the genre, so for instance, in the first book with Boruvka I tried to pass two stories through censorship and I succeeded. One of them is called *Whose Deduction?* and that's a tribute to Chesterton, because the deduction is really God's. Boruvka is conducted to the solution of the crime through a series of accidents, coincidences, which should not happen in a detective story. Coincidence should never help the detective. But in this case, the coincidences help him. You can also see the coincidences as the finger of God who is leading him away from a sin, because at the beginning of the story he's about to commit adultery. But then he's called to this murder and he can't resist a call to duty. Through a series of coincidences he's led to the solution, but in the meantime the girl has left. She's bored, he never showed up, so she left. So he's saved from sin, and the coincidences are really God leading him in the proper direction. Fortunately the censor didn't understand it. He thought it was an interesting story. And the other one is about a political prisoner who is suspected of murdering someone. It turns out that the murderer was the prosecutor who had sent him to jail years ago.

In the second book, *Sins for Father Knox*, the one about the cabaret singer, the idea was that you have this famous decalogue by Father Knox about what must not be done in a detective story. I decided to write ten stories and each of them would violate one of the rules. So the task for the reader would be the normal task: to figure out who the murderer is, and also to figure out which rule has been broken. The sin against the rule is always hidden somehow. You have to figure it out. So that was a sort of game.

HANCOCK

What were some of the rules broken?

SKVORECKY

One rule says that there must be no Chinamen. That refers to the cliché that existed in the twenties in bad detective stories where the murderer always was a Chinaman with a knife in his teeth. So I had a Chinaman in the story. Another rule is that there must be no twins, so I had twins. There must be no secret passage, so I had a secret passage. Or, the detective must always present a clue to the reader when he finds one, so there were hidden clues but in such a way that you could figure them out. It was an intriguing task. Some of those stories are not bad. Another one is that the solution must not depend on some scientific or other specific knowledge, so there is a story that depends on your knowledge of mathematics.

Boruvka also appears in these *Father Knox* stories. But the main character there is the singer, and he falls in love with her in the end. The third book *The End of Lieutenant Boruvka* is set in 1968, after the invasion. He solves a series of cases but then he cannot arrest the murderer because the murderer is either involved with the police or has protection in high places. This leads to frustration. In the last story he helps an American gangster kidnap a Czech girl held by the Czech authorities because her parents are in the States. The parents hired the gangster. But he himself cannot escape. He's arrested and sent to jail for fifteen years. There are alleviating circumstances because of his prior services, so he's not hanged. Otherwise he would be.

The fourth part, which is called *The Return of Lieutenant Boruvka,* is set in Toronto. He escapes from Czechoslovakia and is now a parking-lot attendant in Toronto. He, of course, solves a case. It features a woman who owns the first all-female detective agency, "Sheila's Shamusesses." But she's very incompetent. It's told by a narrator who is a Canadian and who for some reason has very much to do with the Czechs. He doesn't really know why, but there are always some Czechs surrounding him. It's an opportunity to make fun of the Czechs and at the same time to criticize some of the naiveties of Canadians.

HANCOCK

There's a key worry and concern in *The Engineer of Human Souls* that North Americans may be either ignorant or indifferent to political oppression. There's a poignant scene in the novel in which a homesick Czech girl sings a song over the campus radio station, but there's no one to listen. Is that ultimately your deepest concern?

SKVORECKY

Of course it is. This political naivety may be funny, but it's also a very dangerous thing. People who have never been exposed to any real political oppression simply have no way of realizing what it is and what it means. That leads to an underestimation of the danger. There is also what I call "selective indignation." That's not my expression; Kingsley Amis coined it years ago. If something happens let's say in Afghanistan, a very cruel murder — they burn some village — it doesn't really result in too much excitement in the West. You read a story about it, but it's soon forgotten. When a much less cruel thing happens in Chile, there is an explosion and people protest. I'm not against protests against crimes committed by South American dictators. But there should be some balance, because the Soviets are as bad and worse and more dangerous to the world and to peace than some small dictator in Chile. The South American oppressors are certainly nasty people, but they don't present any danger to the world. Whereas the Soviet regime presents a very grave danger to the world. Attention should be paid to Soviet crimes. At least as intense attention as is paid to South Africa or some of the Latin American dictatorships. But here all you read about is the nasty Americans who support these nasty regimes and who govern imperialistically their part of the world. This is simply not true objectively. If you compare American dominance in South America with Soviet dominance in their sphere — there's no comparison. Do you think that the Soviets would ever permit a Nicaragua to happen on their territory? Never. There would be a Soviet army there at the beginning.

What I am irritated by is this saying, "It's exactly like." It's not exactly like. I remember when Vaclav Havel, the playwright, was first jailed. He managed to smuggle to us in Toronto a manuscript of an old Czech socialist politician. At the same time, Daniel Ellsberg stole some classified Pentagon documents and sold them to *The New York Times*. I spoke about Havel in the library to a colleague, a woman who taught in the English department. She said "That's exactly like Daniel Ellsberg." But it's not. First, Havel did not steal any classified documents. He smuggled a book of memoirs, which in any other country would be published. Secondly, he didn't sell these memoirs, whereas Ellsberg stole state secrets and sold them. Thirdly: Havel spent more than four years in jail; I don't know how long Ellsberg sat. So there are differences. If you say something about the KGB and how brutal they are, they say "it's exactly like in the United States. Did you read how they beat up this man or that man?" Again, policemen are similar everywhere, but the difference is in the political system. In America, some of these policemen are as brutal as any other policemen. But they have to play it safe because if they do some nasty thing, they are in danger of being written about and discovered and eventually forced to retire, or even be punished because we still have a free press. Whereas in the Soviet Union, the situation is such where if you are a KGB man, you don't have to be afraid of being written about in the papers and fired for beating up somebody because that's part of your job, and nobody has the right to criticize you.

The important thing is the system. Human nature is the same. The Russian policemen are probably the same type of people as the American secret policemen. But the systems are very different. The totalitarian system simply gives a much better chance to the lunatic fringe, to the bad people. We have Nazi people here in America. They are given so much publicity and are presented as something very dangerous. They are not at all dangerous. They are the lunatic fringe, a few crazies who simply dress like SS men. They have a leader in Chicago who is half-Jewish. So that only shows what type of people they are: lunatics. In a liberal democracy, they will always remain a lunatic fringe. In Toronto, we had this Western Guard. I don't know if they still exist. They never presented any real danger to the society as a whole. They could do nasty things to individuals certainly, but they like the Nazis have simply been discredited by history. Racism, obviously, is unacceptable.

The Communist ideology however, as an ideology, is acceptable. They preach equality, social justice, a sort of paradise on earth. The Nazis never preached that. They were supremacists, Master Race, and so on, and it appealed only to the Germans. How could it appeal to anyone in Czechoslovakia? We were a secondary race. So it appealed again only to the lunatic fringe, the quislings, which in Czechoslovakia were maybe one percent, even less. They were typical lunatic-fringe people. They were pro-Nazis although they were not top-quality Aryans. So this is simply an ideology that has no appeal anymore, except for these lunatics. Whereas Communism, as an ideology — if you forget about its practice, about the murders they commit, about Gulag, about Cambodia, about Afghanistan — as an ideology is nice: brotherhood, equality, social justice. For some reason, because the ideology is so appealing, people have a tendency to close their eyes to what they are doing. Some say this or that was a historical necessity. That's bullshit. We are human beings. We are not animals who would be moved by some necessity. We have reason. We can solve problems without resorting to mass murder and to locking up hundreds of thousands, millions of people. I don't subscribe to historical necessity.

But the tendency is that Communism as an idea is somewhat more acceptable. That leads people to this selective indignation. These South American dictators, they aren't even fascists. I don't think they have an ideology. They're just autocrats who want to hold power and who are against Communism, so they are labelled as fascists. But because they either don't have an ideology, or are leaning more towards the right, nobody likes them. Whereas these different Communist leaders — "After all, they have this beautiful ideal, so all right they may not be perfect." Everybody's proud about being an anti-fascist. But to be an anti-Communist, that's not so good, because you are suspected of being a rightist, a reactionary, maybe a fascist. But this of course is a mistake.

I read a novel by Amanda Cross. She's a professor who wrote a novel, *Murder in a Tenured Position*, a dreadful novel, highly praised by all the critics. At the end of the novel, there is a university gathering and a student gives a speech, and he speaks about the necessity of order and respecting the law and all these things, and everybody applauds. The professors applaud because it's law and order. After the applause subsides, he says, "This is what Adolf Hitler said in 1933." The professor thinks this is an argument against law and order. Well, this is *argumentum ad hominem*, which a professor should never use. Secondly, Hitler very probably also believed that one plus one equals two. Was he wrong? So this is demagogy of the first magnitude. Because Hitler said that one should respect law and order, it's bad. But that's not true. Hitler said many things that are quite acceptable, even true, apart from the things that are not, that are inhuman.

This is simply the attitude of many people: because the Americans do something, it must be wrong. The Soviets, after all, are different people. There is no unemployment, which is not true. People find all kinds of reasons to make excuses. These days they are building a pipeline across Russia. Who builds the pipeline? Vietnamese. And who are these Vietnamese? People from the South, including, apparently, some boat people who never made it to the boats. How many of them volunteered to be taken from their homeland and sent to Czechoslovakia where they've never been, which is a country so different, to be placed in barracks, and work for much less than Czech workers? That's exploitation of the first magnitude. It's really indentured labour. Have you ever read about it? It's ignored. Imagine that Americans would import people from South Korea without their families, and house them in barracks and force them to work for half the pay of American workers, and that not a private firm, but the government would do this. It's unimaginable. What a furor that would cause. So this is what I call selective indignation.

I wrote a letter to *Maclean's* about the Canadian bishops' statement on unemployment. It's nice they are interested in the fate of unemployed people, but I have never read any statement in my fourteen years in Canada

254

about the situation of the Church in the Communist state. These are Catholic bishops. They should show some interest in what happens to their fellow Catholics in Communist states.

I don't like to talk about these things, because people always label me as a sort of rightist, fascist, reactionary. But I am a reactionary in this sense. I believe some values are important and they are now almost forgotten or not respected or not valued. Who is interested in liberal freedoms? Many people just sneer at it. And lawfulness and order, these are not bad things in a democracy. I am reactionary because I believe there are certain traditional values that should not be forgotten, and if they are forgotten, the results may be tragic. As Evelyn Waugh said, a writer must be a reactionary because at least someone must go against the tenor of the age. At least someone must offer a little resistance. And that's counter-culture for me.

MARGARET ATWOOD

My interview with Margaret Atwood took place over two afternoons, December 12 and 13, 1986, in her living room. Atwood lives in a large house in the Yorkville area in Toronto. The sessions lasted about two hours each, and ended when her daughter, Jess, came home from school. The interview was later revised slightly for clarity. Atwood's house is much like her own personality, which I might describe as woodsy. Dark, oriental carpets, large house plants, and a collection of decorative toads (she is incorporated as O.W. Toad, Ltd.) made up the comfortable decor. The interview was both candid and elusive, and her replies were often punctuated with her characteristic laugh.

I had asked her for the interview at a particularly busy time. *The Handmaid's Tale* was a runaway success, winning many prizes, including the Governor-General's Award. A long promotion tour had left her nearly "interviewed out" and in the reams of material written about her, I wondered if I could even come up with a fresh or interesting question.

Atwood is, of course, one of Canada's most prominent novelists, story writers, essayists, and poets. Her fiction includes *The Edible Woman* (1969), *Surfacing* (1972), *Lady Oracle* (1976), *Life Before Man* (1979), *Bodily Harm* (1980), *The Handmaid's Tale* (1985), and her story collections include *Dancing Girls* (1977), *Bluebeard's Egg* (1983), and *Murder in the Dark* (1983). She has also written nearly a dozen collections of poetry, for which she is internationally known.

I began asking her about interviews.

HANCOCK

Interviews can take many forms. They can act as an adjunct to literary criticism, or they can act as literary biography. An interview can get inside a writer's work. Do you think I might learn something about your work which isn't readily apparent from an interview?

ATWOOD

Interviews are an art form in themselves. As such, they're fictional and arranged. The illusion that what you're getting is the straight truth from the writer and accurate in every detail is false. The fact is that most writers can't remember the answers to some of the questions they get asked during interviews, so they make up the answers. A lot of the questions are about things they don't usually think about, or if they do think about them, they don't think about them at the time of writing. Any memory you have of what you did at the moment of writing is just that, a memory. Like all memories, it's usually a revision, not the unadulterated experience itself.

Also, writers quite frequently conceal things. They either don't want them known, or they think of them as trade secrets they don't want to give away, or they are hooked on some sort of critical theory and they wish to make it appear that their work fits inside the perimeter of that theory. Let's just state at the beginning that interviews as the truth, the whole truth, and nothing but the truth, are suspect. They're fictions.

HANCOCK

With that in mind, this interview will evolve as we proceed. Has Canadian fiction caught up to the complexities of the 1980s?

ATWOOD

The short answer is I have no idea because I don't read all of Canadian fiction. Once upon a time, you could, because there was so little of it. In 1960, five novels were published in English Canada by Canadian publishers and Canadian writers. Five! Then, it was easy to keep up. But now, you'd be hard pressed to keep up with all the short stories and novels published by small presses and big presses.

The long answer is that fiction is doing what it always has done. One area of fiction has always to some extent reflected what was going on at the time. Whether it's done badly or well or in what form, is always variable. But there is a connection between what's happening in society and what fiction writers do — to an even greater extent than there is between what happens in poetry and what happens in society. You can have a pure lyric poem, but it's hard to have a pure lyric novel.

HANCOCK

At least in the English novel.

ATWOOD

Or in any language. Because you do have characters still, despite the convention of the self-reflexive narrator, which basically dates back to the 18th century. You still have some voice in the novel that purports to be speaking. A person who purports to be speaking, or various people. These are not disembodied spirits, except in the most rarefied of novels. They are supposed to have something to do with being human on the earth, which means necessarily in a particular place at a particular time. As for "the complexities of the '80s," I'm not totally sure what they are. I suppose writing fiction is one way of trying to find out.

HANCOCK

With Robert Weaver, you've recently collaborated on a short-story collection, *The Oxford Book of Canadian Short Stories in English*. Do you still see yourself as part of what you once called "our tough and sombre literary tradition"? The anthology covers a century of writing. Or, and here's the flip side of the question, do you see a number of writers working in a variety of different directions not connected to a tradition?

When you say "literary tradition" you are not talking doughnuts. You are not saying "this book is a copy of that book is a copy of that book." You are talking about a thread that runs through, you're talking about themes and variations.

For example, the relationship between Money and Divine Grace in American literature has been there since the earliest Puritan sermons. The way the Americans chose to interpret the verse about the rich man finding it difficult to pass into the Kingdom of Heaven, for instance, or the way they chose to interpret, "By their fruits ye shall know them," or the dictum that you should not keep your light hidden under a bushel. Or the two servants, one who hid money away, and the other who put money on the market where it increased. All these things have been taken by the Puritan tradition in general, and by the American Puritans in particular, to mean that rich people have divine grace. Even though it is contrary to certain other verses in the Bible. The verse about the camel, the needle and the rich man getting into Heaven is followed by a verse that says not all things are possible for humans, but for God, all things are possible. So it is possible!

That relationship can be traced through Benjamin Franklin, who tossed out the theology, but kept the thought — "It's more blessed to be rich than to be poor." Let's forget, "It's blessed to be poor in spirit"! We see it in Henry James, with his graceful dying rich heroines who are better than other people. In *The Great Gatsby,* the theme that the rich are blessed is turned upside down, but it's still the same idea that's being played with. Rich Daisy has a sacred iconic life, though it's of a sinister kind.

Canada has tended to have other traditions. Name on the fingers of two hands all those Canadian novels that are about rich people and how wonderful they are. There's rich people in Robertson Davies, but they are not usually shown as wonderful, sacred, and blessed. But it's a different approach. To say there's a Canadian tradition in literature is not to say that all Canadian books are the same. It's to say there are certain ideas that get played with again and again in very different ways. Ideas get turned upside down, stretched, and toyed with. But it does tend to be certain areas that repeat, rather than other areas. The Americans do it with rich people, or their idea of the infinitely expanding frontier. Where is that complex of ideas in Canadian literature? It's certainly there. Students of Canadian literature who are not Canadian have no hesitation in declaring that Canadian literature is a distinct and separate body of work. Otherwise they wouldn't be studying it.

You were thinking about *Survival,* I guess. That was an attempt to say, quite simply, that Canadian literature is not the same as American or British literature. That is now known in the world at large. It wasn't known then, in 1972, not even in Canada at the time. If you read the reaction to *Survival,* some people asked, "Why is she writing a 300-page book about something that doesn't exist, namely, Canadian literature"?

You must believe it exists, because you publish *Canadian Fiction Magazine.* There must be some reason for calling it that, and for putting stories by Canadians in this magazine. If Canadian writing were the same as British or American writing, why put it in a separate magazine? You can say, there's this difference and that difference, and it's changed and gone off in various directions. But you are probably not going to say, "There's no such thing as Canadian literature." That was the attitude of a lot of people only sixteen years ago. The mail I got from ordinary people was, "Gee whiz, I never knew. My high-school teacher told me there was only Stephen Leacock and that was it."

This situation — the need to struggle to assert the mere fact of our existence — is no longer with us. As a Canadian writer, you no longer have to say, either, *I'm going to leave the country to become a real writer in England or the States,* or, *I'm going to stay here to fight and struggle to become known as a writer in a society that thinks art in general is suspect, and Canadian art is doubly suspect, because it's inferior.* That battle doesn't need to be fought any more. Surely we've done enough.

HANCOCK

To change subjects here, the imagination of Canadians takes us North.

ATWOOD

For Canadians, North is a constant. It's one of those ideas that's reinterpreted generation after generation, and by region after region. The idea of North is probably quite different for Quebecers. But "North" is still the thing that's being considered. When the Americans send icebreakers through the Northwest Passage, why do Canadians get so stirred up about et? Not many people go there. It's not as though it happens where they are physically. It happens in their minds. It's a violation of their mental space.

HANCOCK

Though Canadian literature has made great steps forward, in some of your stories you've satirized the Canadian literary community.

ATWOOD

Literary communities are always comic, when they're not tragic: that is, when writers aren't being tortured, shot, and imprisoned. If you take "comic" as that which is divergent from what "normal," "average" people think you ought to be doing with your life, then you, Geoff Hancock, are a comic character. Here you are, running this magazine, devoting your life to this thing which is never going to make any money. It's quixotic of you to do it. You are the Don Quixote of the Canadian literary scene, and so is anybody who runs a literary magazine or a small press in this country. If the society in which you live thinks you should be making millions of dollars playing the stock market or being a doctor and playing golf, which is considered average and normal, then all us artists are defined as whacko.

259

We ourselves may not think that. We may think that we — in general — are the sanest thing around — which I happen to believe. But from the point of view of society — and comedies always take place in that context — we are the "funny people," the eccentrics, the ones who are not in step. And we do have our eccentricities.

HANCOCK

You like to work in a variety of areas. Do you try to understand the processes of each piece of writing, whether it's a poem, a cartoon, a short story, an essay, a novel, a screenplay, or a theatre piece?

ATWOOD

This word "process" is very fashionable. All it really means, as far as I can tell, is "how do you do it?" You have to understand something about the form before you can do it at all. We might include puppet plays, which was one of the things I started out with. Puppet plays for children's birthday parties. Every one of those art forms has a certain set of brackets around it. You can say, *this is what happens within this form,* and, *these are some of the things that don't happen within it.* Some of the most interesting things happen when you expand the brackets. For instance, when we do puppet plays, we don't usually show the live people who run the puppets. What would happen if we mixed up live people with puppets? What would we get then? We would get the Mermaid Theatre, one of the most intriguing puppet theatres around. The brackets were moved over to include live people. We've moved the borders, we've changed the rules.

It's the same with any form. You have to understand what the form is doing, how it works, before you say, "Now we're going to make it different, we're going to do this thing which is unusual, we're going to turn it upside down, we're going to move it so it includes something which isn't supposed to be there, we're going to surprise the reader."

For instance, in the novel, for awhile it was the fashion not to show the author at work. Before that, it *was* the fashion to show the author. Now it's the fashion to show the author again. It was a new thing for the 1960s and 1970s of the twentieth century. It was standard for 1850s novelists to say, "Now, Dear Reader, let me tell you what I think about these goings on. Dorothea didn't know this was happening. But I, the Author, am going to let you, the Reader, in on the secret." If you go back before then, you have the author talking about himself, saying why he decided to write the story in this way and not some other way. Letting the reader in behind the scenes. All of those things are ways of moving beyond the conventions to include things not considered includable. The kind of material thought to be suitable for novels is constantly changing.

This is one of the things that happened to Canada. For a long time, Canadian material was not thought to be suited to "great literature." You could not make a "real novel" out of Canadian stuff. You had to go to the States or England to make a "real novel." Canadian novels *per se* were considered second-rate pastiche, or imitation or embarrassing. John Robert Colombo's poem about "How to make a Canadian Novel" summarized that attitude. Put in some beavers and Mounties and you get boredom. Similarly with women's material. What-you-do-in-the-kitchen-when-the-boys-aren't-there. That kind of stuff was considered not suitable for great writing. It was always dismissed or not used. Then Margaret Laurence, Alice Munro, Margaret Drabble, Marian Engel, and others started using this stuff, and making it work. Lo and behold, it *was* usable, as it had been all along, except that nobody had noticed.

That's one way, for me, of thinking about "process." The other is, what does the author do when he or she is writing? I write by hand. That means I'm very involved with the actual physical texture of writing. I have to have a brain-to-hand-to-pencil-to-paper connection with a page. If my hands were cut off, I would not be able to write. I don't think I would be able to dictate into a machine. I can't type very well, and don't type straight onto the page with the exception of business letters or book reviews. I don't compose much fiction on the typewriter, and poetry not at all. If I get going quite fast, I may get to a point where, when I'm transcribing from hand-writing to the typewriter, I alter and add on the typewriter. But usually I write by hand.

HANCOCK
How do you keep track of where you are in a long-hand manuscript?
ATWOOD
I usually start at the beginning and barrel straight through. It's like CBC "Coast to Coast." I start in Newfoundland, and then roller-coaster across the country according to the time change. If I'm working on a novel, I'll write maybe twenty pages in long-hand. I start transcribing that long-hand into typing, while, at the same time on the back end of the novel I write more. I'm always catching up to myself in the typing while continuing on with the writing. That reminds me of what I just wrote the day before, and allows me to keep track. But some of the stories I'll write in one sitting. When I'm feeling good I can write twenty pages long-hand in a sitting, and transcribe ten on the typewriter. But of course there's a lot of revision.

HANCOCK
Is this a constant method of composition?
ATWOOD
I don't always start at the beginning and go through to the end. Some-times I'm going along and I'll come to a scene which is out of sync. I know it comes near the end, but I'll write it down anyway. It's become quite immediate and I want to get it down before I forget about it. I will have little patches here and there. It's like colouring in a map. It's a form of exploration. (*Illustrates with fingers on table.*) You're going along a river. This is "explored territory" and this is "unexplored territory." But from what you know, there's a pagoda which you should be coming up to,

261

though you don't know what's been here and there. You know you'll be coming to some things you already know about. But you don't always know how to get there.

HANCOCK

Is that the occupational hazard for you?

ATWOOD

I find it the interesting part. If I knew everything, I would get so bored I would stop writing.

HANCOCK

Are you a severe critic of your work-in-progress?

ATWOOD

Let us put it this way. People have often asked me which of my editors is "the real editor". Is it my Canadian editor, my American editor, or my English one? The fact is, it's not any of them. By the time they get the work, it's been through six drafts usually. I used to be an editor with the House of Anansi. That taught me something about editing. Although I write quite quickly in the first instance, I revise slowly.

HANCOCK

Do you find your works "link" together? Is there a larger narrative framework?

ATWOOD

Do you mean does this novel and that novel have something to do with one another? Well, they all have women in them. In *Life Before Man* a male tells one-third of the story. Some of the stories are told from the point of view of men. "Uglypuss" is a case in point: most of that story is told from the man's point of view. The woman comes in at the end. But by and large, my novels centre on women. None of them are about all-male groups. None of them are about miners in the mines, seamen on the sea, convicts in the jail, the boys in the backroom, the locker room at the football game. Never a story have I set in those locations! How come? Well, gee, I don't know! (*Laughs.*)

Maybe it's because I am a woman and therefore find it easier to write as one. Few male writers write all their books from the female point of view. That doesn't mean they hate women.

HANCOCK

You also like paired characters: mothers and daughters, nieces and aunts, such as Elizabeth and Muriel in *Life Before Man*, the Handmaid and her sinister aunts, Joan of *Lady Oracle* and aunts Lou and Deirdre. Could you comment on this?

ATWOOD

Most novelists work in pairs, triplets, quartets, and quintets. (See *Fifth Business* for quintets.) It's hard to have a novel with no characters in it except the protagonist. But I am *interested* in the many forms of inter- action possible among women — just as I am in those possible between

262

women and men. I'm interested in male-male interaction, but can have no first-hand experience of how men relate to one another when women aren't present. For that, you have to ask men.

HANCOCK

Is this a reaction against male authority figures?

ATWOOD

Don't be silly.

HANCOCK

Can a fiction be ideal?

ATWOOD

Do you mean perfect? Oriental carpet-makers weave a flaw into the design on purpose, because nothing on this earth can be perfect.

HANCOCK

Some of your books have come out in elegant and expensive limited editions, like Charles Pachter and Glen Golusca's Salamander Editions.

ATWOOD

Charlie made most of those as an art student. But books as objects have nothing to do with perfection of writing. Perfection is a non-existent thing on this earth. Perfection is an idea. I'm thinking of the uncertainty principle in physics. Even the physical universe is not "perfect," that is, wholly symmetrical, closed, finished. There's something in the nature of things that's against closure. Here's the latest from my nephew — he's the mathematical physicist. They now think the universe is made of little strings, in thirty-two different colours. I said to him if the little pieces of string are so small, how do they know what colours they are? He said, "It's just a manner of speaking."

HANCOCK

A "string" is supposed to be a quintillion quintillion times smaller than the smallest part of an atom, if I remember correctly. The concept was thought up by a Russian physicist. Along with it goes what he calls the TOE Theory, the theory of everything.

ATWOOD

Even better, there's supposed to be seven dimensions, four more than we usually think of. Let's not even ask about perfection!

HANCOCK

Which aspect of fiction writing do you find most interesting or challenging?

ATWOOD

It's all pretty difficult. The most challenging is to do something that surprises me, the writer, and therefore, I hope, will surprise you, the reader.

HANCOCK

Do you like to deal with the large format of a social mythology through fiction?

ATWOOD

I think I used to like that idea. I don't like ideas as a rule —not as *a priori* determinants of fictional modes. Let me put it another way around. I started out in Philosophy and English. Then I switched.

If you're an academic, you have to concern yourself more with "ideas." Ideas make the stuff you're doing a lot more teachable. People find it easier to sit in a classroom and abstract things or turn them into ideas, or consider them from the point of view of ideas. There's not a lot you can say from total immersion in the text. About all you can say is emotional things, like "Wow, it really grabbed me!" Or other reactions that come out in that banal way. *I hated it, I loved it, it didn't do anything for me!* Whereas if you deal in "ideas" you can analyze the structure, the prose, the style, or this and that. But as soon as you do that, you're analyzing, making an abstraction from the actual thing.

Academics have to do that at one level or another. They are in the business of teaching people. One of the things that happens when you teach people is that you say, *Let's look at it this way. Let's look at it structurally. Or mythically. Let's look at the prose, the punctuation, the texture.* But if you are not an academic, you don't have to spend a minute of your time thinking about those things. If you are a practising writer, and that only your engagement is with the blank page and only with the blank page. You never have to toodle off to school. You never have to divide yourself in that way, the blank page at home at night, the day time at school, where you point out how Marianne Moore's poems have little white spaces in them. You don't have to think about that unless you want to.

I used to teach, so I know whereof I speak. I thought differently when I taught. I think differently when I teach from the way I think when I don't teach. It alters how you perceive what you're doing. The mere act of teaching any kind of literature to anybody does that. I'm not making any value judgements here. This is merely an observation on the texture of the inside of your head.

HANCOCK

Do you prefer people to just experience your work?

ATWOOD

Nō, I don't have any of those preferences. It's not a value judgement. You were asking how I went about it, and what my experience was. When I'm not teaching, I don't have to think of my own work in terms of ideas or large social things or any of those concepts. I get right down in the mud, which is what engagement with the page is. It's mud.

HANCOCK

What makes fiction dramatic for you?

ATWOOD

Fiction has to surprise me. If a character is going along doing only what such a person would do, I get very bored. I want to know more. Or other.

Or something else. Or to have them come to a point where they're not what I thought they were. Or that they're not what *they* thought they were. It's probably a form of childish curiosity that keeps me going as a fiction writer. I probably want to open everybody's bureau drawers and see what they keep in there. I'm nosy.

HANCOCK

Whose fiction do you admire?

ATWOOD

Lots of people's! It's the question at readings that always stops me cold. I feel as soon as I start picking those lists, people are going to be hurt because I didn't include them —but it may just be because I haven't thought of them at the time. If you are wondering what I read recently that zapped me out the most, I can tell you three books. One was J. M. Coetzee's *Foe*. That was zappo! The other was Primo Levi's *The Periodic Table*. Another was Ireni Spanidou's *God's Snake*.

HANCOCK

Do you learn anything from books you admire?

ATWOOD

You learn something from everything. But *what* is the question. You often don't know for twenty or thirty years what you've learned. It may appear suddenly a year or two or five years later that you learned something back then that was important to you. I read for pleasure, and that is the moment at which I learn the most. Subliminal learning.

HANCOCK

Could you say something about the writer's "voice"? Is there a distinctive Canadian voice? Could you say something about your own voice?

ATWOOD

I hope there is more than just one distinctive Canadian voice. It would be so boring otherwise. I came across a funny thing I wrote some years ago. The Writers' Union of Canada thought it would improve its fortunes by having all its members write a piece of pornography. Andreas Schroeder was going to put these together into an edited book. This was the genesis of Marian Engel's novel, *Bear,* by the way. It started out as a piece of porn about a woman fornicating with a bear. The Union gave up the idea because they felt from the submissions that serious writers weren't any good at writing pornography. But I think they were looking for the wrong thing. They should have been looking for the kind of parody serious writers tend to produce when they try their hands at this. They would have got more usable material. I wrote a piece called "Regional Romances, or, Across Canada by Pornograph." It's five different pieces, starting with the Maritimes, then Quebec, Ontario, the Prairies, and B.C.. Each one is written in quite a different voice, but quite recognizable. You would know the general area of literature that was parodied. There is not one Canadian voice. There are various voices. But none of them sound particularly

British, and as a whole, they don't sound very American either.

It all depends on where you stand in relation to the forest. If you stand very close, you can see the molecules inside the tree. If you move back a little bit, you see the bark. Move back, you see the whole tree. Move back, you see a group of trees. Move back, you see a forest. Move back, you see a green thing in the distance. Move back a bit, you see a smudge. Where are we standing here? Are we right close to the individual author? In which case, it's the author's voice, not the Canadian voice. Do we stand back a little bit and see a region? Do we say there's a Quebec voice, an Ontario voice? Do we put Alice Munro's stories, Matt Cohen's *The Disinherited*, Robertson Davies' novels, Graeme Gibson, James Reaney, and Marian Engel all together in a corral and say "Southern Ontario Gothic"? This I've done. I've taught such a course twice, once in Alabama, and once in New York. Very teachable. There they are, and yes, they have something in common.

HANCOCK

Would you include yourself in this group?

ATWOOD

No. I'm not from southern Ontario. My roots are the Maritimes and northern Quebec, not Ontario small town. But these writers are different from the West and from B.C. and the Maritimes.

In the west, Edna Alford, Sandra Birdsell, John Newlove, Sinclair Ross, Margaret Laurence are part of a group you might call "western realists." Then someone like Gloria Sawai flies in from left field and writes "The Day I Sat With Jesus on the Sundeck and a Wind Came Up and Blew My Kimono Open and He Saw My Breasts." That's an interesting story because the texture of it is like those other people. The woman talks in the vernacular, very detailed about laundry and household goods. But then in comes Jesus Christ. Within the compass of western realism, this is a variation on it. But it's somebody playing with the convention; it's not a different animal.

And in B.C., there is more than just one group of writers. The Canadian voice contains all these different things. But if you stand back from it all, you can ask, Are these the same things that are happening in the United States or England or Australia? Are Quebec stories and poems *like* the ones from France? Not from what I've read.

English fiction is all about social class. In English life you can't get away from it. Canadians have a great advantage in England because nobody can tell who they are just from talking to them.

Standing quite far back, you can say, yes, there is a Canadian voice. Standing further up, you would say no: only voices.

HANCOCK

And your own narrative voice?

ATWOOD

I would hope it's different in various stories. It's not that I manipulate it.

That would imply something a great deal more conscious than what I do. I can't talk a lot about how I write, because I don't think about how I write when I'm writing. That's why interviews are suspect. I could make something up for you, but it would be made up.

What do you think your strengths are as a writer?

ATWOOD

I used to say, in the usual Canadian way, well, aw shucks, I don't know. We're trained to be modest. But now that I'm middle aged I'm going to allow myself to say, well, maybe I'm good. Not all the time, but enough times, I can get the words to stretch and do something together that they don't do alone. Expand the possibilities of the language.

HANCOCK

And your weaknesses?

ATWOOD

Weaknesses? We can't afford to think about those kinds of things. Most writers are tightrope-walking over Niagara Falls all the time. Look down and you've had it. If I thought too much about weakness I'd block.

HANCOCK

Are you happier with some of your fictions than others?

ATWOOD

My life is full of unfinished stories. It always has been. I start something, get about ten pages into it, and stop. I put it aside.

HANCOCK

Do you ever discuss works-in-progress?

ATWOOD

Hardly ever. I discussed bits of *The Handmaid's Tale* with Graeme. He thought I was going bonkers, I think. That's the problem with discussing works-in-progress. They always sound somewhat crazier than they may turn out to be. He kept saying. "You're going to get in trouble for this one." But he egged me on, despite that.

HANCOCK

Do you see your work as successful in terms of its intention?

ATWOOD

If I didn't think it was somewhat successful — and let us keep in mind my remarks about perfection — I wouldn't be publishing it. Success is different from perfection.

HANCOCK

You don't think afterwards, say at a reading, that you should have taken something out through another draft?

ATWOOD

The book I would write this year is not ever the same as something I would have written twenty years ago. I wouldn't be writing that book now, whatever it is, because I've changed and so has the world. My interests and perceptions have changed. What was of interest to me then would not be of interest to me now. My intentions don't remain constant, so how can a book be expected to live up to my intentions in 1986 when I wrote it in 1964?

HANCOCK

Do you find with each book you learn some new aspects of fiction? How to use backgrounds, foregrounds, language?

ATWOOD

No. I don't think you ever know how to write a book. You never know ahead of time. You start every time at zero. It doesn't count for anything that you were able to pull it off before. It means nothing. A former success doesn't mean that you're not going to make the most colossal failure the next time.

HANCOCK

Does part of the problem perhaps come with the dubiousness of imposing form on the material? One of the great things about the novel is that it ultimately has a form.

ATWOOD

It can't help but be a "form" because it is smaller than its container, which is the universe. Which is itself a form.

HANCOCK

Do you like form? Or are you suspicious of form?

ATWOOD

I don't see why it can't be both at once. That's how I feel about many people, liking and suspicious at once. Why shouldn't I feel that way about form? Let us say that part of the joy is learning to do something you didn't know how to do before. But once you know that and keep repeating it, the joy goes out of it.

HANCOCK

What is the novel to you?

ATWOOD

I'm very suspicious of anything beginning with a capital letter, like Man. Or Woman. Or the Novel. I seem to think from the ground up, rather than from the top down. German is not my natural language. You can nounify anything in German by putting a capital letter on it and making it a noun form. It almost makes the thing exist. The "Novel" for me is the sum total of all men. Therefore, I have a lot of problems with making general statements about them. As for Woman, capital W, we got stuck with that for centuries. Eternal woman. But really, "Woman" is the sum total of women. It doesn't exist apart from that, except as an abstracted idea.

HANCOCK

When you sit down to write a long fiction, which eventually reaches three or four hundred pages in manuscript, do you stop to think about a series of characters in a number of situations that have to be shaped somehow?

268

"Material" has to be shaped because eventually somebody is going to have to read it. Everything has a shape. An amoeba has a shape, though it's rather malleable. There is no such thing as a thing with no shape. It may be a more contained or less contained shape, or an awkward shape, or a graceful shape. It may be sprawling or rectilinear, but there's a shape of some kind which can be described.

HANCOCK

I bring this up, of course, because the novel, or long fiction, or long narrative, as recently as the 1960s went through a phase where it was considered dead and defunct as a form. Then it got revitalized.

ATWOOD

But did that ever really happen? Wasn't it just what a few people were saying? They said the same thing about God. Prove it. They claimed all this dead novel stuff, and all the while people were writing and reading novels, as usual.

HANCOCK

Life Before Man struck me as particularly interesting for its narrative strategy. You had three principal characters, with specific dates as an organizing device. Did you get that right the first time?

ATWOOD

I got part of it right the first time. Some books are a "good read." Part of that book was a "good write." I didn't have to go back to square one as I did with several others. I wanted a triangular structure. From the point of view of A, B and C were wrong. From the point of view of B, C and A were wrong. From the point of view of C, A and B were wrong. I wanted a nice little triangle. That part was not difficult to do.

But *Lady Oracle* was originally written in the second person. It was written as a letter to Arthur. But I realized I couldn't do that, because Arthur already knew a lot of the stuff that had happened to him. I would have been in the rather stupid position of having the narrator tell Arthur things he already knew. It does end up being a story told to somebody else, but you don't figure out who that person is until the end. It isn't Arthur; it's the guy she beans with the bottle.

I took a couple of runs at *Surfacing* in 1964 or 1965. It was the same time I was writing *The Edible Woman*. I've got several beginnings of what eventually turned into *Surfacing*. It was quite different. It was in the third person. The characters were different, though there were four of them. The woman was older. The other woman was her sister. The first complete write-through was quite bad. I had to go back and rearrange things so that there was more going on. My problem is that I get so fascinated by description and details I forget about anything happening. I have several unfinished novels with that problem. They have wonderful descriptions of things, but nothing actually occurs for a long time.

Once I tried to write a novel from the point of view of eight different characters. That was dandy and I had nice descriptions. But after 250 pages, no events had occurred. If I had followed out my scheme, the novel would have been about 1,500 pages long. It wouldn't have worked.

The Handmaid's Tale is organized partly by the repeated "Night" sections. There are periods of action, punctuated by periods of reflection.

HANCOCK
Does there have to be event in a novel?

ATWOOD
Yes, if you want people to actually read it. You can do various "theoretical" works and experiments which will be of interest to a very few people interested in dead ends and what doesn't work. The Andy Warhol movie about sleep is more interesting as an idea than it is as something you'd want to sit through for twelve hours.

HANCOCK
To deal with events, do you have to look carefully at your characters, their motivations, their psychological makeup?

ATWOOD
Characters don't just sit in a chair. Everybody has to get up to pee once in a while. Unless, of course, you want to write a novel from the point of view of someone who has had a total lobotomy. Or has no brain and is immobile. Or is in a catatonic trance. In those cases, if you have anything in the novel at all, it has to be unconscious inner event. But it's still event. Something is still happening.

HANCOCK
Do you try for what T.S. Eliot called "the objective correlative"? To try and reproduce in the reader the same emotional state as the characters?

ATWOOD
That's evocation, rather than representation. Certainly, that's what any successful piece of writing does. It evokes from the reader. It's not a question even of self-expression, of the writer expressing his or her emotions. Who really cares? You can say the writer felt this, the writer felt that. But unless you can evoke that emotion from the reader, it's merely a statement.

HANCOCK
Do you try to do that by entering the wildness of the characters, something that's perhaps hidden even from themselves?

ATWOOD
I don't know if I "try" to do that when I write. I'm not observing it. I don't know what I do when I ski. Ideally, I go downhill. But if I stop to think about it too much, I would probably fall down. I don't think any writer can be in a state of creation and in a state of contemplation about that creation at one and the same moment. If they try to do that, they would certainly interrupt their concentration. Or their state of trance — whatever

you call that place we go to when we write, a place that is not the same as analytical thought. Anybody who claims to tell you *exactly* what they are doing when they are writing is probably lying — maybe speaking from memory, guesswork, possibility. Who knows?

HANCOCK

Does a novelist have a social conscience?

ATWOOD

I never met one without. Even Robbe-Grillet, who was somebody who tried for pure objective value-free depiction, is making a statement. You can't show a character doing anything without expecting the reader to have some view about that, because readers live in a society and make moral judgements. *John took an axe and he chopped off Mary's head.* For you, the reader, is that good or bad? You are going to react one way or another. The way you react to it is going to depend upon what you already know about Mary, about John. You cannot put those words on paper without in some way engaging the reader's moral sense — supposing the reader has one, and I've never met a reader yet who had no moral sense at all.

HANCOCK

Does art have to be moral?

ATWOOD

It is, whether the artist tries to be or not. Even Oscar Wilde was making a moral statement when he said, "Morality is boring, and what I'm after is the beautiful." That in itself is a statement about morality. I'm afraid that engagement is unavoidable. How you handle or approach it is something else again. You can take the Oscar Wilde stance. Or you say, *what I'm after is pure form.* By saying that, you imply the moral dimension is not important to your art. Or you can say, *the social conscience is innate, therefore I will be out on the table about it, and these are the bad guys, let's all spit on the bad guys.* However, the closer you get to that view, the closer you get to propaganda. That doesn't mean that art with some moral sense is inevitably propaganda.

HANCOCK

That argument between form and morality created a tremendous debate in American literature.

ATWOOD

I know, but I found it so unnecessary. Apostles of the obvious. Even fabulist fictions are moral. They are among the most moral of things. What's more moral than a fairy tale? Science fiction is dripping with message. But if something is only that, then we feel we're being preached to and we resent it.

HANCOCK

Let's talk about your short stories. When you work on a story, do you start at any particular point?

271

ATWOOD

As I do in the novels, I start with a scene of some kind. Or an image. Or a voice. I don't work much from an idea. By "idea" I mean something abstract, like *peace is desirable*, or *war is hell*.

HANCOCK

I just read "Walking on Water" the other night, in *Chatelaine*.

ATWOOD

That's one of the "Emma" stories.

HANCOCK

Could you tell me a bit about those stories?

ATWOOD

Emma is a character who doesn't think a lot. She does things, but she doesn't think about them in great detail. She's not an internal character. Sometimes one gets tired of writing the various ratiocinations of the characters and wants to show a character in action, as it were. The Emma stories are very heavy on event, light on Emma's inner world. I have known women like this. Usually, we think of female characters as fearful and timorous. But I have known women who really would do anything. Walk up cliffs, and other foolhardy things. It was interesting to write about something like that. Such people interest me, particularly when they are women, because it goes against their socialization. I don't know if I could write a novel or a whole book of stories in that way.

HANCOCK

Would that be because of market demands?

ATWOOD

Nothing I do has anything to do with market demands, except in the TV script department. That's my substitute for teaching at university. Teaching university has a lot to do with market demands! (*Laughs.*) But I've always felt my writing was somewhat eccentric. It has been *strange* that I have acquired the audience I have. Or the audiences, whoever they may be. Literary writers don't usually get those audiences. But I'm not in the position, for instance, of going to magazines or publishers and asking them what I should write fiction about. I've never done that. I've never had to.

HANCOCK

The story collections seem carefully structured. For example, *Bluebeard's Egg* is nicely framed with the two parent stories. Among many things, these are stories of the natural world framing the urban world of the other stories. Was it planned that way?

ATWOOD

More out of desperation, I'd say.

HANCOCK

Jack Hodgins' *Spit Delaney's Island* is also framed. He needed to do that to wrap up the book.

ATWOOD

I wrote all the stories before I arranged them. It's not a question of having to write this or that to make it nice. I usually spread them all out on the floor and see how they look best to me. It seemed evident those stories should be like that. It's like those psychological tests they give you, with different shapes and colours which they ask you to arrange into a pattern according to shape, colour, and size.

HANCOCK

Would you find the main drama for your characters is in their anxieties?

ATWOOD

The Emma character isn't very anxious. But she gets into situations that would make us anxious. In one story, she almost drowns. In another story, her boyfriend almost drowns. I don't know why they are always almost drowning. Why can't they burn up?

HANCOCK

I was going to ask you a drowning question. Drowning occurs in *Surfacing*, "This is a Photograph of Me," "Walking on Water," the other Emma story, "Death of A Young Son By Drowning," "Procedures from Underground," *Lady Oracle*...

ATWOOD

I grew up by a lake. People drowned in it. I know some people who have drowned, or nearly drowned. Canada is full of water.

HANCOCK

It seems a powerful image for you.

ATWOOD

There's just a lot of drowning going on. Now, if you have your choice about how people die in natural accidents in Canada, it's most likely to be by drowning. Look at the statistics. But you don't have to look at them. Look at your own life. How many people do you know who have burnt up in a fire, compared with those who have died in plane crashes, compared with those who have drowned or almost drowned? Is it not so?

HANCOCK

The women in both *Dancing Girls* and *Bluebeard's Egg* are rich in anxieties.

ATWOOD

Show me a character totally without anxieties and I will show you a boring book.

HANCOCK

This in itself raises questions about what is the nature of fiction.

ATWOOD

What is good fiction? Well, first it has to hold the attention of the reader; not all readers, but what we can call the suitable reader. Once upon a time, a long time ago; I took a course in the 18th century novel of sensibility. I read all kinds of things of the period. One of them was *Sir Charles Grandison*, by

273

Richardson, who had previously written *Pamela* and *Clarissa. Sir Charles* starts out at a cracking pace. The heroine is almost abducted from a stagecoach. Unfortunately, to the reader's great dismay, she gets rescued by Sir Charles. For the rest of this 600-page novel, Sir Charles is perfect. The heroine notices this and that instance of his politeness,his gentleness, his generosity, his perfection, his chivalrousness, but that's about it. I think I've met only one other person who has finished it. I finished it only because I was not going to let this defeat me, I was going to jolly well get through to the end to see if anything of any interest happened whatsoever.

People ask me, why do your characters have these problems? If the characters have no problems, what's the book going to be about? The problem has to be an internal one, or a problem with another character, or an external problem like the Great White Shark, or the end of the world, or the people from Mars, or vampires. Something has to be there to disturb the stasis. Think of a play in which the characters do nothing at all, ever, throughout the whole play.

The question then becomes: granted that something has to happen in a novel, why do certain kinds of things happen in my novels, while other things happen in other people's novels? That's the question, not why does *anything* happen.

HANCOCK

From a content point of view, something has to happen. The "and then, and then," and how and why.

ATWOOD

The "and then, and then" is basic. But if you don't do that well enough, the how and the why aren't going to interest anybody because there will be absolutely no reason to keep reading the thing.

HANCOCK

Do you concern yourself with getting the right scenes in the right order and then the right words in the right order?

ATWOOD

Probably the two things happen at once. I seem to write in quite different ways. Some stories are beginning-to-end straight write-throughs. Others are built up bit by bit. You can tell by looking at "Significant Moments in the Life of My Mother" that the writing of it was episodic. Sometimes you wake up in the middle of the night with a wonderful phrase or sentence or paragraph. You write it down, but you're not sure where it's going to fit. You find out later, or not, as the case may be. My life is filled with pieces of paper with things written on them that I've never used.

HANCOCK

Do you block out the action after you've got all those notes?

ATWOOD

Take for example, *The Edible Woman*. I wrote it on University of British Columbia exam booklets. There was going to be one booklet per chapter. The booklets were white. I wrote that novel in four months, I find with horror in looking back. Then I revised it. Every day I would ask myself, what is going to happen today to these people? In the place where you plot out your exam question, on the left hand side, I'd make a list, a few notes, on what she does today. Then I would write the chapter.

But the point to remember is that nothing works, necessarily, dependably, infallibly. No regime, no scheme, no incantation. If we knew what worked, we could sell it as an unbeatable program for writing master-pieces. Writing is very improvisational. It's like trying to fix a broken sewing machine with safety pins and rubber bands. A lot of tinkering.

HANCOCK

Your short stories are all different. You're not writing the same story over and over.

ATWOOD

The New York Times Book Review called them "wilfully unfashionable" or "wilfully eccentric." But I'm not too sure what is fashionable in the short story these days, nor do I much care.

HANCOCK

The American story writers move in schools, like fish. Right now, it's minimalist fiction, or "dirty realism" as in the works of Raymond Carver and Ann Beattie and Tobias Woolf.

ATWOOD

But as soon as that gets defined, it's already on the fade. To call this the "new fiction" is a marketing strategy. But Canada doesn't work this way. Everyone is equally weird.

HANCOCK

In rereading the stories, I was amazed to find a lot of writing about writing. "Giving Birth" for example, has a strong passage about the problem of communicating through language. That's a central concern with *Murder in the Dark*...

ATWOOD

So it was in *Surfacing*, and to some extent, *The Edible Woman* as well.

HANCOCK

Is that an interest in theory, or post-modernist concerns?

ATWOOD

None of the above. As I've said, I'm not very theoretical in my approach to what I do. As a theorist, I'm a good amateur plumber. You do what you have to do to keep your sink from overflowing. I tried for the longest time to find out what *deconstructionism* was. Nobody was able to explain it to me clearly. The best answer I got was from a writer, who said, "Honey, it's bad news for you and me."

HANCOCK

That's because the text is often deconstructed back to the author.

ATWOOD

What it also means is that the text is of no importance. What is of interest is what the critic makes of the text. Alas, alack, pretty soon we'll be getting to pure critical readings with no text at all.

I don't have to do that, because I don't have to sell my bod on the academic market. I'm not going to get tenure depending on whether or not I'm in the swim. I think I'd just embarras everybody by asking those kinds of questions.

Let me put it this way. One of my early jobs was taking those recondite, verbose market-research interviews written by psychologists, and translating them into language that the average person interviewed could understand. So it was breaking down "psychologese" into simpler units that could be understood by somebody not a professional in the field. That's impossible to do with certain kinds of things. You can get a rendition of advanced physics, but it is just a rendition.

With literary criticism, I really feel that it ought to be graspable. It should not be full of too many of those kinds of words which only the initiated can understand. It's fun for the initiated to have a language which means something to them and to them alone. It means you can one-up people, and it's a closed circle, you can be declared in or out depending on whether you are using the current language. These things do have a habit of rolling over about every five years.

HANCOCK

That criticism aside, with all its inherent truths, your work is starting to be read that way.

ATWOOD

You can read any text any way. You can read it standing on your head. You can use it for toilet paper. It's not a statement about the text. It's a statement about the user.

HANCOCK

To come back to *Surfacing* or "Giving Birth" or *Murder in the Dark,* your own prose draws attention to more than just the story, with a character and a particular situation. The prose itself says there's a problem of communicating through language. It implies a distrust of words, that there's a distrust of language, that language is a distortion.

ATWOOD

Language *is* a distortion.

HANCOCK

Do you mean we can't trust language to get through to "truth"?

ATWOOD

That's true. Although I've used language to express that, it's true. I think most writers share this distrust of language — just as painters are always wishing there were more colours, more dimensions. But language is one of the few tools we *do* have. So we have to use it. We even have to trust it, though it's untrustworthy.

276

HANCOCK

That's an interesting paradox.

ATWOOD

The question is, how do we know "reality"? Hoe do you encounter the piece of granite? How do you know it directly? Is there such a thing as knowing it directly without language? Small babies know the world without language. How do they know it? Cats know the world without language, without what we would call language. How are they experiencing the world? Language is a very odd thing. We take it very much for granted. But it's one of the most peculiar items that exists. People start to feel that there's some kind of inherent meaning in a particular word. Like "apple." People start to think there's something of *an apple* in the word "apple." But if so, why is it called something else in fifty-seven other languages?

HANCOCK

As *The Feminist Dictionary* points out, language is now being re-evaluated, to find out how language has been maligned and changed through usage. For example, the word "gossip" was originally the dialogue between mother and a midwife. And "trivia" is derived from Trivia, Goddess of the Crossroads, where women traditionally exchanged news. But gossip and trivia are now seen as negative terms, when they were once positive.

ATWOOD

Not only is language slippery, but it's limited. The vocabulary we have is limited. There are a lot of things we don't have words for.

HANCOCK

Perhaps there is something "universal" beneath language?

ATWOOD

"Universal"? What does that mean?

HANCOCK

Gabriel Garcia Marquez' *One Hundred Years of Solitude* had an equal impact on Michel Tremblay in Quebec and Jack Hodgins in B.C. (not to mention other writers around the world), though neither read it in Spanish.

ATWOOD

How did it do among the Inuit? Or the Chinese? It's true you can translate things, sort-of, so that they can kind-of be read. But efforts to translate *haiku* have always frustrated me. I know perfectly well that the English translation of the Japanese may give the literal words. Yet the piece is totally lacking in the resonance you get from a knowledge of the tradition, a knowledge of the culture. "Plum blossoms floating down the stream." What does that mean to you? Not a great deal. It lacks a rich cultural compost. Every piece of writing exists in its surround. It comes out of that surround. It has meaning in the surround. You can take it out of there and look at it. An Assyrian sculpture, a figure of a winged bull, with the head of a man, is interesting to look at. But it has nowhere near the meaning for us that it had for whoever made it. We don't know who that person is. We don't know his story. We don't know what magical powers he may have thought the figure possessed. It still has some meaning for us. But it's a different meaning for us.

When we go to India, we find that colours mean different things to them than they mean to us. In India, they don't have snow in the winter, except in the mountains. So the opposite of green is not white, it's brown. If you don't have rains, you have drought. Red means happy in China, but it's blood and passion for us.

HANCOCK

We don't even know how to "read" a Chinese restaurant in Toronto, The dragons on the wall, the Fo dogs which represent Ying and Yang, the tree figures that represent health, wealth, and longevity. There's something tricky about language.

ATWOOD

There's something tricky about "reality," let alone language. Insofar as language relates to a cultural experience of reality, to what extent is that transmissable? To what extent can you translate that into another language and have it understood? I'm now translated into over twenty languages, only two of which I can read, more or less. I have no idea what those other versions are saying, to the people who read them.

HANCOCK

Murder in the Dark doesn't have a "plot," but it does have a "character" in the narrative voice in the four parts. Did you make a decision not to plot the book?

ATWOOD

I was just having fun. Sorry to be so idiotic about this. I know "serious" writers aren't supposed to say things like that. I started writing these little mini-fictions and little pieces of prose that were not connected to a "plot." They were connected in the way that verses in a lyric poem were connected, or like sections in a long narrative poem. It's not a question of A to B to C to D to E. It's a question of these units existing by themselves, but having a certain vibration with the ones they are placed with.

HANCOCK

Did that create any technical problems?

ATWOOD

I wasn't doing them on purpose. I started writing them — fooling around. Then it occurred to me, at some point near the end, that this was probably a book.

HANCOCK

Michael Benedikt, who edited an anthology of prose poems some years ago, claims the prose poem never really settled down in the English language. That it was something exclusively French, Spanish, or Italian. Generally speaking, we don't see that many prose poems in English in Canada.

It's unfortunate. I found they were excellent for readings. Some of them have enough of a plot that you don't have the problem you have with a poetry reading. You can't read very much poetry without people's eyes glazing over. The level of concentration required is so great you can't do it for an hour. I can't listen to a poetry reading for an hour, no matter how good it is. I just can't. My attention gets burned out in the first half hour. Some of the prose poems are funny enough, or have another line that isn't lyrical, so they don't require the absolute kind of distilled concentration that an hour of lyric poetry requires.

HANCOCK

With *Murder in the Dark,* you come back to those concerns that the writer is a liar, that memory is unreliable, that fiction is a distortion, the unspecified narrator. Would I be stretching a point to say there is a connection between this book and *The Journals of Susannah Moodie*?

ATWOOD

Susannah Moodie was a specific person for me. I thought you were going to say *Surfacing,* in which the narrator lies and her memory is unreliable. Susannah Moodie doesn't lie. Nor is her memory particularly unreliable. She has two different sides to her personality. The narrator of the first eight chapters of *Surfacing* is much more an unreliable narrator.

HANCOCK

Are you interested in characters, their names, their psychology, their types?

ATWOOD

I'm very interested in their names. By that, I mean, their names don't always readily spring to mind. I have to go looking for their names. I would like not to have to call them anything. But they usually have to have names. Then the question is, if they are going to have names, the names have to be appropriate. Therefore I spend a lot of time reading up on the meanings of names, in books like *Name Your Baby.*

HANCOCK

What does your name mean?

ATWOOD

"Pearl." And "of the woods." It's an English name. Quite old. Probably 14th century or earlier. From "atter wode."

HANCOCK

"Hancock" is from "hen" and "cock," a poultry farmer. It dates from about the 12th century.

ATWOOD

Keeping the chickens in line!

HANCOCK

When the stories of your characters are unfolding, do you look for that moment when their whole world changes?

ATWOOD

In a novel, you hope there's more than one of those moments. In a short story, there may only be one such moment. And it may not be their whole life changing. It may be one thing they've thought which they can no longer think. It may not be their entire life, it may be just an area. I don't have any thoughts about what *has* to happen in a story beyond the fact that *something* has to happen.

HANCOCK

Do you have to know more about a character than you can actually tell?

ATWOOD

I have to know more than I actually tell. Lots more. I get bogged down in detail. I try to tell too much. I try to tell everything about this person. I try to tell too many things about their underclothing and their breakfast foods. I often have to cut some of that out.

HANCOCK

When the something that is going to happen happens, what is it? Something as basic as an antagonist? Or a social situation?

ATWOOD

It depends on the story. There are hundreds of possibilities, and many ways of arranging them. That's what I was playing with in, for instance, "Happy Endings." You could start at any point in the story. You could start at the end if you wanted to, then go back and show how that end was arrived at.

HANCOCK

In the novels your characters are women who are professionals in their jobs. They suddenly have to assess their life because of changing circumstances.

ATWOOD

You might also say that some of my characters go through periods of craziness. I don't think six novels are so easily reduceable to one formula. It's true I never wrote "the housewife novel." But even "the housewife novel" was the character reassessing her life.

HANCOCK

Professor Elspeth Cameron has written in an essay on your work that your characters are "transformations of imagined persona around an inner self."

ATWOOD

What does that mean?

HANCOCK

In *Lady Oracle*, Joan Foster creates various persona and somewhere in the midst of them all is "Joan Foster." Many of your stories, both long and short, are built around shifting identities, the various personas the characters create. You often organized your books around a split point of view. First and third persons, contradictions within the characters, fractured identities. Is that how you see characters?

280

ATWOOD

Well, maybe. I might see them that way. It would depend upon the character. But probably I do them that way because I get bored with writing in the first person so I switch to the third. I get bored with writing in the present tense so I switch to the past. I get bored with having just a single narrator so I have three instead of one. A lot of this is trying to keep oneself amused, isn't it? I don't like to feel I'm doing the same thing over and over. I would die of boredom if I felt I were doing that. I like to try things that are hard for me. That's despite laziness.

HANCOCK

Do you think human beings are a species to be observed?

ATWOOD

Why would they not be? We observe everything else. Why not ourselves?

HANCOCK

Someone described you as "an anthropologist from another world."

ATWOOD

Most novelists do that in some way. They may treat certain forms of human behaviour as something you should take for granted, more than I do. I find a lot of behaviour very strange. Therefore worth pondering.

HANCOCK

Do you find your various travels reinforce that?

ATWOOD

We have an unconscious assumption that the way we live is normal and average, and that everybody else is strange. I've never been able to buy that. I think we're strange, too.

HANCOCK

Do you keep notebooks when you travel? Photographs?

ATWOOD

Graeme takes the travel photographs. I would if he didn't, though. Right now I tend to go in for family snapshots — the birthday parties, the Christmas trees, and so forth. I used to take pictures of things like fire hydrants, but when you have a growing family, there is an urge to create future nostalgia. As for notebooks, I've tried, but I'm not good at it.

HANCOCK

Someone said that the centre of your work is the power of language to transform our perception of how the world works.

ATWOOD

I'll buy that. I'll endorse that one! I've got to endorse something in this interview. Whoever said that, it's true!

HANCOCK

Are you interested in boundary lines? Is there a point where poetry and prose merge? Become something different? Prose looks a certain way, as do poetry and drama. Perhaps there's a point where they run together?

ATWOOD

Probably there is.

HANCOCK

I mention this because someplace you wrote that in fiction you were "a curious bemused disheartened observer of society," but you felt differently when you wrote poetry.

ATWOOD

Probably I do. But I'm not very good at analyzing what I feel like when I do those things. Probably different parts of the brain are involved. If you could hook up somebody's brain while they are in the throes of composing a poem, and hook up the same brain while that person was writing a novel, I'd expect you'd find brain activity in different areas. I think poetry is written more on the right side of the brain, that is, the left-handed side. That side of the brain is sadder than the other side, according to researchers.

HANCOCK

I'd like to discuss layers and levels in your work. I'll let the explicators get into the depths of *The Handmaid's Tale*.

ATWOOD

They haven't got around to it yet. The book is still on the level of popular reaction. The explicators haven't had time to get in there and explicate it a lot.

HANCOCK

Are you glad?

ATWOOD

None of it has much of an impact on me, to tell the truth. If I were to obsessively read everything everybody wrote on me, I'd go nuts. You couldn't keep up with it and remain sane as a writer.

HANCOCK

Why do you suppose people want to write about you and your work? There's at least five books now, countless scholarly essays, graduate theses, and a clipping file I've seen is about two feet thick.

ATWOOD

You got me. Better to ask them. Why do people collect stamps? There is indeed an impressive amount of work. But I don't put them up to it. This is something they do on their own hook. So either they find it pleasurable, or they find it of interest. But it's not up to me to say why they do it.

HANCOCK

Some people might see you and your work as a nodal point, a focal point of all our interests and concerns.

ATWOOD

It has certainly been seen as that. But it's not something I did on purpose. Or put them up to doing. It's just one of those things. Maybe it's because of my horoscope. Jupiter in the tenth house — very lucky for a career.

HANCOCK

Do you follow astrology closely?

I know how to do it. I can also read palms. I was taught all this by a Dutch art historian whose specialty was Hieronymous Bosch. She had to know these things because they are built into mediaeval works of art. A ring on a certain finger means something. When Hieronymous Bosch paints the Last Judgement with the stars in the sky in a particular pattern, the pattern means something. So there we were in Edmonton, during a winter when the temperature didn't go above zero F. in a whole month; she lived downstairs, and we did this to pass the time.

HANCOCK

Do you want to talk about *The Handmaid's Tale*?

ATWOOD

When I first started thinking about it, I thought it was such a whacko idea I wrote it with some trepidation. It could have been the worst failure you could possibly imagine. I was afraid people would say it was stupid, silly. There was also the risk it would be thought feminist propaganda of the most outrageous kind, which was not really what I intended. I was more interested in totalitarian systems, an interest I've had for a long time. I used to read second world war stuff in the cellar when I was twelve or thirteen, for instance.

HANCOCK

Did the idea that the book is about *now*, written as if it's the future, told in the past tense, complete with epilogue, create a problem? Do you think you might go in a further direction, like Russell Hoban's *Riddley Walker*, and create a new language for the future?

ATWOOD

I didn't think that language would be that different twenty years from now. I would never have written *Riddley Walker* because I don't believe after the big bang, supposing we have one, that there will be anybody walking around. I wouldn't have written a post-atomic-war book. So I didn't change the language much, because in the nature of things it wouldn't have changed much, except for the slogans, greetings, etc. Anyway, the character telling the story was brought up in *our* time, in *our* language.

HANCOCK

Could you tell me about the tape recording as a device in *The Handmaid's Tale*?

ATWOOD

I had to do it that way. The paper and pencil supply would have been quite limited. It also allowed for the discontinuous, episodic nature of the narrative.

HANCOCK

Could you tell me about your use of scenes as narrative units? Characters, suspense, tone of voice, thematic concerns are all compressed into short units. The gap is just as important as the text.

ATWOOD

You're dealing with a character whose ability to move in the society was limited. By the nature of her situation, she was very circumscribed. She couldn't communicate well with people. It was too dangerous. She was boxed in. How do you tell a narrative from the point of view of that person? The more limited and boxed in you are, the more important details become. If you are in jail in solitary, the advent of a rat can be pretty important to you. Details, episodes, separate themselves from the flow of time in which they're embedded —a flow which tends to be monotonous — and become significant, luminous.

HANCOCK

The epilogue was interesting. It was back to splitting the point of view.

ATWOOD

I did that for several reasons. For instance, the character herself was so circumscribed that there were a number of things about the society she could not know. If she started telling us, the readers, about it, we would have thought, *Balderdash, how could she know all this?* The newspapers are censored, TV is censored, she can't talk to enyone, how can she know all this? So there were things the reader had to know that she couldn't tell us. Especially things that took place afterwards. Also, I'm an optimist. I like to show that the Third Reich, the Fourth Reich, the Fifth Reich, did not last forever.

In fact, Orwell is much more optimistic than people give him credit for. He did the same thing. He has a text at the end of *1984*. Most people think the book ends when Winston comes to love Big Brother. But it doesn't. It ends with a note on Newspeak, which is written in the past tense, in standard English — which means that, at the time of writing the note, Newspeak is a thing of the past.

HANCOCK

The Handmaid's Tale is going to be turned into a screenplay.

ATWOOD

Harold Pinter is writing it, which is very interesting. If anybody can do it, he can. One of his specialties is scenes in which people don't say very much, but convey meaning anyway.

HANCOCK

Do you embed things in the fiction? I've noticed all these elements of folktales, gothic tales, fairy tales.

ATWOOD

I sometimes embed private jokes. Or little sketches of people I know; they know I've done it, they get a kick out of it. Sometimes, like Alfred Hitchcock, I make cameo appearances. I put myself into *The Edible Woman* — I'm the female graduate student dressed in black, the one who appears at the party and talks about Death.

HANCOCK

Do you do that after you've got the story-line under control, and the characters are off to meet their destiny, wherever that may be?

ATWOOD

It's more an impulse towards whimsy. It's like the Gothic cathedrals, where the carvers put imps under the skirts of the angels. Those are my bits of "imperfection," I suppose.

HANCOCK

Are characters in a natural environment more religious or spiritual? Is that where you find the gods, or the goddesses, or the God?

ATWOOD

Not usually in church, you'll notice. I can't say the established religions have a terribly good track record. Most of them have quite a history of doing people in — not to mention their attitude towards women.

HANCOCK

Do you want to say anything about the religious and mystical side of nature?

ATWOOD

I don't know if there is one, any more than there is a mystical side to anything. The mysticism is in the eye of the mystic — not necessarily in the stone or the tree or the egg. Or let's say it has to be a two-way street. If we had a sacred habit of mind, all kinds of things would be "sacred." Most are not at present. We would be able to see *into* things, rather than merely to see things. We would see the universe as alive. But you're more likely to find such moments in my poetry than my prose.

HANCOCK

Where does your interest in prehistory come from?

ATWOOD

As kids, we were fascinated with the idea of things that existed before there were any people. We used to build little plasticine panoramas of dinosaurs. As for aboriginal people, and early inhabitants and lost caves, I think that was the fantasy life of children before there was television. *Raiders of the Lost Ark*, with its opening scene of South American jungle temples, was just a throwback to all those stories in *Boys' Own Annual* — the search for lost treasure and whatnot. *King Solomon's Mines, Alan Quatermain, The Man Who Would Be King*, Poe's Antarctic story, *Robinsoe Crusoe, Gulliver's Travels* — I'd read them all before I was twelve.

HANCOCK

And your interest in museums?

ATWOOD

I used to attend the Saturday morning classes at the Royal Ontario Museum. Museums are collections of memories. Each one is like a giant brain. I used to go there with a little girl whose father was an archeologist and worked there, so we used to wander all over the place, by ourselves, after hours.

HANCOCK

You like to work with closed spaces in your stories.

ATWOOD

Some stories do, some don't. It's more likely to be the inner space of the character that's enclosed, not the actual space. *Surfacing* takes place mostly outdoors.

HANCOCK

Are you comfortable with your style?

ATWOOD

I'm never comfortable with my "style" — by which I mean that I'm never sure I have exactly the right words in exactly the right order. But I don't think I have just one style.

HANCOCK

Would you perhaps take your language off into directions suggested by Nicole Brossard or bp Nichol?

ATWOOD

There's more than one way of exploring language. Why do something that other people have already been doing for years and years? If I did what they do, I'd only be imitating them. I sometimes do "experiments," but it's hard to sustain such thing for a whole book-length without repeating Beckett or Jóyce. I wonder if anyone ever asks Alice Munro such questions? Or do they ask bp why he doesn't write like me? People sometimes assume that because I have a larger audience than is usual for a literary writer, I must be writing non-literary books. You do get that form of snobbery from this or that mannikin of letters. But the truth is that I am a literary writer who has acquired, Lord knows how, a larger than usual audience for such things.

HANCOCK

Would you risk losing that audience?

ATWOOD

Since I didn't go about acquiring it on purpose, and since I don't write down to the reader, and since I never expected I would acquire it, it doesn't really concern me. If I lose it, I lose it. Probably it would depress me if I wrote a book that was universally loathed. But you take that chance with any book, don't you? I've never been accused of talcum-powdering the reader...

HANCOCK

One final question: do you have an optimistic sense of resolution? Is there hope in art? In the bigger sense of comedy as life affirmation?

ATWOOD

Hope for what? Let's put it this way. When I finish a book I really like, no matter what the subject matter, or see a play or film, like Kurosawa's *Ran,* which is swimming in blood and totally pessimistic, but so well done, I feel very good. I *do* feel hope. It's the *well-doneness* that has that affect on me. Not the conclusion — not what is said, *per se*. For instance, the end of *King Lear* is devastating, as a statement about the world. But seeing it done well can still exhilarate you.

If you are tone deaf, you are not going to get much out of Beethoven. If you are colour blind, you won't get much of a charge out of Monet. But if you have those capabilities, and you see something done very, very well, something that is true to itself, you can feel for two or three minutes that the clouds have parted and you've had a vision, of something of what music or art or writing can do, at its best. A revelation of the full range of our human response to the world — this is what it means to be human, on earth. That seems to be what "hope" is about in relation to art. Nothing so simple as "happy endings."

It's about other things as well, of course, and it's much more complex than I can begin to analyze. But what you're really waiting for, when you read, when you listen, when you look, when your write, is that moment when you feel, "Hot damn, that is so well done!" An approach to perfection, if you like. Hope comes from the fact that people create, that they find it worthwhile to create. Not just from the nature of what is created.

BHARATI MUKHERJEE

Bharati Mukherjee lives with her husband, Clark Blaise, in a spacious sub-let apartment near Columbia University in New York City. My interview took place there on February 13, 1987, the coldest day of the year. Like Mukherjee herself, the apartment is elegant and calm. On the walls are framed Moghul prints and hangings from China. The tables are covered with books and literary periodicals. The mantelpiece holds framed covers of her books *The Tiger's Daughter, Wife,* and *Darkness,* and printer's proofs of the first story she sold to *Playboy.* With Clark Blaise she has collaborated on two non-fiction books, *Days and Nights in Calcutta* and *The Sorrow and the Terror.*

Bharati is a gracious hostess, a skilled conversationalist, and a writer passionate about Indians in a post-colonial world. She was born in Calcutta and established her career as a writer and teacher of literature and creative writing in Montreal. She now teaches at Columbia and other colleges in the United States. We spent much of a pleasant afternoon discussing India, creative writing, favourite writers — especially Mavis Gallant — and travels.

HANCOCK

Let's start at the beginning. Where did you grow up, and did that affect your later outlook as you expressed it in your fiction?

MUKHERJEE

I was born in Calcutta. Yes, I am positive that Calcutta shaped me. Calcutta is a very special city — it's a world-city, but at the same time it's a small town capable of exciting parochial passions and fiercely chauvinist loyalties. I am what I am because I was born into an upper-middle-class Bengali family in a city where to be Bengali was to be part of the mainstream. I didn't grow up in a multi-racial society in which to be Indian was to be a patronized or hated minority, as did V. S. Naipaul. North Americans don't always understand that an Indian growing up in India as part of the confident mainstream has a very different sense of self than an Indian growing up in a multi-racial country.

India became an independent country in August, 1947, and not long after my parents, two sisters and I made our first trip outside the country. My sister and I went to school in Britain and Switzerland for a few years, so we learned as fairly young children that there was a great big world *out there* that knew little about our native city.

My very early childhood was lived in British-ruled Calcutta. I have only one "colonial" memory, but it's a memory that over the years has become important to me. I can still see myself, feet hooked into the grille-work of the wrought-iron gate of our house — I must have been about four at the time — watching the funeral procession of a teenage freedom-fighter whom the British, very unfairly I now realize, called an 'anarchist.' Everybody had come outdoors to honour the funeral party. Mothers, grandmothers, boy scouts, servants, everybody. It's a heady memory, because what I remember, or *think* I remember, is the mix of fear, that trouble may break out between neighbourhood mourners and the police, and the confidence that very soon India would be free. I feel lucky that I was born just before Independence — I know first-hand how precious liberty is.

New York is my home now, and you know, in many ways it isn't too different from Calcutta. Like Calcutta, New York has a delightfully arrogant sense of itself as the literary and intellectual centre of the universe. And, of course, both cities have sizeable communities of homeless people living on sidewalks. Maybe it's the gradual Calcuttaization of New York that makes me feel so at home here.

HANCOCK

Could you tell me something about your family?

MUKHERJEE

Even more than Calcutta, I've been shaped by my family. I come from a very traditional Bengali Brahmin family. We are an extremely close-knit family. My father, who passed away in 1985, was an absolutely extraordinary man. He was a self-made man. From a one-room laboratory, he built a very successful pharmaceutical firm. He was very much the benevolent patriarch. He was the protector and lavish provider. At the same time, he was a visionary and a great risk-taker. Though he insisted on an almost anachronistically sheltered adolescence for us, he was able to send us three sisters abroad, out of his reach, for schooling. He wanted the best for his daughters. And to him, the "best" meant intellectually fulfilling lives.

Clark's written very affectionately about him in *Days and Nights in Calcutta*. And he is the model for The Tiger in my first novel, *The Tiger's Daughter*.

My mother is one of those exceptional Third World women who "burned" all her life for an education, which was denied to well-brought-up women of her generation. She made sure that my sisters and I never suffered the same wants.

HANCOCK

Are we getting a distorted view of India through such things as David Lean's film of *A Passage to India*, Kaye's *The Far Pavilions* and the TV adaptation of Scott's *The Jewel in the Crown*?

289

Well, we're getting a disproportionate focus on the British Raj in India. The Raj and the machinery of imperialism seem to sell well in North America, but the real India —the India of the Indians —is perceived as being boring or inaccessibly alien.

But I'm pleased that India is finally getting serious media attention. I thought *The Jewel in the Crown* was a remarkably affecting TV series and that it provided a stern, uncompromising picture of British imperialism.

HANCOCK

You've guest-edited recently a special issue of *The Literary Review* called "Writers of the Indian Commonwealth." In your introduction you wrote that "India's children in the new world are a mystery to me that you are eager to discover." Could you elaborate on that?

MUKHERJEE

I am an immigrant, living in a continent of immigrants. I am fascinated by what Clark calls the processes of "unhousement" and "re-housement" in *Resident Alien*. I read voraciously the literature of deracination and assimilation. So it seemed to me natural when *The Literary Review* asked me to guest-edit an issue on Indian literature that I think of Indian literature as being rooted not so much in the geographical entity, India, as in a habit of mind that might be labelled Indian. Until this issue, no editor or critic had thought of Indian literature as a literature of a dispersed people. The Summer 1986 *TLR* contains stories and poems by second- and third-generation Caribbeans, Fijians, Africans, and first-generation North Americans of Indian origin as well as the work of well-established India-based Indian writers.

HANCOCK

Are you also interested in authors like George Woodcock as a journalist and Janette Turner Hospital, who write about India as well, but as non-Indians?

MUKHERJEE

I'm interested in good writing no matter what the author's national origin.

HANCOCK

Who do you see as your contemporaries?

MUKHERJEE

A Third World writer isn't limited as a First World writer is in choosing her contemporaries. Having been born in a city that prided itself as the second city of the British Empire, and having been brought up on British literature, especially on Victorian and Edwardian literature, I feel as close to Jane Austen, Galsworthy, Wilde and Coward as to Bernard Malamud, Alice Munro, Mavis Gallant, Ann Beattie and Raymond Carver.

If you are asking me, do I see myself as another V. S. Naipaul, the answer is: no. The generational gap between us manifests itself more dramatically than the generational gap between, let's say, me and Mavis Gallant. Naipaul seems to have made himself the spokesman for the permanent, and one's tempted to say, the professional, expatriate from the Third World. His characters savour their marginality. I write about New Americans and New Canadians, about belated homesteaders from non-traditional countries. My characters grow and change with the change in citizenships.

HANCOCK

As a professor of creative writing, currently at Columbia, and on various other campuses with creative-writing programs in Canada and America, do you try to keep up to date? What do you talk to your students about?

MUKHERJEE

Every writer has a "given." I try to help the apprentice writers in my workshops discover that given material and find their "voice." More specifically, in a workshop situation we try to zero in on useful questions about narrative strategies. We try to explore the narrative options.

HANCOCK

You said that *Darkness* was written in a quick period of time, within three months, plus a few earlier stories. Do you feel that working in the hothouse confines of a creative-writing department which has students and instructors dealing with matters of form, technique, content, style, details, images, dramatic confrontation, and so on, helped to accumulate all that information for you until it suddenly found an explosive outlet?

MUKHERJEE

No. I like to write, I have always liked to write. I am not one of those writers who dread the typewriter. I wrote *Darkness* as soon as I'd freed myself from the feelings of anger and powerlessness brought on by the racism I experienced in Canada. Right now, my main problem is finding enough time to write. I teach five courses per semester. That's a very heavy teaching load by any standard. If I could afford to live just on my writing, I expect I'd be rather prolific.

But I *do* like to run fiction workshops. Workshops give me a chance to hone my theories about writing.

HANCOCK

Do you talk about things like finding a metaphor for the book, as the painting operates in *Darkness*?

MUKHERJEE

The best discussions are freewheeling. But I hope that I get across to my students my own concern with precision in language and with finding controlling metaphors for stories.

By the way, I don't teach only writing courses. I have a PhD in English and Comparative Literature, and most of the courses I teach in any given semester are straight, academic courses at the graduate or undergraduate level.

As a teacher of writing, though, I want my students not only to write well but to become canny readers of their own writing. So, sometimes, I bring in fiction – it may be just a few paragraphs – by writers I admire, for instance, Cheever or Updike or Munro or Gallant or Blaise – to see how they have solved technical problems.

I have to confess that when I sit down at my Kaypro, I have little idea what'll emerge on the screen.

HANCOCK

You keep a strong dramatic sense, though. Details, gestures work forcefully together in your characterizations. Do you see the characters?

MUKHERJEE

It depends on the work. Yes, definitively, with the two novels. I was mesmerized by the main characters, Tara and Dimple, in those novels. They became companions; I felt that they had lives almost independent of me. Most North American writers start with short fiction, then go on to novels. I started with novels.

Short stories don't always occur to me as being about a character. Sometimes a line or a possible title will set me going. "The Lady From Lucknow," for instance, began with the title. In stories, the hard thing is to find the right "voice," by which I mean locating a centre. Once I find the "voice," I don't seem to need to revise drastically. When I wrote novels, I found myself doing three drafts – the first to find out what the novel was *really* about; the second to sharpen the narrative; the third to catch any infelicities. But nowadays the short stories usually come to me at one sitting. I believe in revision, though. Or rather, I believe that good writing consists of decisions and calculations. One must know why one chooses this word instead of that. I share Isaac Babel's belief that the well-placed comma can stab the heart. I try to make my writing students sensitive to how a word looks and sounds.

HANCOCK

You mentioned encouraging your students to experiment with the page. Do you ever get involved in that big debate that was central in American letters a few years ago, the morality of fiction versus the experiments of fiction?

MUKHERJEE

If by "ever get involved" you mean do I sit on panels that discuss moral fiction as defined by the late John Gardner, the answer is: no. I don't engage in academic debates on this subject. But my own writing always locates a moral centre. The characters themselves may be immoral or amoral, but they operate in a deeply moral world. Some readers have written to tell me that they find my stories scary or unsettling because of this "moral centre."

Do you find there's a difference between the Canadian and the American story?

Yes. I think there's a measurable difference between contemporary Canadian and American fiction. I believe that culture, national mythologies, literary traditions shape both the "inside" and the "outside" of a work. One can detect in choice of syntax, for instance, some cultural assumptions. In the '80s writers from traditional societies, for example India-based Indian novelists writing in English about India, are more likely to feel comfortable using an omniscient point of view than are American writers.

By the way, in my World Literature course at Montclair State College in New Jersey, I always use a novel by a Canadian author. Timothy Findley's *The Wars* works very well in the course. My students certainly feel that in *The Wars* they are encountering a society and a mode of processing that are very different from theirs. They realize that the First World War is central to the English Canadians in a way that it isn't to Americans.

You said somewhere that Canada "fired up your rage."

Yes. My experience with racism in Canada unleashed an anger that eventually led to potent fiction. But initially I expended my energies addressing civil-rights problems. Writing "An Invisible Woman" – the essay for *Saturday Night* – was very painful.

Do you see that your work is equally concerned with form and language as it is with the particular issues of your content?

I'm a careful writer. I am alert to the potency of, and possibilities in, language. English is a language that I have appropriated. At age three, I was sent to an English-medium school in Calcutta. Perhaps we who appropriate English are more aware of the language's powers than are native-speakers. Language gives me my identity. I am the writer I am because I write in North American English about immigrants in the New World.

Have you found where you belong now? You travel widely enough. At the drop of a hat, you cross the continent and the world. That gives you energy.

I like New York City. It's the Calcutta of the Americas. But I can make myself feel that I "belong" almost anywhere – I was happy in Iowa City, and I was very prepared to be happy in Toronto and Montreal. Perhaps, it's because as a Bengali woman I was brought up to be adaptable.

Newness excites me. When I move into a new city, I want to get to know it quickly, and make it my own. I want to "possess" it through my fiction. My characters don't see themselves as lost, marginal people in an unfamiliar city. On the contrary, my characters present an unexpected "insider's" view.

Clark and I have moved around because we must go where there are jobs for us. Yo-yoing through continents isn't my goal; settling-in as quickly as possible is.

HANCOCK

Here's a what-if question. What if you had stayed in Calcutta? Would you have written about something different? The liberation of Goa, the Lucknow uprising?

MUKHERJEE

Who knows! I'd have been a very different person, and therefore a very different writer, if I had stayed back in Calcutta. I still have some close friends in Calcutta, women I went to grade school with. They lead lives of grace, ease, privilege. When I visit them, I realize that outwardly my life in Calcutta would have been much like theirs. But the point is I didn't stay back. My writing has changed over the years. Since *The Tiger's Daughter*...

HANCOCK

I was going to say *The Tiger's Daughter* seemed a British book to me, while *Wife* seemed an American book, and *Darkness*, in part at least, seemed a Canadian book.

MUKHERJEE

My first novel does have, as you remarked, a Britishy feel to it. *The Tiger's Daughter* was written between classes at McGill; actually most of the manuscript was finished during two Christmas breaks and a summer vacation. As a child I was brought up on the novels of Jane Austen, Dickens, Forster, and when I came to write my first novel, the writers I'd read, especially Forster, became models to both mimic and subvert. I couldn't write another *The Tiger's Daughter* even if I wanted to; when I was writing it, the world seemed to me whole and examinable. I was far enough removed from India to look at upbringings like mine with affection and humour, but I wasn't yet integrated enough into Canada to appropriate Canadian issues. What's Britishy about that novel is its authoritativeness — it's hard for me now to write in an omniscient point of view.

By the time I started writing *Wife*, I'd become more North Americanized and that change comes through in the writing. I am not at all an autobiographical writer, but my obsessions reveal themselves in metaphor and language. When I was writing *Wife*, a limited third-person point of view seemed more natural and comfortable than an omniscient one. I was totally engrossed in Dimple. I knew I wanted to stay close to Dimple — an immigrant wife who starts to question her traditional values — and show

294

the immigrants' world through her. And since I was telling the story of the traumatic changes — cultural, psychological — through Dimple, the language, too, was Dimple's; it was more intense, less authoritative and stately, than in *The Tiger's Daughter*.

Days and Nights in Calcutta, which Clark Blaise and I co-authored, was a very hard book for me to write. In my half of the book, I was supposed to write of a sabbatical year we spent in Calcutta in the '70s; I was supposed to write of the upper-middle-class life around me. What I ended up writing, however, was an accidental autobiography. While writing that book, I realized that I had moved from thinking of myself as an emotionally-committed Canadian citizen. The book turns on this self-discovery.

HANCOCK

You worked closely with Clark on *Days and Nights in Calcutta* and your forthcoming account of the Air India disaster, *The Sorrow and the Terror*. Is the collaborative process a great stimulus?

MUKHERJEE

I don't know about the collaborative process itself, but collaborating with Clark is always exciting. We've collaborated in very different ways in the two non-fiction books. With *Days and Nights*, we were essentially writing two separate accounts about overlapping experiences. What turned the distinct accounts into a cohesive "book" was the unplanned converging and diverging of our two points of view.

Our collaboration in the new book, *The Sorrow and the Terror*, is a more concerted one. There isn't a single segment that hasn't been worked on by both of us.

HANCOCK

Do you ever show each other fiction-in-progress? That strikes me as a daunting experience, with two professors of creative writing commenting on each other's work.

MUKHERJEE

Clark's a good sport; he's always eager to see my work, and he makes very helpful suggestions. I should be a better sport.

HANCOCK

Your work has similarities. You both deal with alienation, victims, outsiders, though Clark's is more autobiographical, slightly removed.

MUKHERJEE

I don't think about my fiction as being about alienation. On the contrary, I mean for it to be about assimilation. My stories centre on a new breed and generation of North American pioneers. I am fascinated by people who have enough gumption, energy, ambition, to pull up their roots. My stories are irreverent, and, I like to think, funny. *(Laughs.)* My stories are about conquests, and not about loss.

HANCOCK

In your interview with V. S. Naipaul in *Salamagundi*, you said you admired him for "articulating a post-colonial consciousness without making it appear exotic." You added that you shared that sense of "being cut off from a supporting world," of "reaching across and bringing an unfamiliar society to a different audience." Does that relate to what you just said about pioneering?

MUKHERJEE

No, I don't think so. I admire V. S. Naipaul's early fiction, I especially like *A House for Mr. Biswas.* When I first read him, as a student in Iowa, I thought, here's another writer who isn't British or American and who is writing with feeling about a world that'd be considered "off-centre" by mainstream English readers. But Naipaul and I have had radically different experiences of dislocation, and therefore treat dislocation very differently in fiction. We intersect the Americas at very different points. My characters are not the descendants of indentured laborers. They've been spared, to use Naipaul's phrase, "the overcrowded barracoon" experience. My characters *choose* to uproot themselves from their native countries. For my characters, breaking away is part of maturing.

What interests me about Naipaul now is his appropriation of another people's culture, manners, traditions. In that context – the context of appropriation – I find Conrad, too, totally fascinating.

HANCOCK

Do you see "English" as a foreign language?

MUKHERJEE

That's an interesting question. The process of appropriating – and re-inventing – language became real to me as I was guest-editing the special issue of *The Literary Review.* As I was putting that issue together, I realized how strongly culture influenced not only the writer's use of English, but the shape of her/his fiction.

Of course English is a foreign language for me. My mother-tongue is still Bengali. Let's just say that I think of North American English as my step-mother-tongue!

HANCOCK

Could you elaborate on the parody of Forster that appears in *The Tiger's Daughter?*

MUKHERJEE

I talked about the "parodying" of Forster on a panel at McGill University during an E. M. Forster Festival, and since that talk is already in print, I don't see much point in going over it here. Briefly, in my novel I was trying to subvert the Anglo-Indian literary conventions. For instance, in my novel I shrank Forster's Mau Tank to a poorly-filtered swimming pool. Parody and subversion have energy; mimicry doesn't.

HANCOCK

Do your characters speak for you?

If you are asking, do my characters faithfully articulate my personal views, the answer is: no. My characters, as you know, come from many different social classes and support many different political positions. But if the question is, do my characters speak *to* me, then the answer is: yes. I hear them speak. My head's bursting with stories. The trouble, as always, is to find the time to write them.

HANCOCK
Time is the problem. Like Clark, do you manage to get to retreats or writers' colonies?

MUKHERJEE
I don't have time to go to writers' colonies! I teach summer school.

HANCOCK
Are the voices of your characters bits and pieces of information that you've accumulated through osmosis or clippings or pass along stories or fabrication based on the nuances of the experiences as you understand them?

MUKHERJEE
I write about what obsesses me — the re-housement of individuals and of whole peoples.

HANCOCK
You have used those terms before: re-housement and unhousement. Could you explain them?

MUKHERJEE
Unhousement is the breaking away from the culture into which one was born, and in which one's place in society was assured. Re-housement is the re-rooting of oneself in a new culture. This requires transformations of the self.

HANCOCK
Are obsessions important for a writer?

MUKHERJEE
Obsession is essential.

HANCOCK
Do you have a sense of audience? Or various audiences? Or do you worry about audiences?

MUKHERJEE
I am my ideal audience. I don't have a specific or targeted audience in mind, but I think that as long as a writer isn't writing in her/his diary, she/he assumes the existence of an ideal, maybe phantom, audience.

HANCOCK
Would it be an audience that either recognizes or shares the experience of the fiction?

MUKHERJEE
I know what you're getting at. But I intend to evade the question. Oh

well, all right, let me try to meet your question head-on. When I sit at my Kaypro I don't think of audience. I write because a story has become urgent inside my head. But one is always divided between the person punching the keyboard, and the person reading the screen. That's what I meant when I said that I was my ideal audience. Clark and my editor occupy the next two rows of ideal audiences.

Then when I find out that there is an audience, however small, *out there*, I am wonder-struck. I got quite a bit of mail on *Wife*. There were some really moving letters; I especially remember one from a British war-bride in a New Jersey suburb and another from a German woman in the Maritimes. To know that one's fiction has reached even one person is staggering; it's humbling. I believe in the word. The word creates or locates its own audience. My father, who was a very successful scientist and businessman, too, believed in the power of the word. He was very pleased with my essay, "An Invisible Woman." I had kept that essay from him because I hadn't wanted him to know how pained I was by my racial experiences in Canada. But just before he passed away, someone snuck him a copy of the essay. I am glad now that he saw it.

HANCOCK

Is obsession enough? Or does a writer need ego as well? By that I mean the courage necessary to get the work done, as Norman Mailer once said.

MUKHERJEE

If ego means stamina, I suppose, yes. A writer needs the ability to carry on in spite of rejection.

HANCOCK

Could you tell me a bit about your friendship with Bernard Malamud?

MUKHERJEE

Bernard Malamud was like a second father to us, especially to Clark, I knew him for over twenty years, Clark knew him longer. In fact, I met him through Clark; he was very much a part of the family.

At the same time he was a writer who brought out the best in us as writers. In a way, reading Bern's *Selected Stories* made me want to write *Darkness*. That's why *Darkness* is dedicated to him. There are many dazzling-enough writers, but few works have the compassion and wisdom that Bern's do.

HANCOCK

There's been many changes in the Canadian publishing community as well. Do you see yourself as a Canadian writer, or a North American, or an international writer? Do you see that there's been changes in the Canadian publishing community as well? A new generation of publishers, editors, readers is more receptive to your work now than when it was first published.

MUKHERJEE

I remember some years ago reading about Cynthia Good, the senior editor at Penguin Books, in *Quill and Quire*. The article quoted her as saying — I am paraphrasing what I remember after all these years — that she was looking for Canadian writers who were also international. I remember thinking to myself with relief that finally, thanks to editors like her, Canadian literature has come of age, that it has moved away from the fiercely parochial nationalism of the late 1960s and of the 1970s, that it can now accommodate writers who write of the "other" Canada.

Clark and I came to live in Montreal in 1966, as you know. I taught fiction-writing at McGill and, for a longish time, directed McGill's Creative Writing program, and my first novel, which was published in the States in 1972, did rather well.

What I'm saying is that I got started as a writer — in 1972 I was a Canadian novelist with an "international" reputation — at a time when nationalist Canadian writers were defining Canadian literature by exclusion rather than by inclusion.

HANCOCK

Do you admire writers like Salman Rushdie and others who are bringing a new energy to the writing of India?

MUKHERJEE

I admire Salman Rushdie enormously. Before *Midnight's Children*, writers of Indian origin writing in English were encouraged by convention to write of their world with detachment and irony. Their method was reductive. They treated their characters as though they were uncomplicated. With *Midnight's Children*, Rushdie breaks down those conventions. He aggrandizes, and that's marvellously healthy. The sections on Bombay have a superb excess of energy. Many of the writers before him tried, very unfortunately, to "tame" India for foreign readers. The other interesting thing about Salman Rushdie is that he discards British models. His fiction is closer to that of Günter Grass and Marquez than to Forster.

HANCOCK

That also happened in Canadian writing, as you know, with what I'll broadly call "fiction of the marvellous." Does that particular mode of perception appeal to you as a writer?

MUKHERJEE

In Hindu story-telling — I am talking about the ancient tales from the *Puranasa* and the two epics of the *Ramayana* and the *Mahabharata* — the magical is the norm. All Hindu children, especially children in villages, are told the ancient stories again and again. Shape-changes are common in these tales. Birds talk. Animals practise ethics. It was colonialism that derailed Indian writers from continuing that convention of "magic." I am not eager to use the term "magic realism" because it doesn't precisely convey what I mean about this Hindu oral literature. Colonialism forced generations of Indian writers to value British models and to look down on the native. The British managed to convince Indians that British literature

299

was rational, realistic, and superior, and that Indian literature with its magical qualities was childish. Do I write magic realism? I include "the marvellous" in my fiction, especially in my first novel. My fiction clearly inhabits a space in which there are extra-rational presences.

HANCOCK

Do you find the critics and reviewers sensitive to your work?

MUKHERJEE

Sensitive to my work? I think so. A few *choose* to misread, because they have agendas of their own.

HANCOCK

Could you tell me about the origins of *The Tiger's Daughter*? Was that your MFA thesis in Iowa?

MUKHERJEE

No, I wrote a collection of stories for my MFA thesis. My doctoral dissertation was on a purely academic topic. Let me tell you how I came to write my first novel. When I was a student in Iowa, I wrote a story called "Debate on a Rainy Afternoon" for one of my fiction workshops. The workshop seemed to really like that story. Well, Clark sent off a copy to *The Massachusetts Review*, and my story was published. The story then won an Honorable Mention in the *Best American Stories* for that year. About the same time, editors from three major American publishing houses wrote me, asking to see a novel. The editor from Houghton Mifflin was the most persistent, so I wrote her back that I was terribly busy finishing my PhD dissertation — and teaching full-time, and raising two kids — but that as soon as I had a summer break, I'd get to work on a novel. And that's what I did.

HANCOCK

How did *Wife* begin?

MUKHERJEE

Clark and I were in Calcutta on a sabbatical one winter. We were staying at a place called the Ramkrishna Mission, it's a place where foreign scholars generally stay. The idea is that the scholars will work in reasonably-priced, comfortable enough, hotel-style rooms during the day, and engage in exciting intellectual conversations at meal-times. Clark and I were having breakfast at a long dining-table one morning when a Columbia professor next to me asked, "What do you Bengali girls do between the ages of fifteen and twenty-five?" So I wrote a novel to explain to him what we did.

HANCOCK

You said that *Darkness* came about as a result of your second trip to the United States to live.

MUKHERJEE

Moving out of Canada gave me back my voice. The last seven years or so in Canada I felt I was constantly being forced to see myself as part of an unwanted "visible minority." All I say about the move and its effects on my fiction I have said in the Introduction to that book.

HANCOCK

Ironically, in Canada, you won a National Magazine Award for your honest invective.

MUKHERJEE

In my acceptance speech I said that only in Canada would someone win a prize for indicting the society. I couldn't have written "An Invisible Woman" if I hadn't left Canada, though.

HANCOCK

Are names the metaphor for characters? Dimple seems like such a perfect name, "a small surface depression" as you noted in the epigraph.

MUKHERJEE

Names are very important to me. Dimple, by the way, was a very popular — very chic, if you like — name for Indian girls in the early '70s. But I was also trying to suggest "slight disturbances" through that name.

HANCOCK

Do you see a character like Tara Bannerjee? Or do you slowly create her to fit the demands of the fiction?

MUKHERJEE

Tara wasn't based on any real person. And the novel wasn't autobiographical. But I *was* writing about a small class of people, a passing way of life, that I knew very well. The novel demanded that the narrator figure be passive. So, to some extent, I'd have to say yes to your second question — Tara's passivity was dictated by her dramatic function in the novel. She had to be porous and passive in order to record the slightest tremors in her culture. She had to react rather than to act. The novel centred on the violent passing of an era — and the characters were intended to be fleshed out abstractions. As I was writing, they took on surprising lives of their own. I suppose that because I have a comic vision, most of the characters, even when they are caught in ghastly situations, acquit themselves in amusing ways.

HANCOCK

Do you find that being an academic and a professor of creative writing gets in the way when you work? Do you have to forget all that? When I asked Clark that, he said it was as if none of it existed.

MUKHERJEE

I was going to say the same thing. When I sit in front of the screen, the story takes over. In the first draft, I have no idea where the story's going, what characters will do or say.

Reader-effect is important to me, though. I do know, while I am working — maybe not till the second draft — what I want a reader to feel in any given scene. By reader I don't mean a real person, but the imaginary "other" inside me that we were discussing earlier this afternoon.

HANCOCK

Do you tell your students things about work habits? About doing the work that is necessary to get the job done? Or so many hours a day? About getting a discipline?

MUKHERJEE

I always tell them that writing requires self-discipline. Yes, I warn them about hard work. I tell them that many good writers I know keep notebooks and write every day. But then I tell them that I don't keep notebooks, and I don't have time to write every day.

HANCOCK

One of the things that appealed to me about both your novels was that the prose was so heavily textured. *Wife* had ads, letters, scenarios, various dialogues, the four electric cows. The prose itself was a surprise from page to page. Did you do that on the second draft?

MUKHERJEE

If you are asking me, did I inject "texture" in a deliberate way into the second draft, the answer would have to be: no. Both novels occurred to me in terms of a character — Tara, Dimple — caught in a crisis situation, and to me a character is who she is because of the language she thinks and feels in. My characters are often in the process of forgetting one language and inventing another. The texture of the novel comes from the language used by the focal characters — in that sense, the texture is part of the first draft.

HANCOCK

Does the television act as an ironic mirror to this unhappy story?

MUKHERJEE

Dimple is an isolated woman because she doesn't speak much English. She tells herself that she is learning American English and getting to know Americans by watching TV.

HANCOCK

Dramatically, you establish the direction of *Wife* fairly quickly. You set up the idea of murder in New York, of violence and chaos, and variations on that motif, blood, pin pricks, punctures and other hurtful things of various kinds. Did you plan that part of your narrative strategy from the beginning?

MUKHERJEE

Most of it, yes. I think of plot as an arrangement or a design. The juxtaposition of images, the composition and the framing: all these are important to me. But I hope the ending comes as a surprise. How Dimple settles her problem should shock or at least surprise the reader.

HANCOCK

Is infidelity and murder the only solution?

MUKHERJEE

Dimple thinks so. The ending, I guess, is discomfiting.
Dimple's decision to murder her husband is her misguided act of self-

302

assertion. If she had remained a housewife living with her extended family in India, she would probably not have asked herself questions such as, am I unhappy, do I deserve to be unhappy. And if by chance she had asked herself these questions, she might have settled her problems by committing suicide. So turning to violence outward rather than inward is part of her slow and misguided Americanization. *Wife* is a novel that is very dear to me.

The antagonists your characters face are not evil characters, are they?

MUKHERJEE

My fiction locates very clearly, I think, what's morally right and what's not. But I don't have guys in white hats slugging guys in black hats. There's villainy growing out of misunderstandings and malice, but there's no Devil.

HANCOCK

Your protagonists in *Darkness* are a wide range of characters: illegals, rich, poor, a psychiatrist, a restaurant worker. . .

MUKHERJEE

There are a hundred thousand voices in my head waiting to be heard.

HANCOCK

One reviewer said your characters "bring false ideas of what to expect in the new world, and in defence, create false memories of what they leave behind. As a result, both the old and the new don't exist, and the creators of these worlds become more and more unreal themselves."

MUKHERJEE

I guess I missed that review. I don't know what the reviewer means because I don't have the context. But I do want my characters to be seen as inventing their own Americas and Canadas. The breaking away from rigidly predictable lives frees them to invent more satisfying pasts, and gives them a chance to make their futures in ways that they could not have in the Old World. We're talking, then, about re-location as a positive act. In immigrating, my characters become creators. By creating, they become more real to themselves, instead of unreal.

Index of authors and titles

Short stories by the authors interviewed are grouped under each author's name; all other titles are listed alphabetically.